Understanding Politics

CHANDLER & SHARP PUBLICATIONS IN
POLITICAL SCIENCE

General Editor: Victor Jones

Understanding Politics

The Cultures of Societies and the Structures of Governments

William S. Stewart

California State University, Chico

Chandler & Sharp Publishers, Inc.
Novato, California

Library of Congress Cataloging-in-Publication Data

Stewart, William S. (William Stanley), 1938-
    Understanding politics : the cultures of societies and the
structures of governments / William S. Stewart.
    xiv + 225 p. 23 cm. -- (Chandler & Sharp publications in political
science)
    Bibliography: p.211-214
    Includes index.
    ISBN 0-88316-558-9 (pbk.)
    1. Political culture. 2. Political science 3. Comparative
government. 4. Legitimacy of governments.   I. Title. II. Series.
JA75.7.S74 1988
    306'.2--dc19   88-20431
                                                            CIP

Copyright © 1988 by Chandler & Sharp, Publishers, Inc.
All rights reserved.
International Standard Book Number: 0-88316-558-9
Library of Congress Catalog Card Number: 88-20431
Printed in the United States of America.

Edited by W. L. Parker
Book designed by Jon Sharp
Cover design and art by Jacki Gallagher
Composition by Page One Graphics/Lisa Nishikawa

Contents

Chapter Nine: Leninist Socialism (Communism)   159

Chapter Ten: Fascist Corporatism   181

Chapter Eleven: Understanding Cultural Differences and Political Change   199

Bibliographic Notes   211

Index   215

Illustrations

Preface

This book has been written over the last fifteen years for my students and to work out my own thinking on politics. In 1960, the first year I voted, I was a Nixon Republican. In 1988 I am something of a democratic socialist, but feel that different regimes and the cultures beneath them have different effects, depending upon historic, demographic, and other factors relevant to a particular time and place.

My students sometimes ask how my ideas developed, and I respond with a bit of personal history. After graduate school in English Literature and the Marine Corps as an enlisted man, I was a Peace Corps volunteer in Venezuela. I went there with all the usual American understandings of life, but after a year or so began to suspect that Venezuelans actually had a different culture and different understandings of the truth. My experiences left me scarred and battered, a consequence with which most Peace Corps volunteers will be able to empathize. After teaching high school in New Zealand for a year, I returned to academics in an effort to understand what had happened to me in the Peace Corps. An M.A. in Latin American Studies proved to have very little commercial value, and I ended up as a supervisor of community action workers in Virginia for the Office of Economic Opportunity in the War on Poverty. A year with the OEO convinced me that the problems of poverty and development in Virginia were almost identical with those in Venezuela, particularly in the views the rich and powerful had on the status and motivations of the poor.

How could the United States, a rich and powerful nation which was the envy of the world, and its leader, turn out to be like a struggling Third World country which seemed to be losing its battle with poverty and corruption? I didn't understand what was going on. Dr. Federico Gil had been urging me to return to school at Chapel Hill and I decided to do so, but this time to study the United States as much as Latin America.

While in graduate school I read Fred Riggs's book on prismatic society and Kuhn's on scientific revolutions, both of which are the intellectual beginnings of this book. The idea that all national societies are multicultural, and that economics and politics are dominated by these intercultural dynamics as well as by the contradictions inherent in any one of them was a beginning, but working out the principles of prismatic analysis and giving some content to just what the nature of the more important cultures might be has taken quite a while to develop. This book is the result.

It is not "finished," nor do I expect it ever shall be. The section on morality and wisdom, for example, was added only this last winter, but I feel it is an integral part of what was already there. I have shared my ideas with my students as they have developed, and the work has been very much shaped by the interaction. Classes in American Government and in Latin American Studies have all been a part of it, and, as it more and more approached the shape in which it is now before you, it has become more and more the means by which my students and myself analyze American and Latin American societies.

The first three chapters on prismatic theory have proved to be especially valuable to many of my students, for they are as much applicable to their personal lives as they are to the nation of which they are a part. The chapters on the (semi) different cultures also seem to be internalized by many of them, to such a degree that years afterward they will use the same concepts to understand new situations. Prismatic analysis is conceptually distinct from the patterns of cultures I have described here, but both seem to be relevant and useful to many of my students.

Because these theories and understandings have been developed for and with my students, my approach has not been strictly academic. Footnotes are minimal, and the language as plain as I can make it. At the same time, I have felt no need to talk down to my students, for I expect them to appreciate exactness in the use of language and breadth in vocabulary. New words (to them) have been used when I felt new concepts needed them. To put new wine in old bottles has been considered unwise for a long time, and to use old words for new concepts would be to ask for misunderstanding.

Both my marxist and capitalist colleagues object to this book, for each group feels there is only one truth to human relations and that they know what it is. The philosophical position that reality is not directly understandable undermines their positions, and they react accordingly. Surprisingly enough, they each seem to like the chapter on their own culture but denigrate the value of the rest of the book.

On the other hand, the responses from my students over the years have generally been enthusiastic. An initial period of dismay and disorientation has usually given way to understanding and internalization of the prismatic approach. It has proven particularly valuable in work on Latin American politics, but my classes in the politics of the United States have also been radically affected by the approach. Much that is confusing becomes clear when the notion of a liberal government coupled with an oligarchical national economy is applied to the mass of information we have developed about the United States in political science. Perhaps the most natural use for this book has been in my class on contemporary political thought. It has been well received by my students there and has proved to be a useful tool for the analysis of both American thinking and American structures. On a broader scale, I think it will be useful to anyone who wants to understand the dynamics of people and societies.

William S. Stewart
Chico, CA, March 13, 1988

Understanding Politics

Chapter 1

The Human Foundation of Politics

Understanding politics is difficult for most of us. The trouble is not so much that we can't understand each bit of news when it comes along as that the pieces don't fit together very well. Politicians contradict themselves and each other all the time. Who is to say what we should believe and what we shouldn't?

". . . Know the truth, and the truth shall make you free." But whose truth should we believe? Lying seems to be normal in politics; at least it is not very difficult to read the paper and realize that two statements made by the same politician a few days apart can't possibly both be true. Should we believe our own truth? What if we don't know what's true? How are we to find out if everyone has an axe to grind? No one has the time or the energy to do original research on everything that is important to him or her, and most don't do original research on anything. Because we don't we have to depend upon the findings of others, but how do we know whom to trust?

Most questions in politics (and in many other areas of life) start with these questions. Truth is important to us. Democracy is a farce if the voters don't know what they're voting about and if they can't trust the people they elect. Public trust in the institutions of government has always been low in the United States, but a belief in democracy has been high. This situation is contradictory, but the contradiction doesn't seem to bother people very much. Why, and what it means for politics, is the theme of this book.

Contradiction and self-contradiction are inevitable in life, because we are seldom confronted in our lives with situations in which only one value is important. Usually a number of values must be taken into account,

1

particularly in our relations with other people. The more important the relationship, the more we find those things we value to be fundamental to our understanding and our actions. Whether in family, friends, business, politics, or love, relationships which are livable and understandable in terms of only one value are rare. We have all at times tried to maintain a relationship by concentrating on one value and ignoring others, but we usually fail. In order to understand why, we will use theories of human relations and of the human situation. Theories are more or less useful, and if they aren't useful enough we should have little trouble discarding them. People with theories usually become attached to them, though, for the relation between our theories and our values is much closer than most of us would like to believe.

A "theory" about anything has essentially three functions: it defines what is real and what is not real; what is relevant and what is irrelevant; and possible relationships among relevant facts. Once we know these three things, we have only to find out what the relevant facts are in a specific case and we will then understand what is going on.

Most people distrust theory, basing their lives and actions on truth and pragmatic experience. Under our definition of theory, however, the logical difference between "truth" and "theory" is not great. To know the truth is to be able to distinguish reality from fantasy, relevant from irrelevant, and to understand what the relevant facts mean when they occur. Having a theory serves the same function, but nothing could be more obvious than that the truth is not theoretical.

A theory may be personal and intellectual, but truth is felt to exist quite apart from the individual who believes it. The difference is connotative rather than denotative: as a matter of logic, theory and truth are the same; as a matter of belief, they are worlds apart. We believe that what is true exists in the world external to ourselves, while a theory is an intellectual concept which attempts to describe the truth. What is the difference between them if it is not our own belief in the truth and our skepticism about a theory? Truth, in this context, is simply a theory we believe to be true. The difference is not in its function but in the degree to which we have internalized it and made it a part of ourselves.

Such a logical distinction, however, hardly does justice to the truth. We live by the truth, all of us. Living by a theory is so hard that we would have to reject our own humanity in order to do it. Most of us are not ready for that. The Truth, however painful and ugly it may be, is the basis of our lives, no matter how pretty and attractive are the theories about life which we read and hear about.

Paradigms

In order to avoid the emotional responses built into us, it is useful to use words which will not trigger an emotional response. In this work a theory which a person believes to be true will be called a paradigm. The word has gained respectability in social science circles through Thomas Kuhn's use of it in *The Structure of Scientific Revolutions*,[1] in which he argues that revolutions in scientific thought are founded not upon progressive discoveries about the nature of reality, but by the acceptance of new and different theories about reality. That is, older theories (such as an earth-centered universe) are not "wrong" and newer ones (such as a sun-centered universe) "right," so much as they are useful or not useful for specific purposes. Ptolemaic astronomy, which was earth centered, worked very well and was very useful for some 2000 years. Kuhn states that Copernican astronomy supplanted it more because all the significant Ptolemaic astronomy problems had been solved again and again than because it was considered wrong.

What had begun as a theory had long since become paradigmatic, however, and Copernican astronomy was held to be false for some time. In a religiously oriented age falsity was known as heresy, but we should not let the name obscure the main controversy, which was between truth and falsity. About 400 years later Einstein went the next logical step, which was to theorize that the universe has no fixed center at all; that everything is relative to everything else. That astronomers are still trying to figure out how big the universe is argues that they still believe in the earlier paradigm that there is a universe which is limited and therefore has a center.

Paradigms are theories we believe to be true. Hypotheses are theories which need not represent reality at all in order to be useful, at least to the person using them. In science hypotheses must be capable of being disproved; this requirement leads to the curious result that most hypotheses postulated by scientists are ideas that they don't believe rather than those that they do. The reason is that we really don't believe true ideas can be legitimately disproved, but if we can't disprove them they remain imprecise and scientifically questionable. To disprove what you never believed in the first place can be very useful (particularly if you are trying to convince someone who does believe it) but it is not a method which will ever finally settle the question of what is true.

When a scientist wishes to state a proposition he believes to be true but which his colleagues do not, he will call it a theory. In this way he avoids calling his colleagues either ignorant or stupid and signals that disagreement is acceptable. Both he and his colleagues will then energetically attempt to disprove the theory by examining its implications and attempting to disprove them. The more the theory cannot be disproved the more people will tend to feel that it may be true. If this keeps up long enough the theory will gradually become a paradigm, that is, a theory believed to be true. Since it has never been proved true (it simply has not been proved false) this process usually takes a generation of scientists, for there are always some stubborn individuals who cannot stop believing in the truths current when they first learned about science. Kuhn's explanation for the fact that most original thinkers in science have only one period of originality, and that one when they are relatively new to the field, is that ideas are most easily challenged when they are new to a person. Once they have been thoroughly internalized (that is, moved from theories to paradigms) they are very unlikely to be changed.

The "hard" sciences deal with the physical world rather than with human relations, but it is Kuhn's point that even hard science is founded upon paradigms rather than upon direct knowledge of the real physical world. This is so because of the way human beings perceive physical things. Physiologically we experience both the external and internal world through a nervous system that responds to stimuli through changing electrical impulses within the body. The brain's function seems to be to make sense out of the thousands of messages it is constantly receiving. In essence, it must distinguish between messages originating outside the body and those generated inside, between those accepted as important and those to be ignored, and then deduce the meaning of the important stimuli. That is, the brain must use theories to figure out what is going on.

While it can be said that we experience reality directly through sensory perceptions, it does not follow that we understand it directly. Newborn babies are not stupid; to apply the "stupid" concept to an infant is enough to reveal its absurdity. Infants are helpless not because they are weak (they are surprisingly strong) but because they are unable to make sense of a world that is almost totally new. The sensory stimuli the infant is receiving are radically different from those he or she is accustomed to, and the possible responses to these new items of information are also worlds apart.

The infant has no paradigms through which to make sense of the new world. An appeal to instinct does not get us very far at this point. The only instincts which seem to be built into human babies are a sucking response when touched around the mouth and a grasping response when touched on the hand or foot. These are better than nothing, but they do not materially help an infant's understanding.

An empathic observer watching an infant learning about the world outside the womb is struck not by the baby's stupidity but by the intelligence with which he or she tests what are clearly theories about the new environment. Whether it is binocular vision or figuring out that those things poking at your eyes are hands you can control, infants bring an intelligence to their tasks which is extraordinary only to those who no longer think about them.

Which, of course, is all of us. No one, infants or otherwise, can be consciously aware of all the thousands of sensory stimuli our bodies constantly receive. Growing up is in many ways a process of learning what not to think about. Paradigms replace observation and logic from necessity, not from choice, for only by excluding the vast majority of the stimuli we receive are we able to think coherently about the few we accept as important. People unable to form or accept paradigms are catatonic. They perceive sensory stimuli but are unable to make sense of them. A failure to exclude most stimuli as irrelevant, to distinguish between "fact" and "fancy," or to see relations among relevant stimuli will all result in an inability to function on even the most basic levels.

Logic, unfortunately, is of only limited help. The function of logic is to work out the implications of two or more assumptions. It cannot generate the assumptions themselves. Once we understand how little infants can take for granted we can see the logic in their actions. Logic would seem to be inherent in human beings, for an infant is magnificently logical in testing the implications of his or her assumptions about reality.

While we can label assumptions theories when they are tentative and paradigms when they are accepted as true, their origin is more than a matter of names. Where do we get our truths about the world? Some, certainly, are generated from a physical being's interaction with the physical world. That the sky is above and the mud below for all the people we know and all we have ever heard of implies that gravity is widespread. However, the concept of up and down is not the same as the physical stimuli that produce it. Falling down would seem to be a universal response to any other paradigm in this area. It is easy to see that eventually infants all over the world will learn the same paradigm.

Basic physical actions in general are pretty uniform all over the world, a phenomenon that can be explained by reference to the close and continuous interaction of the physical relations of a human being with the physical objects around him or her. They are based on paradigms which are constantly exercised and found to be useful.

Physical actions, however, are only a small part of the world of human beings. We measure the difference between us and amoebas not so much by the physical differences as by the (assumed) emotional and mental disparities. (It may be, as Lewis Carroll pointed out, that clams spend the time between high tides solving equations of the second degree, but we do not believe it.) Our world is so much more than physical actions that most of our time is taken up trying to decipher what they mean in an emotional and mental context. In order to do this we use paradigms, in this case paradigms about people.

The Family

The first source of our paradigms about people is the family. It is a necessity that human infants be nurtured by others, since at birth we are incapable of keeping ourselves alive. It seems clear that those animals not nurtured by others are precisely those with the most instincts: inborn, presumably genetic responses to stimuli. It is also precisely these animals which are most incapable of learning. Snakes are independent from the egg, but we rarely see trained snake acts. Reptiles in general are autonomous from birth, but they are also considered a lower species, a designation which usually means they cannot learn.

Humans, on the other hand, need to be cared for if they are to survive. We learn from experience, but the experience is almost exclusively that of our family (or a substitute for it) for the first years of our lives. This is so much the case that it is difficult to distinguish the source even of paradigms about physical actions. Are they the result of inputs from direct experience or of inputs from other members of the family? Does a baby learn to walk from experience or from example? The answer is (obviously) from both. Even to pose the question is to exhibit a truly amazing ignorance of the way people grow up. Questions like this lead to rather snide references about "pointy-headed intellectuals" who live in fantasy worlds called ivory towers, so far removed from the real world that their ignorance of it leads them into idiocy.

An implication of the answer "both," however, is that paradigms on a physical level are as much a product of human interaction as of physical experience. If this implication is correct for paradigms about inanimate objects, how much more will it be so for paradigms about people? Human interaction is physical (if we are lucky) but it is also mental and emotional. It is wrong to separate these qualities if we are to understand human beings. Mental, emotional, and physical qualities are implicit in every human act. Though we can separate them intellectually, we find again and again that we cannot separate them in our own lives. The implication is that our paradigms cannot be understood by assuming they are based on separate physical, mental, or emotional factors. Paradigms of physical reality also have emotional aspects. A good example is people who have lived through a major earthquake for the first time. They invariably report being terrified. A paradigm about the earth's stability turns out to have a very strong emotional side to it.

Not even earthquakes can really shake our paradigms about the earth. A few days after the earthquake our paradigm is intact once again and we go right on walking without looking at the ground. Truth exists as it did before the unusual event, because truth is the basis of our lives and personalities. Our understanding of reality is primary to our perception of ourselves and the world around us. Paradigms set the limits of the possible. They separate the dreamer from the realist. The truth makes us free, not our dreams.

At the same time, dreams are highly valued. Although we may scorn the idealist as a dreamer we sometimes worry that we are too limited. This uneasiness with our own understanding of the truth about reality is an old one. It is at the core of Plato's philosophy, of the sophists', and of Aristotle's. The three positions on truth are much the same now as they were then. This persistence is hardly surprising, since human beings do not seem to have changed a great deal in the last two or three thousand years.

Idealists, Realists, and National Cultures

Plato, an idealist, held that truth exists quite separately from those who believe it and that truth can be perceived through intelligence. Rationality and logic, when diligently applied to any subject, will reveal the truth of the matter and allow us to make correct decisions. Far from accepting the theory of paradigms, Plato argued that understanding, scientific or otherwise, was the progressive revelation of a truth wholly external to its discoverers. The ideal (external) truth is more real for Plato than the actual (what we physically perceive). Since truth was by his definition the same for all, laws formulated by those who best perceived the truth would be the best laws for all, and the best political system was the dictatorship of philosopher kings.

The sophists,[2] on the other hand, were cynics to the core. They felt that logic and rationality could be used to prove anything a reasonably intelligent person wanted them to prove. Since logic cannot provide the assumptions about reality upon which reasoning is based, those assumptions (very logically) can be anything the logician wants them to be. The sophists' truth is idiosyncratic to the logician, and each individual is perfectly free to create his or her own truth. Not surprisingly, they felt that each individual would create self-serving truths. The sophists opened schools to teach their debating skills, spreading the doctrine that truth was not external to individuals but was contained within them. Truth was no longer binding since it was no longer universal, and self-interest was the foundation for everything. Every government was based only upon the self-interest of those with power. There was no reason to believe that laws good for the governors would also be in the self-interest of the governed. Indeed, there was every reason to believe that they would not be. Government was tyranny, and that was all there was to it.

Aristotle had experienced enough different forms of government to see flaws and virtues in all of them. After an extensive examination of all the governmental forms he could discover, he decided that the government best suited to a people was that which they considered legitimate. Any other form, no matter how logically correct, would inevitably become a tyranny when it was imposed upon a populace which could not accept it as legitimate. Plato's republic assumed the consent and acceptance of the people. If they did not accept it, Plato's system could not function as he expected it to. Aristotle's point was that most people's notions of legitimacy were a product of their culture, and their cultures were all more or less different from Plato's. At the same time, the sophists were in error when they claimed truth was entirely a matter of individuals. Within a particular national culture there seemed to be widespread agreement on what truth was.

In effect, Aristotle found the source of legitimacy in shared paradigms rather than in perfect external truth or in individual self-interest. Truth is a description we learn from preceding generations. What is legitimate and what is not is a function of the paradigms in which we are raised. What is true about human nature (is everyone selfish or are we faithful to external standards of behavior?) is also paradigmatic. Aristotle located truth in the shared paradigms of national culture.

Roles

A major problem with a cultural approach is the difficulty in distinguishing among paradigms. While we can intellectually differentiate among emotional, mental, and physical facets of human beings we do not normally do so in our own lives. To base an analysis on such functionally artificial distinctions will seriously distort the process of understanding. The concept of roles as the foundations of paradigms is a more productive approach, for it more closely approximates how human beings function. Eric Berne held in *Games People Play*[3] that all of us have a child, a parent, and an adult role built into us. An early exponent of transactional analysis, he felt that our salvation lay in assuming the adult role in our transactions with other adults rather than continuing the inappropriate roles of child or parent. While fundamentally a continuation of Freud's formulation of the id, the superego, and the ego, Berne's approach avoids the cultural judgments inherent in Freud's view, opening new and potentially more productive approaches to therapy.

Our purpose here is not therapy but an understanding of the human situation, and for this we must recognize more than three roles. We all have a number of roles we have learned while growing up, most of them in the early years having to do with the family. As we grow older we experience more and more situations outside the context of the family, as well as observing these situations on television, in books, and from conversations. While it is likely that most of these new contexts are related to the family in order to be comprehended, the result is a multiplicity of roles understandable to each of us — to any individual. Most of these roles will be latent since the individual has not as yet had the opportunity or the need to enact them, but the understanding of the role is there.

Since these roles are, for the individual, truths about how humans act in particular situations as well as how they should act, they are best understood as sets of paradigms. What Berne was talking about was the truth about people as he understood it. His insight was that the truth changes. It changes about who we are and about who others are, in accordance with what we assume our role to be in a particular situation. Consequently, the roles of the others in that situation also change for us.

It would be a mistake to assume that a single situation allows only one role for each for the participants. Berne's point was that in any situation it was perfectly possible to assume a child's, an adult's, or a parent's role. Each different set of paradigms would result in different understandings, different actions, and different consequences. It would also be a mistake to believe that roles are completely separable. Most of us are only one person even if we know how to play many different roles, but multiple personalities in the same individual are not unknown.

The best way to visualize our situation is to use a prism as a metaphor. A prism, as you may remember from high school, will change a white light into the different colors of the spectrum. It is easy to see that the light on one side is a single color and also that the same light emerges from the prism on the other side as distinct and separate colored lights. What is not visible is what is going on in the prism. The prism metaphor as used here takes the concept of self (the ego) as the white light and the different roles we have as the colored lights. Schematically, it looks like the diagram on the next page:

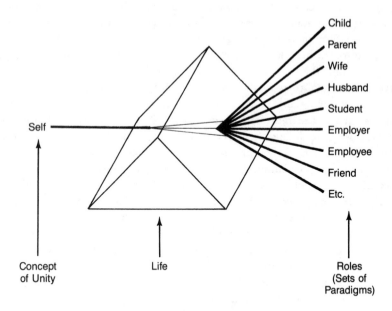

The Prismatic Metaphor

There is only one self/me but that me has multiple roles in life and therefore multiple understandings of what life is. Each role is made up of a number of consistent paradigms which define what is real and what is fantasy in that situation, what is relevant and what is irrelevant to functioning in it, and what relevant facts mean within the context of that particular role and situation.

It is very important to realize that there is no reason why paradigms should be consistent across roles. For example, the paradigms which define a father or mother are very unlikely to be consistent with those which define an employee or a student. It is much more reasonable to expect these paradigms to be contradictory or irrelevant to one another than to expect them to be consistent. An understanding of the implications of this situation is fundamental to our theme. Paradigms are basic to roles and need not be consistent across roles. When two or more roles are involved in a relationship and the paradigms involved are not consistent, paradigm stress is the result. (Another term which describes this situation is "cognitive dissonance.") The conscious reaction to paradigm stress is, very often, to "be logical." That is, in Berne's terms, to "be an adult." At least, this is what we are prone to tell the other person, even if we do not practice it ourselves. The problem with employing logic to solve paradigmatic problems is that it usually cannot do so. The reason is simple: logic is the systematic use of reason to discover the implications of two or more consistent assumptions. Logic alone cannot provide the assumptions, and paradigms are our assumptions about life in a particular role.

Platonic idealism holds that we can arrive at first principles through logic, but Aristotelian logic holds that we cannot. First principles are given; we assume them. The implications of these first principles can be proven (that is, logically derived) but not the principles themselves. When our paradigms are contradictory or contrary, as they usually are, we cannot logically prove one more correct or truer than another. At most we can ascertain that they are in fact contradictory, but this understanding hardly solves the problem. To choose one role as more important than another may help in deciding what to do but it does not resolve the problem. Relative importance in a particular situation does not deny the validity of the less important role, especially as this judgment may well change with time. In fact, unresolved paradigm conflict is the basic condition of human existence.

The normal responses to paradigm conflict are: to simply ignore it; to switch to another paradigm (or even to a completely different role) if the stress cannot be ignored; or to get angry, a tactic which usually results in the needed paradigm switch by converting the situation into a fight. In any good fight, of course, the reason for the fight can be forgotten.

When our knowledge of the truth places us in conflict with ourselves or others, we usually switch to another role and another set of truths. We don't resolve the conflict; we avoid it, at least for the time being. The reason is fairly simple. Our concept of ourselves (our egos) is essentially what we know to be true. To deny our paradigms is to deny ourselves. To lose faith in our knowledge of what is true about ourselves and others is not only to lose faith in ourselves but also to cease being ourselves. We are our paradigms. This explains why psychiatrists have had so little success in "curing" their patients. To "cure" a paradigm that has proved difficult or dangerous for the patient or for others is to change the patient's most fundamental concept of himself or herself. Once something this fundamental has been placed in doubt, upon what basis can we then accept another? While the sophists may have been logically correct, their cynicism leaves us no foundation for our lives. Small wonder that few people are capable of rejecting their own paradigms. To do so is to reject our very selves, while leaving us no logical or emotional reason to accept anything else.

A psychiatrist's general solution is to reaffirm the culture of which he or she is a part. Deviation from the shared paradigms of the culture is defined as "mental illness" and conformity with them as "sanity." Both patients and psychiatrists can see the logic in this and, since few individuals are nonconformist in all or even most of their roles, conformity is possible. (It should be recognized that some deviant paradigms are so at odds with physical reality that they are dangerous in any culture.)

Perhaps to define cultural deviance as insanity is rather hard on psychologists. What happens is that the patient is encouraged to see himself or herself in more "appropriate" roles rather than reject the paradigms themselves. To use Berne's example, there is nothing wrong with being either a child or a parent if you are in fact a child or a parent (or both), but these paradigms may be inappropriate to a relationship with another adult. The problem is that parent/child relationships abound among adults. To point them out may be a risky business but we are all familiar with them. Even at the more comprehensive level of emotional needs (child/id) and behavioral rules and regulations (parent/superego) it is dangerous to get involved in another person's contradictions in a direct and obvious way.

The more usual response to paradigm stress is to change roles. For instance, we have all had the unsettling experience of arguing with someone who constantly shifted the basis of the discussion, usually when his or her position was becoming untenable. While the shift is often between the "should" and the "is," it can involve a whole new subject and obviously different roles. The matter is not so much one of losing at logic as of a paradigm being threatened. Since a different role means a different set of paradigms the stress is avoided, but at the cost of confusion and an often nonspecific irritation for both parties.

The reason for the nonspecific nature of the irritation is that roles overlap. We are inside the prism, where roles are both different and the same. When another person shifts a role, we are seldom conscious of it, perhaps because we so often do the same ourselves. Moreover, there is a powerful tendency in all of us to immediately assume the complementary role. To use the obvious example, when someone assumes a parental role toward us, we have difficulty not responding as a child, even when such a response is negative for us.

A person who cannot easily move from one role to another is usually labeled a fanatic. Most of us will avoid him or her, for the tensions involved in judging all situations by the norms appropriate to a single role are very strong. Fanaticism is quite understandable as a reaction to paradigm stress. To settle into a single set of consistent paradigms, to play a single role in life, is a great relief. It also denies the richness of human experience: the appropriate responses to others in a world made up of a multitude of different roles and different situations. Most fanatics are consciously attempting to avoid hypocrisy, an inevitable and justifiable concern in a prismatic world. They usually descend into even deeper and more serious hypocrisy than the rest of us, however, for to play only one role in this life is both artificial and extremely difficult. Living seems to trip fanatics up, for while thought may be logical, living is prismatic.

In short, the human condition is one of unresolved paradigm conflicts. The conflicts are inevitable because of the different paradigms involved in different roles; the lack of resolution because a solution in terms of one paradigm (role) is a problem in terms of another. To simply give up all roles but one (fanaticism) does not seem to be either desirable or possible. We cannot escape our own inner contradictions and tensions through logic and rationality. Intelligence, if by this we mean the ability to apply logic to problems, is insufficient in itself because it cannot operate on more than one paradigm at a time. Change the paradigm and the results of logical deduction change. Knowledge is the result of the application of logic to particular problems but knowledge cannot deal with paradigm conflicts; for that we need wisdom.

Wisdom combines knowledge with the ability to judge rightly and to follow the soundest course of action. Knowledge is based upon only one paradigm at a time. Wisdom is the ability to balance and to choose correctly among a number of alternatives basing the choice upon understanding, experience, and knowledge. The alternatives themselves are functions of paradigms which cannot be rejected or materially changed.

The only final resolution of paradigm conflict is death. As long as human beings live they will have more than one role in life, and multiple roles make paradigm conflict inevitable.

Chapter 2

Prismatic Analysis and Social Science

The consequences of prismatic theory for concepts of human nature are severe. An exposition on human nature invariably expounds on one quality of human beings as universal, often relating this quality to other animals or to history. "Humans have a territorial instinct," "all people are self-interested," and "all males are aggressive" are such statements about human nature. From statements such as these theorists build concepts of human society which are logical, persuasive, and erroneous.

The problem, of course, is that human qualities are associated with roles. It is true that in some roles males are aggressive. Those roles define aggression as an appropriate or even required response to others. It is equally and simultaneously true, however, that other roles define cooperation as an appropriate and necessary response. If in some roles "all people are self-interested," for example, it is equally true that in cther roles they are unselfish and giving. No single-role theory of human nature is an adequate guide to behavior or understanding behavior in the long run, for it implies that all or most people not only are fanatics, but also that they can sustain their fanaticism without hypocrisy. To deny the humanity of mankind is unwise.

Probably most appeals to "human nature" are in fact devices to help overcome paradigm stress when they are not simply manipulations to overcome someone else's use of paradigms we choose (at the moment) not to recognize. "Ah, but it is human nature to compete" is an attempt to justify competition and, most probably, to deny the legitimacy of cooperation in a particular instance. To reply "Ah, but it is also human nature to cooperate" will lead to a discussion of the roles inherent in the situation under discussion when both the speakers are concerned with understanding, but to an argument about human nature if they are interested only in defending their own or another's actions.

The prismatic concept of the human condition has the same implications for sciences of human behavior. Kuhn[1] defines the scientific method as the systematic application of logic to problems formulated as hypotheses in attempts to disprove theories about reality. The more a theory cannot be disproved the more likely it is to be valid.

A science occurs when two or more scientists accept the same basic theories and can thus rely upon one another's results. The body of knowledge they build up is scientific knowledge. Scientists rely as a matter of course upon the honesty and dedication of other scientists to scientific method, since no science can progress very far if its practitioners are forced to repeat all the experiments upon which their own work is based.

One implication of Kuhn's view of science is that scientists can exist without a science: that is, any person can scientifically explore the implications of a particular theory even if no one else accepts that theory, but that until others do accept it and build upon one another's work a "science" as such cannot be said to exist. It is equally clear that the basic theories of a science operate on the level of paradigms. "Normal" science for Kuhn is puzzle-solving: working out the implications of a single set of consistent paradigms. Scientific revolutions occur when the paradigms of a particular field are changed. Conscientious scientists of the past were just as scientific as those of the present, and their results were equally valid. It is not "science" which has changed but rather the paradigms upon which it is based.

The reason the hard sciences are "hard" and the social sciences "soft" is that physical phenomena can be more easily separated and kept separate than can the different roles which are involved in human behavior. Paradigms about nonliving phenomena are more easily seen as noncontroversial. Moreover, nonhuman phenomena, and especially nonliving phenomena, are much the same across different cultures. An appeal to the reality of physical existence is less subject to violent dispute than an appeal to the reality of human nature.

It is probably accurate to say that physical scientists can conceive of themselves apart from their scientific paradigms, but that none of us can conceive of ourselves apart from our paradigms about people. The application of the scientific method to human behavior (and therefore to human relations) can never result in a science of human behavior because of the prismatic nature of the human condition. While it is possible to isolate a single role intellectually and to recognize the paradigms involved in that role, it is not possible for human beings to live only one role.

Moreover, since conditions inside the prism (that is, in life) are such that while roles are not the same they are not entirely different, either, it is a very chancy business to predict human behavior even in a single role. The result is that while scientific investigation of human behavior is both possible and (at times) rewarding, any social scientist's science of human behavior based on a few carefully chosen, noncontradictory roles will be attacked at its roots by other social scientists who recognize other roles as equally basic, important, and applicable.

Since paradigms are not consistent across roles, no behavioral science can be built up for two reasons. First, since people change roles frequently within any given situation in order to relieve paradigm stress (and often change back once the stress is gone), no theory based upon an understanding of a single role can adequately predict their behavior. Second, since scientists are as human as anyone else, they will in the main recognize the validity of multiple roles and therefore the validity of attacks upon any theory based solely upon the mutual acceptance of a single set of consistent paradigms. It follows that none of the social sciences will ever progress very far beyond the exposition of "new" paradigms as the basis for the future science.[2]

This limitation does seem to apply to social sciences today. It is usually explained away by an appeal to their recent invention (or discovery), but if prismatic theory is accurate they will never progress into hard sciences although they will always attract scientists. It would seem to be more productive to forgo the quest for a single global paradigm that underlies all human behavior, and therefore provides a solid foundation for a science of human behavior, and to recognize that human beings just aren't like that.

Human beings, because they have multiple and inconsistent paradigms, are not scientific. We are unscientific in our lives not because we are stupid, illogical, and passion-ridden but because the application of logic will not solve our problems. It will help us understand them more clearly, but it cannot remove us from a prismatic life. To know how we should act in one role does not invalidate the others, where equally valid logic dictates other and often contradictory actions. At worst, logic compels us to disregard all but one role so we can be consistent, integrated human beings. The problem is that other roles and their paradigms remain, even if they can be ignored for a time. They will reemerge sooner or later, and the problems we thought we had solved will probably be worse rather than better.

The attraction of a social science is easy to explain: it would relieve paradigm stress for all of us by providing impersonal, scientific solutions to societal problems from which we would prefer to be detached and uninvolved. Social science tends to be credible insofar as its results are consistent with our own paradigms. It is most acceptable when its subjects are distant from ourselves, for in that situation we can most easily accept its single-role assumptions. That any science of human behavior fundamentally misrepresents (and misunderstands) the human condition need not be noticed if we ourselves are distant from its application. Social engineering is a far more attractive concept when we ourselves are not the people being engineered.

At the same time, social science has made very positive contributions to our understanding of the human condition. Plato, very much a social scientist, is still read and discussed by anyone seriously interested in understanding human existence. Aristotle, too, speaks to us as a contemporary in the investigation of the limits and possibilities of differing societies. Dating the existence of social sciences from the last century or so, as is often done, is an act of ignorance as much as of arrogance. In every age the problems of cooperation and competition, peace and war, authority and liberty, have been the subjects of both speculation and action. To appeal for their solution to a higher and immutable law, whether that law is the law of Truth, of Religion, of Reason, or of Science, seems a very human and predictable action. Both the reason for and the basis of such appeals can be found in culture.

Culture

Culture is shared paradigms. It is clear that any particular family will have much the same paradigms about the same roles. (For this reason, a person contemplating marriage is always well advised to meet the other family; many of the latent roles of his or her intended spouse will be seen in living, vibrant color at home.) The larger culture exists because the same paradigms exist among a great many people not in the same family.

It is important to note that not all paradigms need be shared. Most cultures seem to have areas where people can disagree about what the truth is without placing themselves outside the society. At the same time, there are clearly some paradigms which must be both believed and acted upon if a culture is to endure.

Cultures, particularly national cultures, inculcate and maintain their fundamental paradigms with extraordinary vigor. School systems, for example, are more easily understood as mechanisms to inculcate paradigms than they are as purveyors of "knowledge." It is not unusual to find schools in this world which do not teach fundamental skills, but it is impossible to find one (or even to conceive of one) which does not inculcate the dominant paradigms of the culture of which it is a part.

It is important to note that what is being taught is paradigms rather than answers to problems. The school's "bad" children learn what is good and bad, what is true and not true quite as thoroughly as the "good" ones. A paradigm separates fact from fancy, defines which facts are relevant, and defines relationships among relevant facts. "Bad" actions and attitudes which are functions of the culture's shared paradigms are understandable, and will never directly result in cultural change even if the majority feels they are wrong.

The reason social sciences function as well as they do is that they are usually limited in their scope to a single culture. Since their subjects share the same paradigms as the investigators it is not surprising that surveys by social scientists find sufficient foundation for their theories to continue them.

Shared paradigms as the basis for social science have their problems, however. Perhaps most obviously, social science's theories will not travel well. What is valid for the United States does not quite do the job in England. By the time we get to non-Western cultures the theories and the results of their applications tend towards the ludicrous. They would indeed be funny if so much of our foreign policy were not justified by these theories. The "stages of development" and other theories of poverty and wealth, for example, are based upon paradigms which are not even particularly valid representations of historical reality in the United States. When we apply them to other cultures the results can be very damaging.

Even so, "truth" is the bedrock of daily living. Time and necessity define our limits, but paradigms define our understanding of life. As we have previously discussed, fanaticism (one role/paradigm) and multiple personalities (one for each role) are debilitating. They have the advantage of doing away with the need for integrating contrary or contradictory roles but for most people they are not satisfactory solutions to the problem. The reason is that human beings are social beings. Having been raised in families and having paradigms which are both products and fundamental determinants of family behavior, people need many different relationships with others. Our most fundamental satisfactions and frustrations most often occur in the context of organizations and involve our relations with others. This explains why the combination of fanaticism and the family (as in "the family of believers" Jim Jones created) can have such powerful and often catastrophic results.

The human condition is one of multiple roles which are neither separate nor the same, all based upon paradigms which define the truth differently. A culture is composed of shared paradigms about many roles. Paradigms define truth in single roles; cultures allow us to function together in multiple roles. While there is a certain amount of mismatch in roles and paradigms among people, the need for their mutual acceptance is obvious if the family and the larger culture are to exist. The strength of cultures is enormous, for they are based upon the deepest knowledge their members possess.

While it may be assumed that cultures are positive for human existence, it does not follow that their members are therefore happy and free of conflict. That paradigms are shared does not imply a positive harmony among those who share them. For example, male dominance/female subordination has for a long time been a paradigm of American culture. Arguing that it provides a basis for living capable of sustaining and perpetuating life is hardly the same as arguing that it makes people happy. It might even be argued that such a paradigm would ensure that marriage will be understood as constant and unremitting conflict if the culture also includes a paradigm which states that all respectable persons are masters of their own fate. Men might be happy in such a situation, but women could hardly be both married and self-respecting.

One obvious solution is to differentiate mightily between women's and men's roles in society, while at the same time making appeals to "human nature" as the basis for these roles. This solution for paradigm conflict states that each sex has different roles, different paradigms, and different truths; that what is true about men is not true about women and vice versa.

It is interesting that such solutions to paradigm conflict are most easily believed when they are most disassociated from physical reality. Men and women are not very different physically, reproductive organs being the only obvious differences. In everything else we are shockingly similar. It is our closeness to one another that leads us to emphasize the few differences. In fact, sexually determined dress, hair styles, movements, and mannerisms are all cultural derivatives from the paradigms of sex roles rather than the result of physical differences.

Paradigms about physical reality such as our understanding of "up" and "down" are constantly and inevitably tested against reality. Paradigms about people are different in that the paradigms create the behavior. No constant and inevitable checking with a physical constant like gravity is involved. In sex roles, where physical similarities could easily lead to paradigm stress, the similarities are disguised or denied while any differences (often totally irrelevant to the content of the role involved) are magnified. When physical reality is not consistent or is inadequate to support cultural paradigms it is denigrated, denied, and its descriptions altered to fit the paradigms. Cultural paradigms take priority over physical reality whenever that ranking is possible.

The general solution is simple: we do not compare our paradigms if we can avoid it. The primary method of dealing with contradictory paradigms is to ignore the contradiction; the most usual way to achieve this is to unconsciously switch to another role. Where this method is not possible or is perhaps too obvious (both to others and to ourselves) we will frequently seek and find others' agreement on the disputed paradigms. Paradigms of such physical phenomena as gravity rarely form the basis of conversations because there is very little need for verification of such a paradigm. We hardly need or look for support from others in our belief that we fall down rather than up.

With paradigms involving human beings, however, we generally need help because of the paradigm stress involved. Paradigms about sex roles, race, or nationalism, for example, seem to need a high level of support. Such support is easiest when the phenomena being discussed are not present. We have all been in single-sex groups in which a good deal of the time was spent discussing the other sex. Upon reflection, it will be apparent that most of this time was given to mutual support for shared paradigms. Given enough support from those around us, we can continue to hold paradigms that are in direct contradiction to physical reality.

A common case is the affirmation of paradigms which are widely shared by both sexes, causing behavior to conform to the paradigms. For example, despite the great successes of female athletes, a great many people still believe that females are less coordinated, weaker, and less able to perform physical tasks than males. Athletic achievements by women tend to be ignored or dismissed as having been achieved by "masculine" women. This reasoning is circular, but the motivation is not so much to denigrate the achievements as to preserve the paradigm of male superiority. That this paradigm is shared by a great many women is a distressing facet of American culture. Exercise for women has become popular for general health and weight reduction, for example, but centers for these activities must be labeled "salons" rather than "gymnasiums," and an almost universal concern of the participants is to avoid building muscles. Paradigms about women's physiques (not strong, don't sweat, thin is good, emaciated is even better, and the like) parallel sex roles and are very much a part of our culture. That they are untrue for the majority of women in the United States seems to be no obstacle to continued belief.

A good example of this sort of thing is the paradigm that women walk differently from men. This belief should be easily dispelled by simply watching men walk and comparing their movements with women's. The only perceivable differences are caused by high heels, which are more common on women than men. Men, however, do not commonly watch other men walk, while they do watch women. Men's movements are irrelevant (the second function of a paradigm) to most men, while women's are not. In fact, most men believe that women walk "the way they do" so that they will be attractive to men (the third function of the paradigm). Most men in our culture have fairly strong inhibitions against watching other men walk, a circumstance which tends to make men's movements more or less nonexistent (the first function of a paradigm). Clothes, too, are often designed to enhance a woman's movements and to minimize men's. All in all, the physical movements accompanying walking seem to have considerable paradigmatic meaning for us. This is all the more remarkable when we consider that these movements have no logical relation to any sex-related physical function.

Even with very strong paradigms such as the one just discussed, men and women still seem to both send and receive very ambiguous signals. Though a man may believe a woman is walking "that way" to be attractive to men, the question remains as to whether or not she is walking that way to attract him in particular. The clothes she has on, or almost on, may be provocative, but does she want him or anyone else to act on that provocation? Women, of course, have the same problems. Is he really interested in me or is he being macho? Is it I or my image he wants, and do I see him or the image he wants to project? Such questions are normal everywhere, but in a culture full of strangers they become both more important and more difficult to answer.

If we lived in a world of single roles, or even of one role at a time, such questions would never be asked. As it is, we all have multiple roles and respond to multiple cues. Shared paradigms may keep us together and allow our society to continue, but they do not protect us from paradigm stress, since a solution in terms of one paradigm is a greater or lesser problem in terms of the others.

The Human Condition

The human condition, therefore, is one of multiple shared paradigms developed through having been raised in a particular family in a particular culture. Though we share our paradigms, each person is different from every other because the circumstances in which they were raised are unique to each. That is, the understanding of paradigms is shared and remarkably stable, but the prismatic nature of our existence ensures that personal priorities among paradigms and the roles available to us within paradigms will be different for each of us.

There is only one of each of us, and each one of us has multiple paradigms. We do not live outside the prism, where all roles are distinct and separate, but inside it, where our roles can constantly change because they overlap and because the combinations of roles involved are also changing.

Appeals to "human nature" are generally attempts to lessen paradigm stress by defining appropriate behavior in a single major role. As such they confuse as much as they clarify, and they generally serve simply to justify the choice of one role over another rather than to heighten our understanding of the human condition. Human nature is prismatic, but while this idea may increase our understanding, by itself it provides no sure guide for action since it gives no reason to choose one paradigm over another.

The ancient and honorable problem of whether humans have free will and can choose for themselves what to do (voluntarism) or whether their actions are determined by factors over which they have no control (determinism) takes on new meaning in a prismatic analysis. We do not choose our paradigms. By the time we become conscious of having them (if ever) they have become our own definition of ourselves, and the possibility of our changing them is very slight. We can and do choose among them, however, and in this sense we are more or less free to choose. The best way to manipulate someone is to maneuver him or her into a role in which the associated paradigms will ensure actions or attitudes which we desire. In this sense we can determine another person's actions, and they can determine ours.

We need not accept the role assigned us, however, especially if we are aware of what is being done. Once we are in a role, our own paradigms will cause us to act in a predictable way, but if we refuse to enter the role we can certainly be said to have free will. On the other hand, some roles are so powerful and the motivations for accepting them so strong that only very unusual people can resist the pressures. People are both determined and voluntaristic. Neither factor is total, and a large part of wisdom is knowing the difference.

Some conditions seem common to all humans, and many are not as open-ended as those we have discussed. Physical limitations, for instance, are constant and do not depend upon culture or the prismatic nature of human existence. The picture of sea gulls captioned "They fly because they think they can" is in error. Sea gulls fly because they are birds. Humans have invented machines which fly and can carry humans, but we cannot fly by ourselves and never will.

Such limitations are so basic that they do not help us a great deal in understanding the differences in human behavior, but they do provide a solid foundation for such efforts. Maslow,[3] for example, has constructed a hierarchy of human motivations which assumes that people must first satisfy basic physiological needs before they can satisfy other needs. Such an approach does not seek to establish relative moral value but simply realizes that some needs are logically prior to others. That is, eating may be a "low" value and self-actualization a "high" one, but if life is to continue, eating is primary. From this assumption Maslow constructs the following hierarchy:

Self-actualization
Self-esteem
Belongingness and love
Safety and security
Basic physiological needs

Each lower need takes priority over the one above it for most people, according to Maslow. Because of this we have a way of predicting which roles will take precedence when differing situations stress one or the other. At the extremes, self-actualization (the desire to become more and more what one is, to become everything one is capable of becoming; that is, independence, self-acceptance, spontaneity, a sense of purpose) will be less important to most people than the need to satisfy basic physiological needs. While some people will not follow Maslow's order, it is reasonable to assume that most people will follow it most of the time. Revolutionary or patriotic commitments during a war, for example, may cause temporary inversions in the higher levels, but in the long run people will tend to give priority to staying alive. If they did not, the human race could hardly have survived as long as it has.

Security in basic physiological needs is clearly next. We not only want to eat today, we also want to be reasonably sure we will eat tomorrow. This is more or less the case for all physiological needs as they are more or less capable of being deferred. For example, food is more important than sex because eating cannot be deferred for very long before starvation begins. Water, by this criterion, is more immediate than either: we will die of thirst before we will starve to death. The situation is still prismatic, however, since none of our needs disappears or is invalid simply because others might be more pressing. Even hungry and thirsty people may dream of sex, although starving people who are also dying of thirst will probably not do so very often. Once we have attained some security in food and drink we find our other needs still there, still valid, and still important.

Most Americans share a paradigm which states that there will always be sufficient food and drink, not only for ourselves but for all Americans. Since this is simply "true" we do not spend any time worrying about it. Whether this inattention is fortunate or unfortunate is an interesting question. Starvation and hunger unquestionably exist in the United States, and if Americans had a more realistic paradigm about food we might take better care of the land and the people. On the other hand, if we did so we might be less concerned with "becoming everything that one is capable of becoming," which would be a pity.

In any case, once basic physiological needs are met Maslow's hierarchy of needs is helpful but not definitive. Different roles are present in all situations, and we all act to fulfill a good many different needs at the same time. Even so, it is probable that security and safety will be factors in a good many roles and will form a part of paradigms which might not at first seem to be concerned with them.

One of our foremost security needs seems to be to ensure the safety of our own paradigms. Since we are our paradigms, ensuring their safety amounts to maintaining our own integrity. Whether our paradigms are negative or positive for ourselves or others, they are the basis and content of our own personalities, and we will defend them. The defense mechanisms mentioned earlier (willful ignorance, denial, and anger) seem fairly standard, and are easily detectable once we become aware of them.

Family Paradigms

While Maslow's hierarchy of needs, and especially its emphasis upon safety and security, is helpful in analyzing prismatic situations other approaches are also productive. A family, for example, is the fundamental and almost universal condition of the early years of human existence. Assuming this, we can derive from it some general paradigms that are likely to be shared to some degree by all people regardless of the particular culture involved.

The first of these paradigms is hierarchy itself. Equality is not a relevant concept in the day to day interaction of infants and their parents, a fact so obvious it is often ignored. To assume or to attempt equality would surely lead to the death of the infant, and it is important to note that in this case hierarchy does not necessarily imply value: infants are usually treasured, parents often making great sacrifices in the infant's interest. They may be lesser in terms of strength, experience, power, wealth, or any of the other factors which can separate people, but they are no less valuable for that. Neither do we value them either solely or mainly for their potential to acquire these attributes. We value them for themselves.

Even so, we accept their position at the bottom of a hierarchy in which we as parents occupy the top position. And though we accept the hierarchy as legitimate the worth of the infant is not generally denigrated by his or her low place in it. The legitimacy does not mean that the parents are "better" than the infant but that there is an order in the family which is necessary if life is to continue past the present generation. The basis for the legitimacy is not logic and rational thought but instead the physiological capabilities and needs of infants. It is simply the way things are.

"The way things are," though, is usually a description of a culture rather than physiological necessity. Parents do not arrive at parenthood with no knowledge of how children are treated in a family: they were children themselves at one time. In learning their roles as children they simultaneously learned the roles of parents, husbands, wives, sisters, brothers, and, most probably, of uncles, aunts, grandparents, and all the other members of a family. True, these roles were learned only within the context of the family, but within that context they were learned so well that they are all latent within each of us. It would be most unusual for any person to play all the roles he or she has learned. Males do not usually become wives, for example, even if they become househusbands, but for better or for worse they know the role of a wife and will expect wives to live it even if for them that role is negative and destructive.

The wife's place in the family hierarchy is learned in her childhood. To change it as an adult is very difficult for both parents, especially if they were raised in similar families. Most people are surprised at their difficulties in being the perfect wife or husband. They should not be. Latent paradigms become actual with marriage, and usually prove to be far stronger than the dreams which preceded them. We all tend to recreate our parents' marriage because that is what we understand marriage to be. Anything else is fantasy and dreams.

Put another way, tradition (which is also called socialization) is what gives legitimacy to most human relations. Physical coercion is a poor substitute for legitimacy and, as Aristotle pointed out, often defeats the purposes for which it is used. The assumption that legitimacy can be achieved through appeals to logic and reason is accurate only when roles can be kept more or less separate and the persons involved believe in reason as a legitimate foundation for action. Reason as a source of legitimacy will be discussed later, but it is obvious that it cannot be considered persuasive for children who cannot as yet talk, and it is highly unlikely that it will be a major influence for some time after that. "The way things are" must be the world of the child.

The family, then, is founded upon tradition and hierarchy. Both of these elements can be challenged (it may even become traditional to believe in reason as the basis for living, and equality as a natural state) but it is very unlikely that such challenges will be successful. The physiological nature of human infants and the consequent need for families is primary in all societies. There are no signs of the family's disappearance despite sporadic attempts over the centuries (of which Plato's Republic was one) to replace it with other institutions.

It is also clear that in most societies in this world, and especially in the economically poorer ones, the family is the basic unit of society. Individualism is a luxury most poor people cannot afford. Most families function as corporate groups with a collectivist concept of wealth and well being: the good of the entire family is fundamental, and the particular persons within it see themselves as defined primarily through their membership in the family. Even in highly individualized societies such as the United States the world of small children is that of the family. To a child of three or four all adults are somebody's mommy or daddy. Within the family vertical integration (hierarchy) and cooperation are normal, while its economy can be adequately described as managed for the welfare of all its members. The parents clearly do the managing, often after some sort of consultation with their children on goals and methods. In many parts of the world this system functions in the extended family as well as in the nuclear family.

To sum up, a family is based upon tradition, is organized hierarchically, and is run through vertical integration and cooperation for the benefit of all its members. Given the kaleidoscopic nature of prismatic society, it is logical to assume that there will always be variations and attempts at change, but the physiological necessities of human infants argue that the family as described here is necessary if humans are to continue to survive.

Chapter 3

Societies and Cultures

To argue that all families, over the course of time, will tend to have the same basic structure and function is not the same as arguing that all societies will be similar. If we define a society as all those people who interact in any way, we are obviously talking about an entity capable of enormous variations. From island societies with no contact of any sort with anyone else, to world societies where both things and people are in constant circulation, the range takes in a tremendous number of possible forms, interactions, and complications.

Perhaps the best place to start is with the size of the society itself. Both historically and archaeologically there is considerable evidence that size has been important in the options available to groups of people. While larger numbers of people allow for greater divisions of labor and the increased knowledge that specialization can produce, larger societies also have problems that smaller societies do not. Generally speaking, the problems inherent in separating roles in a society are much the same as those in individuals. When individuals attempt to separate roles too much their personalities tend to fall apart. The strain of being a different person in each role is too much. When societies separate roles they too tend to fall apart. In both cases the good of the whole becomes increasingly more difficult to even define, let alone to achieve, as the constituent parts become more distinct and different. Many writers have argued that the best size for a society is around 50,000 to 100,000 people, and that all societies ought to be fundamentally self-sufficient. Whether this entity is labeled a city-state or an ecological unit, the reasoning is the same: in order to remain a distinct society the community must exist primarily on resources it controls. Otherwise it will be a part of a larger society, unable to maintain itself.

It is clear that smaller societies throughout history have managed to survive and prosper without extensive government. Governments, in fact, may be seen as inventions designed to maintain societies when numbers have grown to such an extent that without some form of separate governmental structure they would fall apart, because the view of and concern for the whole society will be meaningless for the average member. If this is so, patriotism (a commitment to the whole society and a positive concern for it) is more understandable as an invention of the government than the other way around.

Before considering questions such as this, however, we should consider small societies. Being small, they will probably be well integrated; the paradigms about society and the place of the individual within it will be shared by all its members. It will be obvious to all of them who and what they are. Their paradigms will most likely be those of the family. Beyond the family itself, there will be little need for extensive or separate governmental structures, since traditions (the shared paradigms) will be binding on all. Given the close and continued contact of all the society members, peer pressure as well as individually held paradigms will hold things together. These are anarchist communities.

Since there are no strangers in these communities, there is no need for paradigms governing relations between strangers. Values such as honesty, for example, are almost irrelevant in small societies where everyone not only knows what everyone else is doing but has to go on living with them. These values are paramount in larger societies where anonymity and strangers are common. Members of large societies find it difficult to conceive of a cooperative and productive life without a separate structure to hold society together.

Small societies, often as small as a hundred or less, see no need for these structures. Consequently, there is a curious inversion of values in them from the point of view of members of large societies, who often find government a coercive force that constrains the actions of individuals more than allowing for them. A lack of government is seen as both desirable and terrifying, in that the alternative would seem to be freedom for chaos and violence as well as freedom to create and expand. In anarchistic cultures, however, traditions rule rather than government. The cohesive and authoritative elements of life are not laws passed by a legislature but traditions which are not seen by the members of the anarchistic culture as limiting so much as defining. The shared paradigms of the society are so strong that anyone who seriously defies them places himself or herself outside society. Anarchist communities have historically not killed or imprisoned those who act against their traditions; they have exiled them, a fate that in the eyes of the community is at least equal to the former punishments.

Many Indian communities in North America are (or were) good examples of anarchism. They were usually small, often fewer than 500 people, and culturally very stable. Tradition, custom, and a tremendous sense of self characterized the differing tribes, and while warfare between tribes was common, violence within a tribe was very rare. "Chiefs" were chosen for specific purposes, and the chief's authority was dependent upon its voluntary acceptance by the members of the tribe. The people were highly integrated, not only among themselves but with the world in which they lived. They generally considered themselves members of a community that consisted of all the beings in it, whether those beings were animate or inanimate. Self-sufficiency was a condition of life for small tribes, and the reliance upon immediate others led to a heightened sense of the dependencies involved.

The European, upon contacting these tribes, often asked "Who's in charge here?" The question had no answer, since no single person was in charge. The shared paradigms of the society itself were "in charge," but since they were shared by all they were not perceived as onerous or as imposed from without. Custom and tradition required that each male child should have a vision which would define him as an adult, and to which he should be true all his life. Since the elders of the tribe assisted in interpreting the visions, tradition, custom, and individuality were integrated. It is interesting that by European standards these societies were almost excessively individualistic, largely because Europeans tended to overlook the power of tradition to govern conduct.

The bases of the continued existence of these societies were manageable size and self-sufficiency. American Indians rarely functioned together in large numbers. When special circumstances were involved, large joint efforts could occur but the necessity for self-sufficiency in a hunting and gathering society quickly broke them up again. Settled agriculture, of course, would have produced enough food for large groups to solidify, but the larger groups would have resulted in profound changes in culture. It is clear that many Indians, at least in the Eastern and Mid-Western areas of North America, were hunters and gatherers by choice rather than by necessity. Given the culture, existence in small bands was positive rather than negative, and the total population size was hardly large enough relative to available resources to drive them to agriculture.

Where the physical conditions were different, cultures more similar to our own developed. In Mexico, Guatemala, and the Andes, scarce resources, fixed boundaries, and large populations led to large societies based upon agriculture. Game is scarce in these areas, and tropical diseases confine most people to the highlands. Very early corn and potatoes were invented through selective breeding, and governments through sheer necessity. Large societies with all the basic paradigms of contemporary large societies were developed. The culture of these peoples was radically different from those of the anarchist cultures to the North, South, and East, where smaller groups were not faced with the necessity of holding together people who did not know each other. It is interesting to note, in this context, that empire (the domination and control of other peoples) is consistent with the principles of large societies but not with those of anarchist societies. Both the Aztecs and the Incas were imperialistic. The Mayans were quite as advanced in every area but do not seem to have developed a coercive empire, so while empire was possible and consistent with the paradigms of these large societies it does not seem to have been necessary.

Cultures of Large Societies

In the rest of this work we will be concerned with the different cultures which are common to large societies. While anarchism has both negative and positive aspects (a very rigid culture combined with great personal freedom within that culture, for example), it is not usually capable of existing in large societies. With the technology of communication and transportation that exists today, and that shows every sign of becoming both more available and more intrusive everywhere in the world tomorrow, it is unlikely that small societies will be able to continue in existence without taking on at least some of the attributes of the large societies around them. Attempts to recreate these communities (such as those which occurred on the West Coast during the 1970s) generally either break up or evolve into communities with governments, police, and most of the other attributes of large cultures.

An exception to this rule would be the Amish communities of Pennsylvania and Ohio. These communities have managed to maintain solid anarchist values through a policy of self-sufficiency in both material and spiritual spheres. Seen in this light, their use of horses and other early technology is not a result of their rejection of contemporary technology but their rejection of a dependence upon the society which produces it. If the Amish were to use the "advanced" technology of American farming they would quickly become dominated by the banks, repair and parts systems and other aspects of the larger society, and lose the sovereignty necessary to the continuation of their culture.

The popular conception of anarchism as chaos, savagery, and criminality is consistent with what happens in a large society when government breaks down. Different sorts of cultures have evolved in large societies, all of them with governments that prevent anarchy. We will discuss seven of them (Tory Corporatism, Oligarchy, Classical Liberalism, Radical Liberalism, Democratic Socialism, Leninist Socialism, and Fascist Corporatism) as if each was produced from the one described before it. While they are easier to understand and to explain with this procedure, it is probably not the case that such an evolution actually took place. It is much more sensible to assume that all seven have existed for as long as people have existed in large groups, but that in different ages different cultures have dominated.

Since cultures are made up of paradigms, it is not surprising that historians of each culture have not only assumed that their paradigms defined "civilization," but have also written or rewritten the histories of other ages and other cultures as if that were the case. Indeed, if they did not do so they would be rejected by their colleagues and misunderstood by their other readers, if any. Even so, a reader sensitive to all of the cultures usually has no trouble identifying groups and individuals in these histories who clearly held other paradigms than those of the dominant culture. When autobiographies, journals, diaries, and other primary sources are read, the clash of paradigms is even more obvious.

It is a fundamental assumption of this work that large societies are prismatic, not only because their dominant paradigms tend to contradict one another (as they do in individuals) but also because within large societies there are always subgroups or individuals who believe in cultures other than the one (or ones) that tend to dominate society. Their presence is usually unacknowledged or seen as subversive by those who dominate. It is the old problem of heresy, expressed in the United States as being "un-American." The assumption is the same: that those whose paradigms are different believe in things which are not true. At best they are foolish: at worst they are actively evil and should be suppressed.

In analyzing different cultures, both dominant and nondominant, we will use six concepts to help structure our thinking: legitimacy, organization, basic units, concept of society, government, and economics. These are hardly all that we could use, but six is a manageable number and the concepts broad enough to cover most of society.

Legitimacy: Tradition, Rationality, and Charisma

It is interesting that in dictionaries the primary definition of "legitimate" has to do with the family. A child is legitimate, of course, when his or her mother and father were married at the time the child was born. Put another way, legitimacy has to do with being publicly accepted and acceptable as a member of a particular family within a particular culture. Only a secondary definition refers to political legitimacy, and even that usually contains references to monarchs and the principle of legitimacy through birth. Indeed, by the time we get to "legitimate" as "in accordance with law and custom" we have been reduced to the third or fourth definition of the term. The family aspect still seems primary, even in this American age of the nuclear family, which a good many people feel is itself only a crumbling relic of the past.

It is not a relic, of course, and never will be. As Robert Frost's Mary said, "Home is the place where, when you have to go there, they have to take you in." In other words, you belong there. What interests us is why. One answer is "because." Because you were born there, and even more (much more) because you were raised there. The family's paradigms are your paradigms. No matter how pleasant or unpleasant it is, in a very real sense they are you and you are them. What holds you together and perhaps simultaneously keeps you apart is the family culture of shared paradigms.

"Legitimacy" in a large society refers to the noncoerced acceptance of government as authoritative. That is, people obey the government because they know they should, not because they are forced to. Since all governments of large societies use coercion to some extent, the question of legitimacy is not so much whether a particular regime is legitimate or not but rather how much legitimacy it has. That is, how many people in the society governed by that regime accept it as authoritative without coercion, and how many do not? Large societies inevitably contain people who do not accept their norms, customs, and laws. Small cultures easily spot such people in the rare instances when they occur and expel them if they refuse to conform. Because constant personal interaction among all the people in a big society is neither necessary nor possible, dissenters are both less easily identified and produced in larger numbers.

Since this is the case, some basis for the coercion of these people must be found. The simplest is to condemn them because their behavior or thinking is different. That is, because they are not in accordance with tradition and custom or, in our terms, with the shared paradigms of the dominant culture. We should distinguish here between behavior or thinking that is in accordance with the shared paradigms of the culture but considered wrong, and behavior or thinking that is not in accordance with the culture. The former is considered criminal and the latter treasonous. Criminal behavior, no matter how much it is deplored, will not change a culture and in large societies is accepted as inevitable. Public authorities seek to control it rather than to eradicate it, and criminal groups are often an accepted element of society. Treason and subversion, on the other hand, are far more serious matters to the authorities, for they imperil the legitimacy of the regime.

Even so, if criminal behavior is present to such an extent that citizens lose all sense of security, the government will lose legitimacy, for in large societies one of the functions of government is to keep respectable citizens reasonably safe from criminals. Governmental coercion is quite acceptable as long as it is mostly practiced on the "nonrespectable" members of society; that is, upon the poor and powerless.

It is doubtful that any regime can sustain itself in the long run through coercion alone, although there is an interesting twist to this situation. A regime which can sustain itself over enough time will gain legitimacy through the simple fact that coercion itself will have become a tradition and custom of the culture. Once people have been born and raised under a particular regime it will tend to be accepted because "that's the way things are."

There are limits, however, to what people can accept. Any regime which cannot provide or allow for most people's basic physical needs is skating on very thin ice, as is one which cannot provide at least minimal security in these needs. Regimes seeking legitimacy trade security for acceptance. If they cannot do this, they will generally fall. If they can provide security for everyone who accepts their authority, they will be very strong. As new regimes gain legitimacy they will use coercion less, generally reserving it for the treasonous and, to a lesser extent, for the criminal.

Treason, defined as nonacceptance of the regime, is a constant preoccupation with revolutionary regimes. These regimes exist for the purpose of changing the paradigms of the culture; of inculcating new beliefs about the truth of human existence among the people who live in that society. The question for everyone involved is this: Upon what basis should I accept these new truths? Revolutionary leaders obviously cannot expect the culture itself to provide for the acceptance of their ideas, even if (interestingly enough) some cultures with a great deal of experience with coercive regimes tend to grant legitimacy to the revolutionaries themselves. Their problem, in this case, is how to convert their legitimacy as leaders into legitimacy for their ideas.

In the long run, the answer is time itself. If the revolutionaries can impose a new system over a generation, younger people will accept it as traditional. Their paradigms will have been formed in the new culture, and it will be fundamental to their own self image.

It is hardly coincidence that every revolutionary regime that deserves the name has placed great emphasis upon the family. Some have attempted to abolish it, others to control and influence it, but none have been indifferent to it or could afford to be. The family is the primary organization both for sustaining the life of infants and for providing them with the paradigms which will define them. It is by definition a profoundly traditional institution.

The basis for changing the paradigms of adults can hardly be tradition, the basis for the paradigms they already have. Coercion, while it may be used to produce conformity of actions, can hardly in itself be the source of new ideas. Generally speaking, the source of new ideas is to be found in old paradigms that are applied to other roles than the ones with which they were originally associated. The method is rationality. As we have already noted, living both separates and mixes up our roles, but people generally find their personal integrity to be best maintained by keeping roles and their paradigms separate and distinct. Because of the overlapping of roles this behavior tends to be "irrational," a situation most of us cope with by ignoring our own contradictions. When we choose not to ignore them, or are forced to recognize them by others or by circumstance, we will often be "rational." That is, we will follow the logical consequences of a single set of consistent paradigms eve.. if the result is the denial of other paradigms we also believe.

The result is revolutionary thinking, justified in the name of rationality. Things have not changed much since Plato's time, when he based his revolutionary republic upon reason, pure and simple. A paradigmatic analysis reveals that his "new" republic was based upon the rule of a leader who denied the legitimacy of any political input from non-leaders, and that the basis of the new republic was to be reason rather than tradition. Plato had his chance to produce. The king of Syracuse admired Plato greatly, and asked him to convert the kingdom of Syracuse into the new society. The result was a resounding failure. Plato had assumed that his new culture would be accepted because he found it reasonable. It was not accepted.

The problem with reason as the basis for revolutionary change is that any society is prismatic. For the same reason that the scientific study of people will never result in a social science, revolutionary ideology will never result in a wholly new society. The more dogmatic and logical the revolution, the more difficult it is for ordinary nonfanatical human beings to integrate it into their lives. While the people who actually make the revolution are quite likely to be fanatics, particularly if the struggle is a bloody one, fanaticism cannot be the basis for the new society. Those revolutionaries who depend upon widespread fanaticism to create the new society either fail completely or find the results of their revolution very different from those they desired.

The longer the revolutionary struggle, the more likely its leaders will recognize the prismatic nature of human beings as inevitable, and evolve doctrines which will allow for it. Mao, for example, was a member of a revolutionary group that had endured twenty-five years of civil war before gaining control of China. During this time he had extensive experience with government in circumstances where losing the support of the people meant betrayal and death. It is hardly surprising that Mao evolved a revolutionary ideology that accepted contradiction in the revolution and in the future society as both inevitable and potentially productive.

Relatively short revolutions which are either bloodless or in which the violence does not lapse into widespread civil war also seem to allow for revolutionary regimes willing to accept logical contradiction and prismatic situations as legitimate within the new society. The worst situation seems to be a relatively short but widespread and bloody civil war which hardens the fanaticism of both leaders and followers without giving them either the experience or necessity for modifying their fanaticism. The collapse of the old regime in these circumstances leaves the winners with a great deal of experience in war and conquering but very little in governing, a very dangerous combination for everybody.

In any case, the basis for the new regime will be rationality insofar as it is revolutionary. If we are correct in our assessment of the human condition, such a basis will be neither complete nor lasting. By the time the revolutionary generation is gone the "new" society will have as its basis tradition and custom, just as the old society did. Revolutionary leaders have at most fifteen or twenty years to change the paradigms of the people, and probably far fewer. If they are wise, they limit their changes to those areas of life they consider most important, giving continued and obvious support to traditional paradigms in other areas (and in particular to those which are the bases for their own ideas) and by doing so contribute to their own legitimacy.

One further source of legitimacy should be discussed. "Charisma" has become not only a common attribute of popular people but the darling of political scientists, who are otherwise at a loss to explain the success of leaders who deny paradigms the academics accept as the truth. In these contexts it is little more than a slur upon the credulity (or bad taste) of the masses or a tribute to the personal magnetism of the hero of the hour.

The term was originally a religious one but it is now generally understood to mean a quality of leadership which captures the imagination and allegiance of the people, a definition easily connected with popularity.

It is much more than simple popularity. Charismatic leadership and followership occur when conditions in a society are so chaotic or unusual that the shared paradigms of the culture no longer provide accurate guides to behavior and understanding. In some degree this situation is always present but usually our paradigms, particularly those we share with others, are adequate both for day to day living and for understanding ourselves and our society. When society breaks down to such an extent that this is no longer the case (as it did in Germany between the two World Wars) people have lost the very foundation of their lives, that is, their faith in their own paradigms. In such times people have to believe in something and it will often be a person. If we no longer believe in our paradigms, we no longer believe in ourselves either. Some people commit suicide when this occurs; a good many more escape to alcohol and drugs, particularly if the majority have not lost their faith in their own values. When paradigms are widely and openly doubted, however, mass movements frequently occur.

The fundamental requirement for a leader of such a movement is complete and utter belief in himself or herself. If we have been forced to reject our own paradigms there is a terrible attraction to a person who not only has not lost his or her own faith but who believes totally and obviously in his or her own paradigms. We must believe in something or we have no basis for living. Through our faith in the charismatic person we more or less borrow the paradigms we need to make sense of the world and our place in it. Quite naturally, we usually get it a little wrong, simplifying it too much and distorting some of the meaning. The important thing, though, is that we can believe in ourselves again, and can therefore go on living with ourselves.

Charismatic movements are as much a matter of charismatic followership as of any quality in the leader. If the fundamental paradigms of a culture remain undoubted, there will be no charismatic movement no matter how available and visible the charismatic leader.

The nature of a charismatic movement seems to be a function of the amount of time the basic cultural paradigms have been called into question. If the crisis is relatively short and can be attributed to forces outside the culture, a clarion call to the "historic" values of the culture is most likely. That these values are mythological rather than historical is of little consequence. They serve to reaffirm the faith of the people in themselves and to attribute the crisis not to any problem in the culture but to alien forces that can be identified and opposed while national values once again become strong and believable.

If the crisis continues past the first charismatic movement, however, such appeals to the very culture that is being questioned become less and less believable with the ineffectiveness of each new movement. In this situation a truly revolutionary movement is possible. If it is based upon at least some of the basic paradigms of the culture it will be more likely to effect a permanent change, but almost anyone with a fervent faith in himself or herself will find a following. Legitimacy, at least for the moment, is to be found in people with deeply held paradigms when the majority of people have come to doubt their own.

Organizations of Cultures: Hierarchy and Equality

Any society is organized upon both hierarchical and egalitarian principles. Although these concepts are opposites, the prismatic nature of the human situation allows for their combination despite the resulting confusion and contradiction. Consciously, however, one or the other is usually dominant and held to underlie all aspects of society. Such a position greatly simplifies thinking about society. "Hierarchy" refers to organizing things or people from higher to lower. Rank, grade, and class are concepts that are based upon hierarchy. In a hierarchy equal things or equal people are equal in that they have the same rank or grade in a hierarchy. A statement such as "all men are created equal" is different. Here hierarchy is simply not applicable to the creation of men.

It is obvious that hierarchy is consistent with the family as we have described it. In fact, it is one of the family's basic characteristics, since infants and parents are unequal in almost all their functions. By extension, we can expect to find hierarchy in the larger society and to see it legitimated by paradigms rooted in family life. Absolute equality in this case will be limited to spiritual value. That is, all members of the family are believed to be equally important as particular persons, even if they are unequal in every other way. It is interesting that anarchistic cultures emphasize the differences among their members far more than their "equality." When everyone is known and tradition rules, there is no need for the concept of absolute equality to ensure either rights or responsibilities. Each person can be seen as a particular case within the context of an unquestioned system of rights and responsibilities. American Indians, for example, seemed excessively individualistic to Europeans, who had difficulty understanding the principles of anarchistic societies. For members of large societies, law, order, and discipline are necessary to hold together groups of people who are not committed to one another through the culture. In anarchistic societies such commitment is normal, necessary, and automatic. Given that commitment, "equality under the law" is an irrelevant concept, both because there is no law and because every person is known, and therefore obviously different from everyone else. "Equality," in fact, is perhaps best understood as a concept for thinking about strangers.

Hierarchy, on the other hand, is a concept which may apply equally well to strangers and to people we know well. Whenever we think of "better" and "worse," of "more" and "less," of "higher" and "lower," we are thinking of hierarchical concepts.

Although we can distinguish among a great many hierarchical and egalitarian roles, we will concentrate on a few. In hierarchy we shall emphasize those roles based upon birth and those based upon merit. The difference is clearly related to the differences between tradition and rationality. Indeed, those cultures that claim to be thoroughly rational have a difficult time dealing with hierarchies based upon birth. Usually they end by simply living with at least a limited amount of inherited status in their society, coping with it by ignoring it when possible and denying its importance when it cannot be ignored. Traditional cultures usually do the same thing about merit when the same contradictions become very obvious. In a general way, traditional cultures find room for merit and rational cultures tolerate inherited status, despite the contradictions involved.

Basic Units of Cultures: Corporate Groups and Individuals

Cultures vary in their assumptions about the basic unit involved in living, and therefore about the unit which is the proper concern of the government. Both individuals and the family are units of society, and we will differentiate cultures along these lines.

An individual person would seem to be very basic. While it is possible and quite normal in some cultures to see people in terms of only one role at a time (thus more or less dividing the person), the focus is still on the individual. Interestingly enough, people from cultures which feel the family is the basic unit usually feel role separation is illegitimate: each person should be seen as a whole, whether he or she is an employee, an employer, a friend, or simply someone you meet in the street. The first effort made in a new relationship in these cultures is usually to find out something about the new person's family.

Individualistic cultures see people as unconnected with others and therefore free to take any role they choose or in which the situation places them. "Familial" cultures, on the other hand, see each person as meaningful only within the context of a larger corporate group, primarily the family. Since a large society often has many corporate groups in addition to families, we shall speak of corporate and individualistic cultures, depending upon whether members of those cultures consider corporate groups or individuals more basic to society.

Within a corporate culture, the association of persons occurs within the corporate group itself and is governed by whatever standards of behavior are practiced within that group. Individualistic cultures are presented with a grave difficulty in this area: what standards of behavior will govern their relations? Since individualists hold a corporate group to be illegitimate, accepting group standards for behavior is also illegitimate. On the other hand, it is clear that some mutually acceptable standards are necessary if any other than individual action is to occur.

The general solution found in individualistic cultures is that of free association: the individual accepts the association's standards for behavior with the proviso that he or she may quit the association at any time. The source of the standards themselves may be those of the association as it is (tradition) or they may be created by its members, presumably on rational grounds.

While corporatists experience no paradigm stress simply from being in a group (indeed, their stress occurs when they are not in a group), an individualist will clearly be in a conflict situation: in order to achieve individual goals cooperation is necessary, but cooperation entails limitation on individuality. Any solution involves role separation, and the basic contradiction will remain. Moreover, the fundamental principle of free association — that any member may quit the group at any time — may prove impossible and will often involve some sort of negative result. The first of these may well be the sacrifice of the results expected and hoped for when the individual joined or helped create the group.

The question of correct and legitimate relations among people is a fundamental one. It will be answered differently by corporatists and individuals. In doing so, they will be expressing their concept of themselves.

Concepts of Cultures: Cooperation and Competition

Cultures vary in how they conceive of proper relations among people, a variable clearly connected with roles. In this study we will concentrate on cooperation and competition. While both can be seen in any culture they have very different consequences when they are raised to the level of guiding principles for general behavior. In this they are analogous to hierarchy and equality. Just as hierarchy is fundamental to the family while equality is not, so without cooperation a family could not exist, but competition is not necessary. It is even possible to conceive of a family or other corporate group without competition, however "unnatural" or "unhealthy" such a group might appear to those from individualistic cultures, but no group can exist without some sort of cooperation.

It also seems that no group is so cohesive and cooperative as when its members are faced with a common problem. While this might be a "natural" problem such as winter or floods, wars and other intergroup competitions can also be occasions for corporate solidarity and cooperation. In this way cooperation and competition are often intimately related; prismatic contradictions are clearly present in this area of life as well as in the others. To be both cooperative and competitive with the same person at the same time is both possible and, in some cultures, normal, just as we can be traditional *and* rational or concerned with hierarchy and equality at the same time. Paradigm stress is involved, but that is also a normal condition.

When cooperation in a group has as its goal the welfare of the group as a whole, the group may be termed "collectivist." Collectivism itself may be structured in different ways. In groups that value hierarchy it will entail vertical integration and cooperation, with competition seen as evil and obedience to authority considered positive. When things are going fairly well in such a culture, paradigm stress will be low, particularly when the group and its hierarchy are traditional. On the other hand, when things are not going well and the difficulties are clearly attributable to errors, bad judgment, or competition within the upper levels of the hierarchy, paradigm stress for everyone concerned is liable to be rather high.

Groups which value equality also have a difficult time when things go wrong, for their only logical method of making decisions and implementing them is consensus. Any other method will entail sanctions of some sort, a situation that implies a hierarchy. Even if this hierarchy is that of a majority over a minority, it still implies a power situation with one person or group having power over another. Democratic forms of government seek to solve the problem by the use of free association on single issues, assuming that a "free floating" majority with constantly changing members will prevent the appearance of a permanent majority and a permanent minority. The very existence of the coercive power of the majority, however, weakens the principle of equality where it does not destroy it.

For this reason anarchistic groups have seldom if ever been "democratic." Consensus rather than voting has been the basis for their decisions, and discussion has prevailed over debate. In large societies, however, such methods are extremely difficult if not impossible. Without a positive acceptance of hierarchy as an organizing principle any large society attempting to be collectivist would seem to entail severe paradigm stress in making and implementing societal decisions. Representative democracy, as a solution to this paradigm stress (collectivism vs. egalitarianism), does not solve the problem so much as displace it to the legislature. While this solution may have the virtue of allowing the majority of the population to ignore the contradiction, the paradigm stress remains. Egalitarian cooperation in large groups is thoroughly prismatic, for it involves contradictory paradigms when, as in any very large group that seeks to accomplish anything concrete, some must take orders from others.

Governments

Government, contrary to a popular assumption, does not exist merely to allow some to give orders to others. Its primary purpose in all but revolutionary societies is to maintain society as it is. Anarchy, with its absence of government, works in small societies when they consist of single cultures cohesive enough to maintain themselves through shared paradigms, social pressure, and family ties. Larger societies need separate structures with the power to use physical sanctions because large societies are invariably multicultural. The multiplicity of cultures means at least some important paradigms are not shared. The presence within a single society of persons who are recognized as members but who do not believe the same things creates two related problems.

First, social pressure is less effective in limiting disintegrative behavior. Since the society is so large that family ties are very limited, people raised in different cultures (which do tend to be consistent within families) feel little need to conform to the standards of other families. This lack of cohesiveness is usually compensated for by a fictional "family of the nation-state" in our times, but without the coercive powers of the government to limit deviant behavior the nation would soon break down to the smaller communities within it.

Second, the presence within society of people and groups with different cultures makes it more difficult for people to cope with their own paradigm stress. All cultures have contradictory paradigms (although some have more acute stresses than others) but when all people have the same contradictions and more or less the same way of coping with them the personal stress involved is reduced. When other people living in the same community do not have the same problems and often seem to have an easier life because of the difference, people find it much more difficult to maintain the old values. Rationality tends to replace tradition, with all its consequent effects. When paradigm conflict becomes overt, rationality demands logical solutions, which usually means trying to abandon one or more of the contradictory paradigms. A result of this attempt is a loosening of the ties that hold people together.

Government is a more or less artificial means of holding a society together in the face of a continual tendency to fall apart. The more a society is consciously and overtly based on the small communities within it, the more stable it will be, since these communities tend to have the opposite tendency: they hold together, constantly renewing themselves through the generation of new family ties and the consequent regeneration of shared paradigms. The more a society denies the legitimacy of the smaller communities and the validity of their cultures the more it will tend to disintegrate, and the government will have to be strong and active to hold it together.

Over time, however, all governments will tend to function as maintenance organizations with the primary purpose of keeping things as they are. Since this function reinforces tradition, the tasks of governments in stable times boil down to the control of deviants and the continuation of whatever was done in the past. In these cases "government" will not be much of an issue in people's lives, and the people in government will tend to be the gray bureaucrats of legend.

In times of crisis, however, the latent divisions within society will become actual. Paradigm contradictions across cultures will become the subject of debate and contradictions within cultures more difficult to bear. Governmental leaders (who very much tend to be members of a single culture) will predictably appeal for national unity, by which they mean a positive acceptance of their own culture, its goals, and its methods of coping with stress. Since any reference to contradictions within the society tends to exacerbate them, the basis of this appeal is almost always to an external enemy assumed to be the common enemy of all within the society. When the cause of the crisis is actually within society itself (an increasingly unequal distribution of wealth, for example, or an increasingly severe abuse of one segment of society by another), the people who point this cause out tend to be identified with the external enemy and thus not legitimate members of society. The result, of course, is increased repression and heightened tensions.

If this goes on long enough the result may well be chronic governmental instability, but this should not be considered the same as societal instability. The crisis of government may itself become traditional. Changing governments and the consequent appearance of change may be the way people in a society cope with paradigm and cultural contradictions which do not change and are not expected to.

Economics

The last of the variables we will use to define cultures is their set of paradigms about the production and distribution of goods. Goods must be produced in all societies for life to be maintained, and how those goods are distributed among the members of the society is a function of the paradigms involved. Each culture has different beliefs about the correct economic roles of its members. When all the members of a society are members of the same culture they will agree on what should be produced, who will produce it, and who will consume how much of what. When a society is multicultural, however, it is unlikely that agreement will exist. Moreover, since economics has to do with living and dying as well as with how well we live, disagreement in the economic area will be important and lasting. The hierarchy of needs discussed earlier placed the fulfillment of physiological need first and security in those needs second. Economics is fundamentally how we fulfill our needs for food and shelter.

While economic systems vary considerably among the cultures, they can generally be analyzed by looking at who manages the system (if it is managed at all) and at how and upon what basis the goods are distributed. In an activity as basic as economics, we may expect to find economic values and roles closely related to legitimacy, basic units, and concepts of society.

Morality

Morality may be defined as the principles of right conduct, and as such it is related to wisdom. Wisdom, it may be remembered, is the ability to balance and to choose correctly among a number of alternatives basing the choice upon understanding, experience, and knowledge. To judge rightly and to follow the soundest course of action is something which is difficult for all of us, and our success at it can be judged only by the outcome of our actions.

Morality is simpler, for it does not have to do with our ability to forecast events so much as with limits upon what we will and won't do. The human situation is one in which a great many roles and their associated paradigms give us guides for understanding and action. Unfortunately, many of the paradigms are contradictory: specific roles often give insights and require actions which are wrong according to other roles and their paradigms. While wisdom is foresight into the consequences of our actions, morality simply sets limits. We need something like this to guide us in our actions, for without it we are going to do serious damage, both to ourselves and to those around us.

The source of a moral sense is the corporate group in which we grow up. The family not only teaches us our paradigms but also gives us a sense of how far they can be trusted on their own. Morality is a feeling rather than a logical idea because the use of pure rationality traps us in a single paradigm or role. The essence of morality is that it is a feeling for all our roles at once; not what we should do in a particular role, but how we should integrate our roles.

If we were wise enough to see the outcomes of all our actions perhaps a moral sense would be unnecessary, since we would then be able to use rationality to calculate the impact of our actions. This is not possible for the same reason that a science of human behavior is not possible. People are constantly forced to make so many conscious and unconscious choices that no one can predict the outcomes with perfect certainty.

The social sciences, of course, say little about morality and use it even less, for it is unscientific, and therefore relegated to the realm of superstition and myth. It may be unscientific, but it is the surest guide we have in setting limits on our behavior.

It is clear that a moral sense is most necessary where tradition and custom are weakest. Anarchist cultures, for example, can rely within their group on tradition and custom as guides to action without fear that the results will be unacceptable to them and those around them. In this sense, morality in an anarchist culture is a small factor in daily living, since there is almost no need for it. In individualistic, rationalistic cultures, where tradition and custom are logically unacceptable reasons for action, a moral sense could hardly be more important. Tradition prevents even a stupid person from acting stupidly, but in rationalist cultures there is nothing to mitigate the results of the actions of the stupid and it is difficult for even intelligent people to act intelligently. Unfortunately, it is precisely in these cultures that a moral sense is most likely to be lacking.

This situation is partly alleviated by the likelihood that no matter what individualists think is the basis of their actions, they are in actuality going to base most of them on tradition and habit. Moreover, there is a quality of individualists that is lacking in anarchists. Anarchists almost always make a great distinction between those in the group and those outside it. While violence inside the group is usually almost unknown, the most outrageous cruelties to outsiders may be quite normal. The individualist, recognizing no group as limiting him or her, is most likely to apply whatever moral sense he or she possesses to all people.

Morality is necessary if we are to avoid the worst consequences of paradigm contradiction. In the individual, a lack of morality can easily lead to fanaticism and harm both to the person who lacks it and to those with whom he or she comes in contact. In cultures and societies, lack of shared morals will most likely lead to a breakdown of the groups involved. The paradox that those cultures most in need of a shared morality are precisely those least likely to possess it remains, however, as does the irony that by looking to science for answers the members of these cultures are preventing themselves from using the moral sense that they do possess.

At the same time, it is difficult to see how a reliance upon tradition can be consciously built up in a culture which denies the validity of tradition. Throughout the discussions of the cultures that follow, the reader will do well to remember the function and problems of morality in human living and attempt to define for himself or herself the morality likely to develop in each of the different cultures.

Summary

Cultures are shared paradigms, so in describing a culture we are describing the various paradigms which consistently occur together. In presenting cultures in a certain order, in relating each to those previously described, and in locating them within a particular historical context we are essentially dealing in myth, for the seven cultures presented (eight counting anarchy) have coexisted for a long time.

To identify a society by its dominant culture or cultures is easy to do but not very helpful, for by doing so we ignore the intercultural dynamics which are vital to understanding it. This is one of the reasons why the leaders in dominant cultures often present their own culture as the only possible one, all others being considered pipe dreams at best and cruel frauds at worst. As long as no other culture is felt to be possible, the leaders' own dominance is greatly reinforced. Morality is then defined as the morality of the leaders. This situation is not necessarily or even probably a deliberate hoax on the part of the leaders, for it is quite normal to believe that the truths we know are universal and everlasting. Platonism is far more common than Aristotle's outlook even today, and probably always has been.

Political Cultures

Paradigms	ANARCHIST	TORY CORPORATIST	OLIGARCHY
Theoretical Source of Legitimacy	TRADITION	TRADITION	TRADITION / RATIONALITY
Organization of the Culture	HIERARCHY (age and merit)	HIERARCHY (birth and merit)	HIERARCHY (birth and merit)
Basic Unit of the Culture	SINGLE EXTENDED FAMILY	CORPORATE GROUP (self-governing and self-sufficient)	CORPORATE GROUP (rulers) / INDIVIDUALS (nonrulers)
Concept of the Culture	COLLECTIVIST	COLLECTIVIST (vertical integration and cooperation for the good of the whole)	COLLECTIVIST (rulers) / COMPETITIVE (nonrulers)
Government	NO SEPARATE STRUCTURES OR INSTITUTIONS	MONARCHY (advised by leaders of corporate groups)	PARLIAMENT (leaders of ruling group)
Economics	MANAGED ECONOMY / WELFARE FOR ALL	MANAGED ECONOMY / WELFARE BY CORPORATE GROUPS (judge by wealth of poorest)	MANAGED ECONOMY (for benefit of ruling group; judge by wealth of rich)

Political Cultures

CLASSICAL LIBERAL	RADICAL LIBERAL	DEMOCRATIC SOCIALIST	LENINIST SOCIALIST	FASCIST CORPORATIST
RATIONALITY	RATIONALITY	RATIONALITY	RATIONALITY	TRADITION / RATIONALITY
HIERARCHY (merit)	HIERARCHY (merit) ELECTORAL EQUALITY	EQUALITY (elected political hierarchy)	EQUALITY (authoritarian political hierarchy)	HIERARCHY (merit and birth)
INDIVIDUALS (free association on single issues)	INDIVIDUALS (free association on single issues)	INDIVIDUALS (free association in functional groups)	INDIVIDUALS (associated in functional groups)	CORPORATE GROUP (self sufficient under dictatorship)
COMPETITIVE (all against all)	COMPETITIVE (all against all) /INITIAL EQUALITY OF OPPORTUNITY	COLLECTIVIST (egalitarian cooperation for the good of the whole)	COLLECTIVIST (egalitarian cooperation enforced by party)	COLLECTIVIST (vertical integration and enforced cooperation)
CHECKS AND BALANCES (elected by rich individuals; vote conscience)	CHECKS AND BALANCES (universal suffrage, single-member district)	MAJORITARIAN (universal suffrage, proportional representation)	SINGLE AUTHORITARIAN PARTY (party selects new members)	DICTATORSHIP (self-government for fascist groups only)
FREE ENTERPRISE (no regulation or management; judge by wealth of rich)	FREE ENTERPRISE (regulation vs. monopoly; welfare for children of poor)	MIXED ECONOMY / WELFARE STATE (judge by wealth of poorest)	MANAGED ECONOMY / WELFARE STATE (equal wealth for all; state owns all)	MANAGED ECONOMY / WELFARE STATE (fascist groups manage)

Chapter 4

Tory Corporatism

The basic difference between a small society and a large one is that in the latter some method must be found to keep strangers functioning together in a cooperative way. In anarchy, family ties and their constant reinforcement through personal contacts hold the small, single-culture society together. In corporatist cultures the assumption that responsibility to the group is more important than individual needs and desires serves the same purpose. The leader, whether a traditional monarch or a charismatic dictator, symbolizes the head of the societal "family," in which everyone is included. The family responsibilities that are continuously present for the anarchist become symbolic to the corporatist, and because they are less immediate and real they are both weaker in their effect and easier for leaders to manipulate. At this point differences between responsibilities to family and to the larger society (the monarch for tories) can develop, and morality becomes more important.

We shall discuss two types of corporatist cultures, the tory and the fascist. In both, the immediate family ties of the anarchist are the symbolic basis of society, but the tory is a settled and ongoing culture while fascism is the attempt to create such a culture through the use of force. An absence of a large police force and a reliance upon existing shared paradigms characterizes the tory culture. A pervasive secret police and strenuous government efforts to create shared paradigms characterize the fascist. Because in our age fascism is usually justified as a reaction to leninist socialism, we shall describe it after we have discussed that culture.

Theoretical Source of Legitimacy

The legitimacy of a tory culture, in theory as well as in practice, is tradition. "The way things are," "our way of life," and "that's how we do things around here" are all appeals to tradition and consistent with tory cultures. While rationality is present and important, the culture is not justified by appeals to logic and rationality but by appeals to tradition.

This does not mean that a tory culture cannot be rationally justified, or course. Edmund Burke in his *Reflections on the Revolution in France*[1] pointed out that while the logic of the proposed new society in France was excellent, its goals laudable, and its justice exemplary, all these were theoretical. He felt that the foundation of a society was tradition and that the revolutionaries would find logic and reason insufficient to grant them the legitimacy they needed. Without legitimacy, the basis of the revolution would be coercion, a system that would develop its own momentum and logic. Events proved him right. While it may be argued that the common people of France were better off after the revolution than before, it is beyond doubt that the revolution did not develop as its planners thought it would and should, and that French society was not and is not what they envisioned.

That Burke was not totally enamored of his own society is evident in his assessment of the rich. At their most stupid, bigoted, and cowardly, however, he felt they were the ballast in the vessel of the Commonwealth. "Men of ability" would eventually triumph with their reforms, but not too soon. Tradition, which he was straightforward enough to call simple prejudice, was all-important in the maintenance of society. Reform ought to be delayed until the reform itself had gained the legitimacy of tradition.

Burke's position is shared by all tories. While not blind to the drawbacks of tradition, particularly where inherited power is concerned, tories feel tradition is and ought to be the basis of society. Ambitious people, who by definition seek to change their place in society, are considered dangerous. This is partly because by changing their own place in society they affect everyone around them, but even more because the personal qualities associated with ambition are felt to be harmful. Greed, covetousness, bullying, and meanness are all qualities tories associate with an ambition to get ahead, qualities which they feel tend to tear society apart rather than hold it together. A laudable ambition to a tory would be the desire to be good at whatever it is you were born to do. A farmer's son, for example, should want to be the best farmer he can be; a merchant's son, to be the best merchant he can be. To change the position into which you are born is a serious matter, and one which is generally suspect.

Merit, nevertheless, must be recognized and allowed for somehow, or society will decay. The maintenance of a healthy society itself requires the recognition and support of hard-working, efficient, and strongly motivated people. Fred Riggs has termed the combination of birth and merit normal to tory cultures "attainment."[2] When eligibility for a position is determined by birth (an ascriptive criterion) those who have not inherited the proper position in society are simply not considered. Among those eligible, however, merit should determine who gets the position, and individual (or corporate) achievement is supported. Attainment allows for some mobility in positions while preserving the basic structures of a traditional society. Ambition is not crushed but it is very closely channeled so that nothing fundamental will change. Farmers will still be farmers and aristocrats will remain aristocrats.

Organization of the Culture

Tory aristocrats exist in a social and economic hierarchy based upon birth that is fundamental to tory paradigms. The family has a hierarchy based on birth and age, one which is inherent in its functioning and an inescapable part of family life. The tory culture has applied this principle throughout society as natural and inevitable. A tory sees hierarchies of birth everywhere, and believes that all societies are based upon them. Equality is not only impossible, but is also a very dangerous illusion. If those who seek equality gain power they will end by replacing a legitimate hierarchy with an illegitimate one, to everyone's detriment. To a tory, hierarchy is the skeleton of society, and the problem is to control it for everyone's benefit rather than attempt to cure its abuses by destroying it. One does not try to cure a person with a broken bone by removing his skeleton.

True aristocrats will use their power and influence for everyone's benefit. Because unrestrained ambition often leads to selfishness, and even more often comes from it, ambition must be limited by birth. At the same time, merit must be allowed to function. "Attainment" and patronage are the vehicles through which merit can aid society, but a tory believes that a just and lasting society must be maintained more through tradition. The hierarchy of birth, which is the source of all legitimacy, must take precedence over merit whenever the two are in serious conflict. The alternative, to a tory, is the terror of a revolution that has no basis other than coercion and no guide other than the logic of coercion.

Basic Unit of the Culture

Quite naturally a tory culture believes in corporate groups. Whereas anarchy could allow individuals a great deal of scope because their society was limited to a single cohesive family, tory cultures emphasize families themselves as the basic units of society. Each family specializes in a particular task (aristocrats govern, of course) and in this way the whole society can achieve in ways not possible for anarchy. Functional specificity by families allows for teaching to occur within the basic unit, thus making the system self-perpetuating. By and large, the extended families of a tory culture are self-governing and often self-sufficient. Certainly the geographical regions are self-sufficient, the towns being supported by the surrounding countryside.

Just as the whole of a tory society is seen as a large family by tories, so the smaller regions are seen as smaller families. While corporate groups interact, there is a limit to the patterns of interaction. Physical proximity and shared histories are fundamental to the villages and towns of tory cultures. Farmhouses, for instance, occur in groups rather than singly, and towns tend to be frequent and small rather than large and widely separated.

An important point to note here is that while individuals last only their own lifetime, a family has the potential to last indefinitely. For individuals the world begins when they are born and ends with their death. Individualistic cultures, whether they are liberal or socialist, tend to see an adult's lifespan as the maximum time available for anything. For individualists, utopia or any other goal must be achieved now (or perhaps tomorrow) because that is all the time they have. Tories tend to see time as indefinite because they measure it much more by the life span of the family than that of any particular person in it, including themselves. Consequently, they tend to plan and build for the indefinite future. Conservation, which has only recently become a major concern in the United States, is a basic facet of tory thinking. Short-term goals aimed at immediate profit are unusual in tory cultures because such goals usually sacrifice or ignore long-term interests. Since the tory considers his or her family more important than himself or herself, such a sacrifice is immoral, even if it involves only family members as yet unborn and unknown to the person involved.

The self-governing and self-sufficient nature of the units in a tory culture also tend to give tory persons a broad sense of efficacy and worth. Their work is obviously and closely connected with the good of the whole, and since the decisions affecting their work are made within the unit, there is a feeling of control. The fact that these decisions and the perceptions of difficulties are largely defined by tradition is not a problem when the person making them accepts tradition as a part of himself or herself in a positive way. The possibilities for stability tend to be the same as those for stagnation, but since so many decisions are made within the basic corporate units of society it is likely that their needs will be met and the society will be maintained. Individualists will tend to see a tory culture as restrictive, unimaginative, and unduly cautious, but tories will see it as secure, well-ordered, and prudent.

Concept of the Culture

It follows from the nature of the corporate group that cooperation will be considered far more important than competition in a tory culture. Given the positive acceptance of hierarchy, cooperation involves vertical integration and its goal is the good of the whole. The good of the basic unit in society, the corporate family group, is assumed to be consistent with the larger family of the whole society. This assumption also works the other way around. When natural catastrophes (or unnatural disasters, such as war) dislocate daily living to such an extent that local groups cannot cope, leadership from above is seen as natural and beneficial.

Vertical integration and cooperation for the good of the whole is natural and right for the tory. One of the reasons such a system does not result in a totalitarian dictatorship is the self-governing nature of the corporate groups that make up tory society. Each group has its own hierarchy, its own skills, and its own rightful place in society. Within its place, it governs. Farmers, for example, are the technocrats of farming; the same people who do the work control the technology of the trade. Management and labor tend to be the same, while any technological change comes from those doing the work rather than from a different group.

The paradigms of "ownership" are quite different in the tory view from those of individualistic cultures, and technology and its goals are also seen differently. "Ownership" in a tory culture is not vested in individuals but in corporate groups. This follows from the concept of the corporate group as the basic unit of society. The principle of hierarchy, however, puts the control of resources in the hands of particular persons. The combination of these two principles is seen in the concept of "usufruct," the personal right to use something as long as the use does not harm or destroy it. Resources are to be used for the good of members of the present family but not to the detriment of the future family. The same principle applies to the larger society. Resources are to benefit the whole as well as the particular part.

Since tradition largely governs goals and methods of production, in normal times the system tends to run itself.

Security in the system is very important. While particular people may be disciplined, or even executed, they and their families will not usually be dispossessed by losing their right to property. For instance, authority over an area may be vested in a particular family, but they have no traditional right in tory culture to evict anyone unless that person is guilty of abusing his or her position by destroying the land or other property they have in their çare. Farmers are not "renting" the land, and they have the same rights of tenure as the lord of the area.

Tenure in universities, in fact, is a tory right of membership in a community that cannot be violated unless it is proved that the tenured person has abused his or her position to the detriment of the academic community. The reason academic tenure is controversial today is that it is a tory value existing in a largely individualistic society. Since the paradigms of most of the people in universities and colleges in the United States are individualistic rather than corporate, just as in the larger society, academic tenure is widely misunderstood and misused.

The right of tenure in tory culture is universal. All people are members of corporate groups and no person may be denied this right. While imprisonment, exile, and execution are possible in extreme cases, the more usual process when a wrong has been committed is to hold the corporate group of which the malefactor is a member responsible for his or her behavior. This method relies for its efficacy on social pressure and traditional paradigms of responsibility to the family. As long as society is cohesive and is dominated by tories, it works very well.

A second characteristic of the tory combination of collectivism, hierarchy, and corporatism is that technology is usually very slow to change. Groups are identified with existing trades and the trades themselves are taught through tradition. Unemployment in an individualistic definition is impossible, since everyone has tenure. Work is motivated by feelings of responsibility to others, pride, corporate need, and tradition, but not by threats of individual dismissal and starvation. Given this situation, labor-saving devices will be valued only when there are not enough people available to accomplish traditional work by traditional methods. Generations of skill and pride are invested in all occupations, and tories see no reason to radically alter them as long as they are accomplishing their corporate goals. Stability in the culture produces, and in many ways depends upon, stability in technology.

That tory cultures are capable of great and successful technological changes is illustrated by the history of the Japanese in the last century and a half. The Japanese have always been tory, although contemporary

Japanese are finding it necessary to make increasing efforts to maintain their culture. These efforts are nothing new, for the closing of Japan to Western trade and influence in the 1600s was a successful attempt to do the same thing. When Japan was forcibly "opened" in the 1850s by the United States Navy under Perry, the Japanese aristocracy realized that without similar or superior military technology they would be unable to maintain their culture. Firearms had been banned two hundred years earlier when their culturally disruptive effects became apparent; now they would be necessary. It was soon also apparent that Western industrial technology would also be necessary if Japan was to have any chance of remaining independent.

Within sixty years Japan became a major industrial power without the misery and massive cultural changes that accompanied the industrial .revolution in the West. The corporate, cooperative, and vertically integrated Japanese culture not only did not change, it was the structure by which Japan industrialized. Western experts in development and change consistently miss this point precisely because their paradigms are those of Western cultures, where change in dominant cultures accompanied industrialization. Quite naturally, they have concluded that industrialization requires cultural change.

It is possible, however, that changes in technology were made in order to maintain the dominance of the new culture. Put this way, it is equally logical that a later, reactive industrialization would be required to maintain a tory culture threatened by the different, industrialized, dominant culture of the West.

Japanese industrialization had the very unfortunate consequence of requiring raw materials from outside Japan, a circumstance that resulted in Japanese imperialism as the only way to combine the maintenance of the dominant Japanese culture with control over the resources which industrialization needed. The larger point in the present context, however, is that tory cultures are clearly capable of profound technological change when the culture must make such changes to maintain itself. Lacking such a threat, it is also logical that tradition, corporatism, and collectivism will all combine to maintain a stable and largely unchanging technology.

Government

The governmental system of a tory culture is as much like that of the family as possible, but the differences a large society requires are important. Hereditary monarchy is as close to the paternal status of the leaders of a family as it is possible to get, but the resemblance to the authority structure of a family is more symbolic than actual.

Where a father or mother is a constant physical presence within a family, consciously giving legitimacy to decisions made by the children when the parent does not make those decisions, the monarch is only symbolically present. Decisions are continuously made throughout society without the knowledge of the monarch. Given the functional specificity of a large society, the vast majority of these decisions are also not understandable to the monarch. A farmer or a weaver, for example, teaches his children his profession and therefore understands the decisions his children will make. The monarch is most likely neither a farmer nor a weaver, and therefore does not have the basis for understanding why and how technical decisions in those professions are made.

On the other hand, he or she claims a special knowledge and understanding of government that experts in other fields are not expected to have. The aristocrats in general have government as their profession, in exactly the same way farmers farm and weavers weave. Just as the aristocrat is not expected to know the professions of other corporate family groups, so it is self-evident to them that they do not know the aristocrat's.

The result is a society made up of family-based corporate groups which are internally self-governing and are in control of the technology necessary for their professions. The function of the aristocrats is to coordinate the differing groups when it is necessary and to provide leadership in times of crisis. Tradition provides standards and values for interaction that are known and accepted by all. The contradictions in interests among groups are adjudicated by the aristocracy when they are not settled at the source by tradition. The judgments handed down are naturally based upon tradition, a system which tends to keep a balance among the traditional rights, privileges, and responsibilities of the various groups in society.

Two points stand out. First, "government," if that is understood as a centralized, pervasive, and rationalized making of decisions for all society, will exist only in times of crisis, and then only to the extent necessary to reestablish society as it was. The competing logical requirements of differing paradigms are controlled by referring to tradition rather than pure rationality, a situation which lessens any impulse toward centralization. As long as corporate units produce enough of their products to maintain both themselves and the greater society, they are expected and required to govern and provide for themselves.

All members of society have tenure; their rights and privileges cannot be denied them as long as they are meeting their responsibilities. A large part of the monarch's function is to receive petitions from groups who feel their rights and privileges are being threatened by other groups and to be ready and able to help maintain them as tradition dictates. Government in a tory culture is highly decentralized, with the central government providing only coordination, adjudication, and crisis leadership.

The second point is that the aristocracy is the only corporate group in society that is expected to be able to see society as a whole. If a tory culture is functioning well, aristocrats will be educated to understand, coordinate, and adjudicate in the interests of all corporate groups. It is important to understand that the difference is one of function rather than of intelligence, value, or moral worth. In theory a farmer is not considered less intelligent, less valuable, or less moral than an aristocrat. Each is to be honored and respected insofar as each fulfills his or her place in society. A peasant may be wise and intelligent without wanting to join the aristocracy.

Legends about wise and honorable peasants are frequent in tory cultures, but almost entirely lacking in societies that individualistic cultures dominate. The cruel question "If you're so smart why aren't you rich?" makes no sense in a tory culture, where tenure protects people from poverty and security is associated not with individual wealth but with membership in a corporate group and in the culture itself. It is interesting in this context to note that the only "wise peasant" legend in the United States of which I am aware is that of Uncle Remus, a slave. Perhaps wisdom is allowable in social and economic inferiors only when there is no risk that they may use their wisdom to change their place in society.

In any case, it is an error to assume that there is only one hierarchy in society and that all people either wish to climb it or are lacking in ambition. In a tory culture each corporate group has its own hierarchy. A proper ambition is to excel within your own group, not to desire to change groups or to destroy them. In a well-functioning tory culture the monarch respects and honors a master craftsman quite as much as the craftsman honors the monarch. Each has his or her place, ambitions, privileges, rights, and responsibilities and is judged by how well these are fulfilled. The individuals are not equal or the same, and it is precisely this lack of equality that allows them to respect one another. A good carpenter is better than a bad king, a fact that can be recognized because they are not in competition. In the United States today, even a bad president is honored far more than a good carpenter because both are considered to be in a single hierarchy. Rank is considered an achievement in itself, quite apart from what was done to attain it or how the power and influence of that rank is used.

Which brings us back to government. In a tory culture "government" is the domain and the responsibility of the monarch and the aristocracy. Only the aristocrats have been raised and educated to understand the whole society and only they are in a position to see it as a whole. The perspective of all other corporate groups is that of their own profession and family. The aristocrats' lack of any other profession allows them to see the whole. An aristocrat "in trade" has in fact abandoned his trade, which is to govern in the interests of the whole. Upon entering another profession he or she will inevitably develop a narrower point of view, one which in a governor amounts to sacrificing the whole in favor of one of its parts.

The reason tory cultures depend upon a monarchy is not because other corporate groups in society are considered stupid or greedy but because their perspective must be that of a particular part of society. While wisdom, honor, and respect are possible for all, it is place that determines perspective. Only an aristocracy whose sole function is to govern in the interests of all will be in a position to do so.

The main problem, of course, is that the aristocrats may in fact govern in their own interests. Oligarchy, the next culture we will discuss, is the logical result. Within a tory culture, however, there are numerous safeguards against such a development. The major one is the fact that the same tradition which grants the monarch legitimacy also makes the various corporate groups functionally separate from the monarch. They are self-governing and provide for themselves. In normal times the monarch and the aristocracy have little to do. They are not involved in the many daily decisions and tasks that are the heart of any culture, and unless there is a crisis they do not expect to be. They have the leisure to read and think, to patronize the arts, and to prepare themselves for their duties as leaders should they be needed.

Foreign affairs is the natural aristocratic function, although even here the mundane details of commerce are the function of merchants. If the culture is working properly, the role of the aristocracy and the monarch is to react to petitions brought to them rather than to meddle in the daily affairs of the other groups. If they should attempt to do so the most likely reaction is an immediate appeal to the traditional rights and privileges of the corporate group involved. Individuals as such have little protection and no place in tory cultures, but as members of corporate groups they have both.

A further protection against abuse of power is the parliament of leaders who advise the monarch. The aristocrats in the parliament generally come from different parts of the country and are felt to represent the different corporate groups within their areas. The traditional, functional independence of the corporate groups themselves is far more important, but the parliament does have some traditional maintenance functions. Perhaps more importantly, it is the structure that is central to tory democracy, a form of government and culture that can function within a society containing strong individualistic cultures.

The theory of tory democracy is that while members of nonaristocratic corporate groups cannot know what is good for the whole society because of their restricted perspective, they certainly know what is good for their own group. When voting, they are expected to vote either for or against the existing government according to whether or not its policies have benefitted their group. If the government's policies have benefitted the majority of groups, the government will be retained; if not, it will be replaced by another group of aristocrats who promise to follow different policies. The competition and the individualistic voting that contemporary Western democracy entail are contrary to tory paradigms, but most of tory culture can continue to exist within such a system.

Economics

Tory systems of government are moderately flexible, then, but the basic culture remains one of hierarchical collectivism based upon largely self-governing corporate groups. The economic aspects of the culture are fairly straightforward. The economy is managed by the various corporate groups. Production controls are centered in the hierarchies of the producing corporations, while consumption is a function of membership in a corporate group. It is a decentralized system that depends for guidance upon tradition and the coordinating function of the aristocracy. In this sense, it is managed but not planned, since no one sits down and rationally maps out new policies for the whole society.

Tory economics also includes welfare, but the unit responsible for the welfare of particular people is not the central government but the corporate group. Each person has tenure in his or her group, which in this context means that economic needs are provided for by the group. In return people fulfill their own responsibilities, which very much include working and producing. One of the reasons that tory cultures are not usually innovative in their technology is that labor-saving devices are often counterproductive. If workers must be fed, clothed, housed, and otherwise provided for, replacing them with machines accomplishes very little. Only in labor-short situations will new technology make sense, and even then it will have to conform as much as possible to tradition. The emphasis in tory economics, as in any other part of the culture, is upon the maintenance of society rather than change. "Improvements" are suspect, perhaps most importantly because all of their consequences cannot be anticipated.

The distribution of goods in a tory culture is, of course, unequal. Hierarchy exists in economics as well as in other areas, and some are wealthier than others. Everyone should be provided for, but the question of "who gets how much" is settled by tradition. On the other hand, no one should go hungry. The quality and type of food may vary with a person's station, but everyone should have enough.

Tories judge a society by the condition of the least wealthy in it. If the least wealthy are well-fed, well-clothed, and well-housed, the tory is not disturbed by the coarseness of the food, the roughness of the clothing, or the humbleness of the houses. The fisherman's clothes are not suitable for the court of the king, but the courtier's clothes are hardly suitable for fishing, either. It is assumed that fishermen like to fish, strive to excel at it, and are satisfied with their lives. In tory cultures human economic wants are not insatiable and few yearn to be aristocrats. The distribution of goods may be unequal, in that every person does not have the same things as everyone else, but people have what they need and, given their acceptance of their place in life, they should have most of what they want if they work hard and well at their professions. Each corporate group provides for its own, as much in the definition of what is good and desirable as in the provision of those goods. The important thing is that no one starve. Poverty has no place in the tory culture.

Two Contradictions of Tory Cultures

If this exposition of the tory culture has seemed utopian, it is because it is the first culture to be described. In the real world at least, the seven cultures we will deal with all exist at once. The most a tory could hope for is a society dominated by tory paradigms. At the same time, difficulties arising from the nature of tory culture itself can be distinguished from difficulties created by the presence of other cultures. At this point we will deal with the former, leaving difficulties with other cultures to be dealt with when we discuss those cultures.

The first problem, and the one most obvious to individualists, is the relative lack of mobility in a tory culture. While everyone is encouraged to develop and achieve within his or her corporate group, the corporate group itself limits the options available. Moreover, sex roles in a tory culture are usually strong, well defined, and pervasive. While there is no theoretical reason why male dominance should prevail, it usually seems to do so.

On the other hand, dominance is relative to the role involved. For instance, many Latin women do not understand what is going on in the United States with women's liberation. Militant feminists in the United States tend to be individualists who see only one hierarchy and a single competition. All places in society are found in this hierarchy, and any self-respecting person should strive to climb higher, or at least resist being placed in a low-status position. Latin women, coming from societies dominated by tory paradigms, see themselves in a world made up of a great many different hierarchies. In some of these hierarchies, women have high status while men are relegated to lower positions. Moreover, since women and men can be perceived as belonging to different hierarchies, they can respect one another without feeling any need to be "equal."

Even so, the lack of mobility in a tory culture can create many difficulties, especially when crises do not seem to be handled well by the aristocracy. Tory culture emphasizes stability and security at the expense of mobility; when insecurity is strong, mobility becomes more attractive. While different tory cultures respond to this problem differently, medieval Europe had a particularly interesting way of handling it. The church as an institution could be joined by anyone from any group. The church itself, and especially the religious orders within it, then became the person's "family." Since the church had a great deal of moral and material power, and since all within the church were eligible for promotion to positions of power and authority within its hierarchy, this amounted to social, political, and economic mobility.

Such opportunities were not to be had without sacrifice, of course. In order to maintain mobility based upon achievement within the church and to maintain access to it from other groups, its members had to remain celibate. If they were allowed legitimate offspring the principle of inherited station and tenure would have applied, and the church would quickly have become simply another sort of aristocracy.

As it was (and is), the church provided tenure, security, and the possibility of upward mobility for its members while remaining consistent with tory paradigms. It is interesting to note that the smaller corporate groups within the church are those which, over the years, have maintained the greatest independence from secular authority. The Franciscans, Dominicans, Jesuits, and other orders are tory in everything except birth and inheritance. In Latin America in particular, it has been these orders which have helped maintain tory paradigms. By doing so, they have implicitly and at times explicitly exposed those elements in society which got wealthy by using poverty as a threat and a punishment to coerce labor from the poor. The regular clergy (those priests not members of the orders) in colonial Latin America were hired and fired by the Spanish king, and were more likely to take the side of the rich against the poor. The religious (the members of the orders) were physically and emotionally maintained by their orders, and far more able to resist the threats and bribery of the corrupt. The religious orders became not only a release from some of the negative aspects of tory culture but also a strong support of that culture. Today these same orders have generated the liberation theology which demands that the lives of the poor have priority over the needs of the rich.

The Chinese also developed systems for dealing with the problems and contradictions inherent in tory cultures. Confucius is identified with these stratagems, although they were developed before him. The structure most directly analogous to that of the church in the West was the Chinese bureaucracy. Administrators were chosen from those who passed the examinations for admission to the bureaucracy, and everyone was eligible to take the examination. It was very strict, very difficult, and very honest. Inevitably there was a bias toward the children of aristocratic families, since they were those who could most afford the tutors and the books necessary for preparation. Even so, everyone was eligible and the bureaucracy provided the mobility lacking in other parts of society. It also ensured that at the least public officials were intelligent and well aware of the requirements and goals of tory government, since the texts of Confucius himself were often the subjects of the examinations.

Another Chinese device to handle the difficulties of tory culture was (and is) the "Mandate of Heaven" concept. Tory tradition requires the cooperation and support of all people for the monarch. The question of a bad monarch immediately arises. Do the people owe allegiance to a monarch who is not a tory? If the monarch exploits his subjects, breaking down the self-governance of corporate groups, denying them their rights and privileges and impoverishing their members, are they still bound to respect and obey him?

Confucius felt that all governments will eventually become corrupt. The metaphor he used was that of the seasons, with Winter representing the lingering death of the old government and Spring the establishment of the new. The difficult phase, of course, was right around New Year's. The Mandate of Heaven was the traditional endorsement of tradition for the existing government. A government lost the Mandate of Heaven when it was overcome by rebels, who then received the mandate in their turn. Confucian subjects, very much including government officials, were to resist bad government but not to rebel against it. When those who did rebel against it defeated it, the good citizen (and the good government official) immediately accepted the new government as legitimate.

The morality of those who rebelled was not the point: society itself would suffer less if they were accepted as legitimate and (a very important point) if they knew they were accepted. The tragedy of Vietnam, from a Confucian point of view, was not that the government changed but that the period of civil war was so long and so inconclusive. Left to themselves, the Vietnamese would undoubtedly have made the shift in a relatively short time, with the new regime receiving the overwhelming support of the people simply because it was the new regime.

Foreign interference by forces that neither shared nor understood tory culture made the transition long, tortuous, and miserable. The problem was not whether to accept or reject the new regime, but to distinguish which of the many factions involved would be the new regime. When that question was finally settled its legitimacy (for Confucians) was not an issue.

Generally speaking, however, both Western and Chinese tory philosophers came to the same conclusion: while people could and should refuse to administer immoral (that is, nontory) laws, they should not actively rebel or aid a rebellion against a monarch. Both St. Thomas Aquinas and Confucius argued that rebellion would probably cause more immediate harm and suffering than a bad monarch. Aquinas, however, argued further that any successful rebellion would have no legitimacy. Its victors would be forced to coerce obedience and would be constantly suspicious of competitors for power, a circumstance that would almost guarantee bad and bloody government for years to come. Logically enough, both men based their arguments on logic, since it was tradition itself that was called into question.

Aquinas, however, did not believe that rebels could be blessed by God with a mandate. Such a belief would have upset the balance of power between the church and the temporal rulers of the time, many of whom were only marginally influenced by the church as it was. For the church to grant potential legitimacy to rebels would be too much. Aquinas' arguments, while focused on this world rather than the next, were addressed to citizens of a world which accepted two spheres of authority, the spiritual and the temporal (material). The split was prismatic, of course, and the overlapping nature of the roles tended to create a good many prismatic contradictions. If the ultimate superiority of the spiritual realm was never in doubt, the immediate reality of the material realm was never in doubt either. Aquinas' best solution was to resist unjust authority without rebelling against it, relying upon time and the eventual (peaceful) death of the unjust ruler to improve the situation. The Mandate of Heaven concept does the same, but is better prepared to deal with a successful rebellion.

Summary

We have discussed the contradiction between security and stability on the one hand and individual mobility and ambition on the other. The prismatic situation of opposing paradigms, both of which are necessary and legitimate parts of human life, does not permit a solution, and the tory culture does not provide one. It does, however, have a distinctive way of dealing with the problem, a way heavily weighted in favor of security and stability.

The church in Europe and the bureaucracy in China were carefully defined ways of providing legitimate outlets for ambition, limiting its scope and directing its energies for the good of the whole. Of the two, the European was the more flexible, for the only qualifications for entry into the church were faith and a willingness to accept the discipline of the church. Moreover, one could join at any age, a circumstance that was very positive for a good many people. It was not uncommon to enter the religious orders after a career in a secular profession and after raising a family. The life of the church was not necessarily limited to contemplation and prayers, either, for many of the clergy were responsible for the administration of church properties. With the expansion of Spain to what is now Latin America, this function often became the administration of entire regions involving the introduction of European values and technology to non-European peoples.

The Incan, Mayan, and Mexican cultures were most definitely tory, and in those areas the religious orders of the church were very successful in protecting and promoting tory values wherever they were able to maintain their authority. The monarchs of Spain, who had the right to name the clergy within their domains, originally used the religious orders as the administrative structures for Latin America. Within a few years it became apparent to Spanish monarchs that the tory culture represented by the orders (particularly the Franciscans, the Dominicans and the Augustinians) was in contradiction to their need for money.

Profit is supposed to be a subordinate value in tory culture when it clashes with the security and well-being of corporate groups. Since almost all profit from the new world involved the labor of the indigenous peoples, it was soon clear to everyone involved that protecting the rights of the Indians was in opposition to the creation of wealth for the monarch and the aristocracy.

The stage was set for a continuing struggle between tories, generally represented by the religious orders and their aristocratic allies, and the oligarchs, those among the rulers who put their own benefits before the welfare of others. The struggle is still going on in Latin America with very nearly the same participants.

The contradiction between traditional legitimacy and corrupt government also continues with a much broader scope, at least in the forms of opposition. While historic corporate bodies still exist in the religious orders of the Catholic Church and the Chinese bureaucracy, the legitimacy of a corrupt government is a question in all societies, even in those that have "solved" the ambition/stability problem by legitimizing almost all forms of ambition. Corruption of the system occurs in all cultures, even if its definition and the problem of how to deal with it differ.

There are many other contradictions in tory cultures, most of them analogous to the problems arising in the family. Of all the cultures of large societies we will discuss, the tory is the closest to that of the family. Its safeguards, such as the legitimacy of corporate groups within society and the primacy of the welfare of all of them, are logically similar to the welfare of particular persons in a family. Individuals and corporate groups are not identical, however, and it is this difference that becomes crucial to the next culture we will discuss, that of oligarchy.

Chapter 5

Oligarchy

Oligarchy occurs when a particular corporate group in society promotes its own welfare by exploiting others. Since the aristocracy and the monarch exist in a tory culture to coordinate and control the other corporate groups, it is clear that they are also in the best position to exploit them. Indeed, all other groups are expected to have their vision more or less limited to their own requirements and processes because of the need to focus on their own work. Having no other work than government, the aristocracy can see society as a whole, and therefore how it should fit together. This vantage point is also useful for exploitation.

Theoretical Source of Legitimacy

Oligarchy is the natural corruption of a tory culture. At this point we will assume that oligarchs come from the ranks of the aristocracy, differing from them essentially in their definition of family. Where the anarchist identifies family and society because his blood relationships make up society, and the tory accepts the paradigm that all of the large society is his or her family, even those not related by blood or marriage, the oligarch accepts a great division between his or her family and the rest of society.

The oligarch, who is definitely not an individualist, strongly accepts family responsibilities and the time sense that goes along with them. Individual selfishness is abhorred. Self-centeredness, egotism, and the rejection of family in any way are regarded with repugnance, as is the placing of short-term profit over long-term family loss. The oligarch, in short, is a tory as far as his or her own family is concerned.

Nonfamily members, however, are regarded almost as nonpeople and exploited for the good of the family. Because of their position in society, aristocrats have numerous opportunities to exploit others, especially in times of societal crises when all groups are expected both to follow the leadership of the aristocracy and to make sacrifices for the good of the whole. The aristocrats who order sacrifices for others while arranging for the enrichment and protection of their own families have become oligarchs. Since it is highly unlikely that the other corporate groups in society will knowingly accept such a situation without coercion, oligarchs usually lie about both the situation and their intentions. A thorough oligarch, in fact, will use his leadership position to create and exacerbate crises rather than avoiding them, all the while urging the other corporate groups and individuals in society to continue their sacrifices for the good of the whole.

Tradition is the source of the oligarch's legitimacy. In terms of the oligarch's own family this is quite enough, just as it is for the tory. Other groups in society, however, will be very unlikely to accept oligarchs as legitimate if they see them for what they are. Oligarchs must therefore present themselves as something other than oligarchs if they are to rule with a minimum of coercion.

If society is dominated by tory paradigms, oligarchs will represent themselves as tories, a strategy that is especially effective in their own minds since they are tory within their own family. From the broader point of view they accept themselves as the legitimate rulers of society but do not accept other corporate groups or individuals as having legitimate rights, privileges, or tenure. They reserve these concepts for themselves. The deception necessary to rule without coercion is a potential problem for oligarchs in that there is always the possibility that their children will believe the public statements rather than the private intent, and act contrary to the narrow interests of their family.

Organization of the Culture

Hierarchy will remain as the organizing principle of society and government because it is hierarchy that simultaneously gives the oligarchs security in their own position and the opportunity to exploit others. To oppose hierarchy would be lunacy in an oligarch.

The basis of hierarchy for oligarchs will remain inherited status. The family is all-important, being not only the object of enrichment but the justification for everything the oligarch does. Birth is the criterion for in-clusion in the ruling group and those included will remain a corporate group.

The reason other groups accept the oligarchs as rulers is tory tradition. First, it assures the followers of the aristocracy that government is in the interests of all corporate groups in society, and therefore of their own. Second, tradition also ensures that the rights, privileges, and tenure of each group in society will be maintained. Oligarchs will seek to discount and discredit the second tradition at the same time they attempt to rein-force the first. This is a tricky business, for any attempt to change tradi-tion tends to undermine all tradition.

Oligarchs have some room to maneuver because, ironically enough, the oligarchical tendencies of tory aristocracies have been recognized for a long time. When Aquinas and Confucius counseled patience and passive resistance, what they were thinking of was a proper tory response to oligarchy, its natural corruption. Burke spoke of the dangers of relying upon rationality for legitimacy, a tory/oligarch reaction to individualism. He also counseled patience in redressing wrongs. Any reform of society was to take place only when the reforms themselves had gained the legitimacy of age and familiarity.

The patronage of aristocrats (or at least of the wealthy) for men of merit becomes an interesting issue in this light. While the Catholic Church in Europe and the bureaucracy in China were (among other things) struc-tural devices to harness the power and energy of personal ambition in sys-tems which could not recognize any individual ambition that transcended its possessor's corporate group, the "sponsoring" of individuals of other groups by aristocrats achieves the same ends but without the same safeguards.

The principle of attainment limited ambition by restricting eligibility: every person could strive to achieve a high and honored position in his (in-herited) corporate group, but could not hope to change groups. The European church and the Chinese bureaucracy allowed for change but simultaneously required allegiance to the new corporate group. Patronage, however, creates a situation where the receiver may give loyalty to the donor as a person. It can be individualistic, and while it has the virtue of being able to recognize and reward merit quickly and individually, it can be used for a great many purposes inconsistent with tory culture.

Merit, the second criterion for hierarchy, can be expected to be em-phasized by oligarchs outside their own corporate group. By appeals to merit, they can recognize people as individuals and encourage the breakup of the corporate groups whose members they seek to exploit. At the same time, a contradiction is created: If people are distinguished by merit, how can oligarchs justify their own inheritance of wealth and power? Oligarchs may be satisfied with their inherited status, but why should anyone else accept it?

The temptation and the need of the oligarch are too great to avoid the problem. Merit is the best criterion to follow if the traditional rights and privileges of subordinate groups are to be broken, and they must be broken if the oligarchy is to profit at the expense of others.

Basic Unit of the Culture

The basic unit for the tory is the corporate group. In tory cultures people not identified and defined by their inherited membership in a corporate group cannot be accounted for and are outside society. The oligarchs continue the same paradigm. "Society" shrinks to themselves; the individuals created by merit and the destruction of their corporate groups are not considered to be members of "society." Where the tory measures the well-being of society by its least wealthy members, the oligarch reverses the focus. If the oligarchs are prosperous and safe, then everything is fine. The poor become irrelevant to "society," which is now judged in terms of wealth and conspicuous consumption.

The national society, which in our terms includes all the people living within the geographical boundaries of the state, is now divided. Where the tory saw a kaleidoscopic, interrelated system of self-governing corporate groups, all functioning for their own good and the good of the whole under the general supervision of the aristocracy and the monarch, the oligarch sees only two groups: the corporate group of the rulers and the individualized nonrulers. The ruling corporate group is self-governing within itself while the individuals outside it are governed by the oligarchs. Instead of working primarily for the benefit of their own corporate group and for the whole society secondarily, workers now labor primarily for the benefit of the rulers and then for their own individual benefit. Instead of living securely within a corporate group small enough so that all its members have been known since birth and who work cooperatively for the immediate, visible goals of corporate prosperity and maintenance, individuals now have to buy their security each day with work that benefits people they neither know nor care about.

Concept of the Culture

The concept of society held by the oligarchs has changed from that of the tories, but there are points in common. Cooperation for the good of the whole remains a positive and honored value within the ruling group, but does not extend to anyone outside. The collectivism of the rulers is reserved for themselves. All others in the larger society are expected, encouraged, and forced to compete with each other, for it is only in this way that the oligarchs can break the power of the other groups and their control over the resources that have been traditionally theirs. Once the solidarity of the other corporate groups has been broken, the oligarchs despise the masses for their individualism, citing their selfishness, egoism, and irresponsibility toward one another as proof of their inferiority.

In a tory system, competition was closely regulated and channeled by tradition. In an oligarchy, ambition is considered natural and proper in nonrulers (if despicable), the only limit being their ineligibility for membership in the ruling group. Attainment is still the method by which rulers are chosen, since eligibility for ruling positions is limited to membership in the oligarchical families.

Nonrulers are expected to accept the traditional authority of the ruling group and the hierarchy that defines it, but they are not to be allowed the corporate unity and collectivist actions, also traditional in tory cultures. This discrimination results in paradigm conflict, although it will certainly be more marked in nonrulers than in the oligarchs themselves. "Oligarchy," in fact, usually refers to the rulers as much as to the entire system. This reference is generally accurate because nonrulers have little reason to accept oligarchy as legitimate if it is easily recognizable as oligarchy. Oligarchs therefore represent themselves to nonrulers as members of some other culture, usually as tories or liberals.

Government

The structure of government changes when oligarchs dominate, even though they rely upon traditional tory support to give them legitimacy. The change comes about because the position of the monarch in a tory culture reinforces the monarch's tory values. As the focus and symbol of the family values inherent in tory culture, the monarch already has the highest position possible in the hierarchy, as well as the wealth and power that go with the position. If neither of these are absolute (and they are not) they certainly carry immense prestige and security. The monarch would have little to gain and much to lose from a change to oligarchy, for it would entail strong possibilities for insecurity and decreased prestige. Moreover, if a tory monarch became selfish and individualistic the most logical development would be the reinforcement of his own power and wealth, and the most likely source would, at least in the first instance, be the aristocrats.

Foreign wars and succession crises certainly offer opportunities for power struggles within the aristocracy, and the resulting civil wars a fine opportunity for oligarchy to prosper. The result of a strong oligarchy is usually to weaken or eliminate the monarch, replacing him or her with a parliament made up of the dominant members of the families constituting the ruling corporate group. A similarly defined group advises the monarch in a tory system, so there is traditional justification for its existence. What is important is that the cabinet of oligarchs is more powerful than the monarch, who remains as a puppet or is done away with altogether.

The ties between a monarch and the people tend to be very strong, a circumstance very undesirable from the oligarch's point of view. Such ties bypass the oligarchy, providing less powerful corporate groups direct access to the monarch in their attempts to preserve their traditional rights and privileges. Better to get rid of the monarch than to allow him to frustrate the enrichment of the oligarchy.

Government also becomes centralized, as the oligarchs gather all the facets of power into their own hands. Just how centralized depends upon how united the oligarchs are, for at least in the beginning there is no guarantee that the many different aristocratic families will all turn to oligarchy, or that all who do will be united. In the long run, however, the oligarchs have far more to gain by supporting one another than by competing, and as intermarriage creates a single extended family the state will become more centralized.

Economics

The economic system of the oligarchy is quite simple. It is an economy managed by the ruling corporate group for the benefit of the ruling corporate group. It is much simpler than the tory economic system, which involves decentralized management by each producing group for the benefit of the managing group and for the rest of society. The coordination of such a system is made possible by the use of tradition as a basic guide. Very intricate interdependencies can work quite well with this system, even if they are logically very complex, providing for a bewildering array of needs and wants across a very broad spectrum. No one is bewildered because no one ever tries to logically understand it all at once; people respond only to particular needs at particular times. Their education emphasizes the whole system and the reasons for its existence, but tradition is seen as both the glue that holds society together and the guide for actions that will perpetuate it. The one thing undeniable about traditional ways of doing things is that they work on at least a maintenance level. When things have been done a certain way for hundreds of years, it is a fairly safe bet that continuing to observe tradition will not make things worse.

It will probably not make them better, either, and the oligarchy wants things to be better for themselves. Since the traditional tory way of managing the economy is very unlikely to result in any major change for the better in the status and wealth of the oligarch, it must be changed. The management of the economy must be centralized in the oligarchy's parliament, although what this often amounts to in practice is simply the mutual support of the oligarchs for the exploitation of each one's geographical area. During this period the "masses" are created, since the oligarchy sees the rest of the population not as an intricately interrelated system of corporate producing groups but as a great mass of people differentiated only by their personal qualities.

A further consequence of the oligarch's change of focus is that the day-to-day management of production and distribution cannot be left with the traditional hierarchies of the corporate groups involved. Indeed, the whole point of the reorganization is to strip these groups of their power to manage their own affairs. If they retain their management powers they will also retain their wealth, which will therefore not be available for acquisition by the oligarchy.

Summary: The Oligarchical System

The differing paradigms of oligarchy are fairly easy to understand. They may be summed up as "all power and wealth to the oligarchy." Paradigm conflicts would seem to be minimal for the ruling group, for they combine the close and constant interpersonal contact and reinforcement for group solidarity of the anarchists with the material goods available to larger societies through functional specificity (one person or group specializing in the production of one thing). If other people in the society have problems, both paradigmatic and physical, the problems are of no concern to the ruling group, for its members have paradigms that limit their responsibilities to their own corporate group alone.

If internal paradigm conflict may be low for the oligarch, conflict between the ruling group and others will certainly be high. If only the tory and oligarchical paradigms are strong in society, oligarchs may seek to minimize the conflict by presenting themselves as tories, but their actions in exploiting the other members of society tend to undermine these efforts.

If a monarch is retained as part of this charade, the possibility of his actually developing enough power to rule is always present. Insofar as the monarch has no power, his credibility as a tory declines, but if he is allowed power there is no guarantee it will not be used against the oligarchy. The assertion of all power to the monarch, for example ("absolute" monarchy) is consistent with the denial of power to subordinate groups but inconsistent with the collectivist paradigms oligarchs have for their own group.

The destruction of the internal hierarchies of the other corporate groups which accompanies their atomization places all managerial functions in the hands of the oligarchy. This concentration vastly increases their power and at the same time opens the way for its further concentration in the more narrowly defined government itself, a circumstance favorable to the development of dictatorship, which at this point would take the form of absolute monarchy. The tradition supported by the oligarchy to legitimize their own power can just as easily be used by the monarch to justify his.

Property, too, changes its character with the change to oligarchy. Tory property is meant to produce goods for the benefit of its users and for the use of others. A hierarchy of skills, experience, and authority closely linked to the governing hierarchy within the producing group both produces and uses property. The focus is upon the finished product and the conservation of the capital goods involved. Generally speaking, each product is made from beginning to end by the same person or group, and the quality of the product is the responsibility of its makers. The whole process both depends upon and generates owner-operated shops, farms, and other industries, although ownership is better understood as usufruct, as we have seen.

If the oligarch is to extract wealth from the production and distribution of goods over and above what the aristocracy traditionally receives, the system of ownership must be changed. Where tenure is universal, rents and taxes have different meanings from the same terms where eviction and condemnation are normal procedures. The payments that trickle up to the aristocracy in a tory system are probably better understood as tribute, which often takes nonmonetary forms and combines a good many positive roles at the same time. Work exchanges, community projects, harvest festivals, birthday celebrations and other community events may all contribute to the position of the aristocracy without being the same as rents and taxes. Generally speaking, tory cultures tend to include as many roles as possible in whatever is being done. The overlapping paradigms involved tend to support one another and the system as a whole.[1]

Oligarchs, intent upon increasing the wealth and status of their families and denying any responsibilities to those outside the family, tend to separate roles among the nonrulers as much as possible in order to increase the possibilities for manipulation and the destruction of traditions which do not benefit them. Tribute or tithes can be converted to taxes and rents by the logic of an ownership role isolated from the network of responsibilities to all others which defined "usufruct." Once the principle of private property is established, property is no longer seen as only one binding aspect of collectivist responsibilities but as something quite isolated from the community, subject only to the needs and desires of the private owner. In this situation the oligarch's tenants clearly have no rights of tenure, for they do not own the property, even if their families have occupied the same farm or house for generations. Nonpayment of rents becomes cause for eviction, and it is the owner who sets the rents. The connection between the user of the property and the lord now becomes a monetary connection between a tenant and a landlord. The only criterion relevant to the isolated connection is money, for only an abstract commodity like money can be separated from the web of reciprocal responsibilities of the old system.

The enclosures of the commons in England during the seventeenth and eighteenth centuries offer a good example of the process by which oligarchs can gain control over a tory culture. The commons were lands adjacent or within each village which were used in common by all the families in the village for their own immediate sustenance. Each family cared for its own domestic animals and gardens on the land their family had always used, although changes in family size could lead to adjustments in the size of the plots involved. Generally speaking, the commons were distinguished from the other lands in the area by their use for immediate sustenance rather than for raising crops or animals for export to other areas. As such, they represented nonmonetary income for the villagers, not all of whom were farmers. Blacksmiths, shopkeepers, and all the other inhabitants of the village used the commons as a matter of right. It was an integral part of the tory culture of self-government and self-sufficient corporate groups.

To "enclose the commons," that is, to fence them in to keep the villagers out, accomplished two things at the same time. First, it reduced the nonmonetary income of the villagers, rendering them more dependent upon money — and money was largely controlled by those who had the most of it: the oligarchy. Second, it made the common land available to the landlord to be used for commercial production, which in the English case during this period was usually the production of wool. When this happened fences within the commons were prohibited so the sheep would eat anything planted by the villagers.

This second function can easily be overemphasized, for it is often subordinate to the creation of the cheap labor that the villagers were forced to become. Cut off from the commons, they must now work for money in order to live. The cushion of at least partial self-sufficiency being removed, they now had no option but to seek employment wherever it was offered.

Several implications of successful oligarchy are relevant here, beginning with the split between public and private. No such split exists in a tory culture: everything is both public and private at the same time. Such a distinction is in fact nonsensical to a tory, since he conceives of all people as having both constant responsibilities to all others (public) and constant personal rights and privileges (private). The two factors cannot be separated for a tory.

Oligarchs, however, claim their own rights and privileges as universal, but their responsibilities as limited to their own families. This is the beginning of the public/private dichotomy, but for the oligarch it is not a limitation on the powers of the state. Since he and his family are the overt ruling group they have no reason to limit the public power of the government.

What is limited is the claim of nonrulers to their welfare. Nonrulers become "private," in that their welfare is of no concern of the state. The oligarchs have defined "society" as themselves, and judge the success of the government by their own prosperity.

Oligarchs are wealthy because they have redistributed the available money and goods from others to themselves. In doing so they create poverty and need where it did not exist before. The poor, oligarchs say, are always with us, and are no one's responsibility but their own. Relations of the nonrulers with rulers become those of subjects rather than citizens. They have responsibilities but no rights. The members of the ruling group expect nonrulers to conform to a network of traditions and laws that favors the rulers, but the only connection in the other direction is money. Money is what links the nonrulers to food, clothing, and all the other necessities of life, and money is their only security against the loss of these things.

In order to create this situation the oligarchs must make deep and important changes in tory culture, especially changes in the management and technology of the production of goods. Merely changing the patterns of distribution is not enough. If the physical producers of goods and services retain control over the management and technology of production they can simply stop or slow down production when they find it benefits no one but the oligarchy. Their self-government and partial self-sufficiency allow them to continue to function with less money, particularly since a good deal of a tory economy is based on barter. The oligarch's control of money is not, at first, the same as control of the economy. In order to make it so he must change management patterns, a change with great implications for technology.

The master craftsmen and the guilds of tory culture must be broken and replaced by systems that prevent the working person's control over the process. This replacement entails technological change because tory technology is both owner-operated and (usually) designed to make the entire thing produced. Tories do not make parts of things; they make the things themselves. Moreover, they make them in their own homes and shops rather than in factories. This practice limits both the number and nature of the goods produced, but since tory cultures are basically stable and maintenance oriented rather than dynamic and expansionary, these limits impose no great hardship. Goods are made to last as long as possible and inheritance passes them on to others.

The factory system of mass production usually destroys the tory system of production and replaces it with one meeting the requirements of the oligarchy. That it need not do so is demonstrated by Japanese industry, which adopted the structures of mass production but adapted them to their own tory culture. Nevertheless, there are clear connections between the factory and the needs of the oligarchy.

In a factory workers are under the constant supervision of management, and the rate of work can therefore be set and maintained by management. The workers being visible, any idleness can be seen and punished. The production line, where the object being produced is transported past work stations, allows management to vary the rate of production by varying the speed of the line. Instead of each worker producing the whole product, he or she now performs only a single function, repeated each time another product comes by the work station.

With this system, the design and technology of the product is no longer in the hands and minds of the workers but in a new element of society, the engineers. What they design, they do not produce, while what the workers produce, they do not design. This is the general strategy of the oligarch in his efforts to break down a tory society: to divide and separate the "factors of production" in order to gain control over the process. At every point, processes and people are divided and set against one another. Competition within and across jobs is introduced to maintain the divisions and to keep up the rate of work. Money in the form of wages is the main connection between management and the other people involved in production. The income of the workers is no longer directly connected with the quality or price of the product, a circumstance that allows management to absorb the profits when prices are raised and to fire workers when sales fall.

Whole classes of people are created by these changes, for the unitary modes of production characteristic of tory cultures combined all of these differing functions in a very few people. Foremen, hiring offices, personnel managers, engineers, and all the others involved in a factory operation were unnecessary before. Generally speaking, these are the people who will form the "middle" classes. Tory cultures have a kaleidoscopic arrangement of corporate groups, each having its own hierarchy. There is no middle class since there is no single hierarchy by which everyone is measured.

When oligarchs destroy the corporate unity of all the other groups and institute a system in which money is the most important connection among the resulting individuals, they have also created a single hierarchy of wealth and power. The middle of this hierarchy consists of people who can be fired from their jobs at any time. Unskilled labor, or course, is at the bottom of the hierarchy, and therefore constitutes a lower class.

The unemployed may be described as the lowest class, and it would be a great mistake to leave them out of the hierarchy. They are, in fact, the motivating factor for the employed as well as the mechanism that keeps wages at a minimum. The income of workers is no longer related to the value of the product or their membership in a corporate group, but to the minimum amount of money necessary to keep them at work.

In slavery, this amounts to food and sometimes food alone. Here there are no unemployed to act as a reserve labor force, keeping wages down by their desperation. Simple coercion ensures the slaves' labor. Some oligarchs engaged in slavery argued that they would "take care" of their slaves because they owned them, and therefore had an interest in their health if not in their welfare. The Jamaica system shows the fallacy in assuming that corporate, tory values would continue to function in an oligarchical system.

On the Jamaican sugar plantations in the seventeen hundreds, the English owners followed a policy of deliberately working their slaves to death, replacing them with new slaves. The immediate cause of death was not starvation but disease, overwork, exposure, and malnutrition which left the labor force in no position to resist. The plain fact (to management) was that it was far cheaper to capture healthy workers in Africa and transport them to Jamaica than it was to take proper care of the workers already there.

Such a policy was possible in Jamaica because the original inhabitants had been annihilated and the slaves were in no position to impose their own culture upon the planters. The plantation system was essentially the factory system applied to agriculture, so the other factors of production have already been described. Such a system was impossible in England because of the tory culture there. It began to develop in Latin America but was stopped through the imposition of tory values through the monarch and the Church, although many substitutions for slavery were developed there and in England to circumvent the law.

Debt peonage in both areas was one of the primary mechanisms used to coerce nominally free labor. In this system management makes loans to workers, who must then work to pay off the loan. A legal system to enforce the contract through imprisonment for nonpayment must exist, as well as management's control of the opportunity to work. Sometimes the conditions leading to the need to borrow must also be manipulated (for example, a money tax), while the "company store" (a system where workers must buy food and supplies from a store which management controls) can be used to maintain the debt. This last mechanism has the virtue of allowing the company to pay high wages without having high labor costs, since the money is recovered through the even higher prices charged by the company store. The actual net wages turn out to be simple subsistence for the workers.

It is important to note that once these structures are set up they may be run by "paternalistic" employers who do in fact pay higher than subsistence wages. These employers may claim to be tories. They may in fact be tories, but the situation is fundamentally different from the primary tory culture we have already described. The workers exist within a factory system, they do not control the technology or rate of production, and their privileges and security exist at the option of their employer rather than as a matter of tradition and law.

The oligarchical system would seem to benefit the oligarch enormously and does, but is not without problems for its managers. We have already discussed its difficulties with simultaneously relying on tradition for legitimacy and destroying the traditional rights, privileges, and way of life of the nonruling groups. A similar problem exists with the technical innovation involved in changing technology. The engineers who create the new technology are unlikely to completely accept tradition as the sole criterion for legitimacy, especially where that legitimacy underlies the authority to use and manage the new technology. The paradigm stress is obvious, and is likely to prove difficult for the oligarch.

Environmental concerns are also a problem area, for the oligarch would like to preserve a healthy and attractive environment for his own family. While the simple expedient of living in enclaves where the poor and miserable are not permitted will work well for awhile, the pollution created by a system that feels no responsibility for the greater part of the population is unlikely to be confined to the areas in which they live. The pollutions associated with fossil fuels, atomic power, and invented substances is especially difficult for the oligarch, for their effects are very widespread.

A second long-term problem in the oligarchical system is that the patterns of production and distribution which so benefit the oligarch tend to stop unless the system expands. High unemployment, low wages, and a disregard for the welfare of anyone but the oligarchs themselves creates an immensely productive system, in that prodigious quantities of goods are produced that then belong to the oligarchs, but it simultaneously destroys any mass market for these goods. If workers are paid subsistence wages, they cannot buy more than a minimum of food, clothing, and housing. At the same time an innovative class of engineers and inventors continues designing more goods and more "efficient" ways of producing them. The system will logically stop as unsalable/unpurchasable goods accumulate.

The solution is to expand. Oligarchical wars are usually wars of expansion. Imperialism is a logical solution for at least some of the oligarch's problems. Expansion provides the markets that have disappeared at home at the same time it allows for an even greater division of the factors of production. When cotton is grown in India but spun into cloth in England, it is very unlikely that the two labor forces will combine against the oligarchs. If either group does successfully revolt, it will be left with meaningless assets, for it is the combination which gives value to the parts. Cotton mills are not worth much without cotton, and it is very unlikely that the government (the oligarchs) will lose control of the links between the two factors.

Imperialism brings with it new problems. Competing empires and the resistance of the imperialized create imperial wars, while the complexity of the larger system may threaten its continued management for the benefit of the oligarchy alone. The middle class tends to grow in numbers and becomes more difficult to control. People in that middle position have enough status and enough money to be an independent force. Since they are necessary to the oligarchy, they cannot be eliminated. the most vocal may be fired, but the rest will continue to think.

Working-class people think too, but are not in much of a position to change the system from within. Unions and other forms of rebellion are met with force. The very coercive forces that control both the employed and the unemployed part of the working class create more elements of the middle class. The bigger the system, the bigger the middle class and the greater the opportunities to change a system based upon tradition and the continued dominance of inherited wealth and power.

Chapter 6

Classical Liberalism

Generally speaking, classical liberalism makes virtues of the changes brought about by successful oligarchy. The individualism, the competition, and the repudiation of corporate group responsibilities (which tories see as unmitigated evils and oligarchs as the necessary conditions of life for nonrulers) are transformed by classical liberals into positive values necessary for living respectable, honorable lives. Moreover, classical liberalism is the first of our cultures to feel the need for a wholly rational, logical explanation for society. This need is imperative because tradition supports the tories and oligarchs. Any appeal to tradition ends up being an appeal to tory or oligarchical values, and classical liberals seek to establish themselves as quite distinct from the previous cultures.

A name for the new culture presents some difficulties, most of them involving its relative place in Western history. "Liberal" is derived from the Latin word for "free," and, if it retained this meaning, it would be a very fitting term. Classical liberals hold that their culture is based upon liberty, that its paradigms are all consistent with the utmost freedom feasible for human behavior, and that only through a consistent application of their principles can freedom become and remain an accomplished fact. As we shall see, classical liberalism contains its own internal contradictions as well as basic contradictions of the human condition, but as a general statement about the culture, "liberal" is not bad.

Unfortunately, "liberal" has also come to mean "favorable to reform and progress," so that where classical liberalism has become dominant the term "liberal" is applied to those who would change it. The culture we will discuss in the next chapter, radical liberalism, is called "liberal" in the United States for this reason as well as for its inclusion of many liberal paradigms. Indeed, the "classical" part of "classical liberal" came into use when it was necessary to distinguish between the older, established liberalism and the new, radical liberalism that sought to reform a society dominated by its predecessor. In the United States liberalism has come to mean radical liberalism, while a socialist is generally described as an "extreme liberal" or a "radical leftist."

We will assume that the oligarchs have had some success and have succeeded in dominating at least parts of the national society. In doing so, they have created both a "lower" class of individualized working and unemployed people and a "middle" class of foremen, engineers, managers and the like who maintain their privileged status only if they maintain their employment, an "if" that generally depends upon their usefulness to the oligarchy.

The individuals in the lower class generally see their salvation as a return to tory culture. Their lack of power, the effect of the situation on their families, and their often miserable living conditions leave them little hope of solving family problems by individual effort. Moreover, their memories of tory culture (either immediate or historical) lead them to trust the aristocracy as well as to consider aristocratic leadership necessary. The problem is to distinguish the tory aristocrat from the oligarch; the two share family connections, names and status. For the tory aristocrats themselves, the same problem exists, but their position is cushioned, materially at least, by the oligarch's upholding the traditional status of the aristocracy.

During this period the oligarchs represent themselves as tory, holding that crises occurring in society (unemployment, misery, the new factory system, the loss of traditional rights and status by producing groups, and the rest) are caused by wars, natural disasters, international economic pressures, and the like. Imperial wars sometimes offer possibilities for emigration as well as opportunities to appeal for tory solidarity in the face of foreign threats, both circumstances that favor the oligarchs. All in all, individuals in the lower class will be most likely to seek out and support tories, seeing individualism as a trap.

The new middle class is in a different position. Middle-class individuals, dependent on the oligarchy as the source of money and valuable to the oligarchy precisely because they do not feel responsible for the welfare of those beneath them in the single hierarchy of wealth the oligarchy has created, are able to fulfill their responsibilities to their own immediate families. Moreover, they will generally feel that it is their own individual effort that has enabled them to do so, for in order to attain their middle position they have had to compete with many others who also wanted it. They must continue to compete in order to hold their positions, and the fact that the competition is judged by the oligarchy tends to be obscured by the achievement itself.

It is irritating, however, to find the way to further achievement blocked by inherited wealth and power, and to be continually judged, rewarded, and punished by those who themselves do not compete. It is more than irritating — it is dangerous, for when only money is security (and the oligarchs take great care that all except themselves have no other security) there is never enough: when constant competition is the price of membership in the middle class, no amount of money is sufficient to ensure the future. We will all grow old and incapable of effective competition some time, and when that time comes middle-class individuals can expect younger, more effective competitors to take not only their positions but also their money.

In short, the position of the middle class is privileged but precarious. Being winners supports their self-confidence but security is always out of reach. Maslow's hierarchy would predict that such a situation is unstable, or at least that people in it will try their best to get out of it. Working-class people tend to be tory in this situation, since their success is limited and their status low. If they accept tory responsibilities to their extended families their status will remain low, since no matter how hard they work for low wages, there will always be more mouths to feed than money for food to fill them. The only positive change possible is a change in corporate status, and the best resource at this stage is the remaining tory aristocrats.

The middle-class individualists trust their own ability to win at competition and to individually benefit from winning, but their security is low. Corporate groups to them are represented by the oligarchy above them, not by any remaining tory groups in society. Out of this situation comes the classical liberal culture.

Theoretical Source of Legitimacy

Since tradition supports the tory/oligarchy combination, the classical liberal believes in rationality. This is supported by the nature of the work of the new middle class, which is both innovative and unprecedented. Competition and the need for innovation reward logic, while the single dominant hierarchy of wealth tends to submerge the paradigm conflicts that impede the ruthless use of rationality in the tory culture. Tradition, if used as a guide by nonrulers in a society in which the rulers are oligarchs, simply traps middle-class individuals in a web of relationships and responsibilities that not only prevents them from rising but, on the contrary, continually drags them down toward the bottom of society as the poverty and want of the extended family and (former) corporate group drain their resources.

A tory response is possible, but for a middle-class person very costly and hazardous. It is unlikely that the oligarchy will be defeated once in power, and if the oligarchs are defeated by tories the position the middle-class person fills in society will disappear. Far more rational to accept the situation and make the best of it. Both self-interest and logic support such a strategy, and the classical liberal is essentially a platonist, arguing that logic and intellect are infallible guides to action.

The problem with this approach is that it is not consistent with how we live. The human condition is such that logic cannot solve our problems, for any problem involving human relations is sure to be both paradigmatic and prismatic. Our earlier discussion of the human condition emphasized the difficulties in believing that science is the solution to all our problems, or even the more important ones. Logic, like fire, is a good servant but a bad master. Classical liberals have falsified the human condition in assuming rationality to be the source of legitimacy, and many of their problems stem from this basic assumption. To found a government and an economic system on logic when the vast majority of people simply accept traditional beliefs is to ask for trouble. Not surprisingly, a good many of these paradigm conflicts also occur in the classical liberal's family. The family, however, is not the classical liberal's basic unit of society.

Organization of the Culture

The classical liberal believes in a hierarchy of merit, and no other. The problem with this belief is that even with the exclusion of the hierarchies of the tory corporate groups a good many other hierarchies remain. For example, each profession has its own hierarchy of skill and achievement, families retain their hierarchies of age, social relations are often hierarchical, and even sports have their hierarchies. The prismatic nature of society stubbornly remains, and in persisting disrupts the classical liberal's assumption that all people may be placed in a single hierarchy of achievement.

The solution is characteristically platonic. Plato believed that the ideal was more real than the actual: that the intellect, through logic, can conceive of truths more stable, logical, and understandable than the world around us, which is continually growing and decaying. The classical liberal believes in merit and in an associated hierarchy of achievement that is more stable, logical, and understandable than the actual prismatic world, where the human condition produces people who are meritorious in one role and failures in others. Just as Plato believed that all ideals, when fully understood, were one, so the classical liberal believes that all merit (and therefore all merit hierarchies) are ultimately the same. In order to measure the same merit across different hierarchies, the classical liberal relies upon the abstraction that the oligarch has forced upon the rest of society as a means to its exploitation: money.

For the classical liberal merit will be rewarded by wealth, a very different assumption from that of the tory, who knows that wealth is simply an attribute of membership in a corporate group. It is not very far, however, to the assumption that merit is wealth, and the next step is even easier: wealth is merit. To judge all humanity by a single criterion (merit) is very difficult when people not only function in different hierarchies but when each of them functions in a great many hierarchies at the same time. How much more productive (and simpler) to assume that merit and wealth are functionally the same.

Such an assumption allows individuals in differing hierarchies to be compared and their worth to society immediately perceived. If the wealthy are meritorious and the meritorious wealthy, there is little need to understand all the differing facets of society in order to evaluate other people. If the other people involved are also seen as individuals rather than as members of differing corporate groups, then the use of a single standard for evaluation and judgment is even more logical.

Before discussing the individualism fundamental to classical liberalism, we should pause at this point to recognize that the use of wealth as a measure of merit involves the classical liberal in a major difficulty: the oligarchs are also wealthy. Any standard that measures merit by money will necessarily find oligarchs meritorious; but classical liberals also know that oligarchy is wrong, for it is based upon tradition and inherited wealth rather than "earned" wealth.

As long as the oligarchs continue presenting themselves as tories the paradigm stress is not great, but oligarchs are not (necessarily) stupid. There is nothing to stop them from representing themselves as classical liberals if it is in their interest to do so. If they do, and if they hold high positions in financial hierarchies, how is the classical liberal to deny them merit? But if oligarchs are meritorious, how can the classical liberal destroy the oligarchy that is oppressing and manipulating him? Put another way, how can the classical liberal find security in merit if the very group that keeps him insecure is made up of meritorious (wealthy) individuals?

The same problem occurs in the other direction. Nonmeritorious people should not be wealthy, but what about the classical liberal's own children? Certainly when they are adults they may be denied any wealth they have not themselves earned, but how should children be regarded? A five-year-old cannot be expected to earn large amounts of money, but does this make him or her less meritorious?

Basic Unit of the Culture

Thinking about classical liberal merit brings us rather forcefully to the next paradigm of classical liberals. Individualism is fundamental to the culture, both because all people are to be seen, evaluated, and judged as individuals and because individual self-interest is assumed to be the motivation of all actions. In other words, selfishness is now a virtue (or at least reality) and egocentric behavior is expected and rewarded.

The immediate problem is that this paradigm directly contradicts many of the paradigms developed in families. The most obvious conflict is with parent-child relationships in the immediate family. It is difficult to see what the parent gets out of the relationship if selfishness is the key motivating factor involved. Even if some of the work of raising a child can be seen as catering to a parent's feeling of self-importance, it would seem that any really selfish parent would either abandon or murder the child when things get difficult. The very survival of human beings points out the paradigm conflict inherent in any culture based upon individualism, and classical liberalism hardly escapes this dilemma. Where tories and oligarchs find their greatest satisfaction, the classical liberal finds the most intractable problems and moral dilemmas.

The plain fact is that families and individualism do not mix well. The cooperation and caring for others essential to a harmonious family directly contradict the egocentric, achievement-oriented, and money-measured life of the classical liberal. Pregnancy can be uncomfortable and is often downright painful. Babies should be avoided, aborted, or abandoned by rational and logical classical liberals, and classical liberals believe in rationality and logic.

Among other problems, children and families reduce the freedom of individuals, and personal liberty is fundamental to classical liberals. Without freedom from imposed or inherited responsibilities, individualism remains the individualism imposed upon nonrulers by oligarchs: an evil that furthers exploitation by preventing any corporate resistance to the ruling group. The "liberty" of the individual to reject corporate responsibilities is imposed by the oligarchs on nonruling tory groups, but avidly sought by classical liberals bent upon rising in this world.

Social climbing, the great sin of tory cultures, has become the great virtue of the classical liberal. In this climb to the top, an extended family is impossible, and even a nuclear family is more a hindrance than a help. The self-made man is the ideal of the classical liberal. Anything that stands in the way of his rise to wealth, and therefore to high status and power, should be cast aside.

Naturally, a few problems remain. First, the individualism of truly successful classical liberals seldom lasts, at least in their relations with their families. While the possession of great wealth may not prevent the classical liberal from denying it to his children, thus ensuring that they will make their own, individual way in life, it is not generally done. Even if it is, by the second generation a more corporate approach to family life is likely to develop, and by the third generation oligarchy will have been recreated, if it was ever destroyed in the first place.

It is most likely, in fact, that it never was destroyed, since the wealth of the oligarchs tends to make them meritorious in the eyes of the classical liberal. The practical goal of the classical liberal is not so much to destroy the oligarchy as to join it. The old saying "from shirt sleeves to shirt sleeves in three generations" would in this case refer to a family that was unable to convert individual wealth into the corporate status of oligarchy. It assumes that oligarchy does not exist and that individual achievement is always as necessary for the retention of wealth as for its creation.

The second problem with the individualism of the classical liberal has to do with the concept of liberty. It is paradigmatic to a classical liberal that all individuals are free to achieve. Slavery, for example, is morally reprehensible to a classical liberal, for it obviously prevents the slave from achieving greater wealth. That is, it contradicts the paradigm that merit and wealth are the same. Generally speaking, anyone in a classical liberal culture who is not rich, or at least affluent, is considered to be without merit. Since individual effort and achievement create wealth, anyone without wealth must either be lazy or too defective to achieve. If the rich deserve to be rich because of their individual merit, then the poor must deserve to be poor because of their individual lack of merit. It is their own fault they are poor. Liberty gives each person the right to succeed. If they do not succeed something must be wrong with them.

Liberty, however, tends to contradict the classical liberals' paradigms about hierarchy. A hierarchy involves the lower members accepting the authority of those above them, but insofar as they do so they have given up their liberty and their individuality. If it could be assumed that all people freely cooperate for their own good, as in the tory culture, the problem would be solved, but the classical liberal does not assume this at all. The classical liberal paradigm of relations among people is that their individualism leads them to compete with one another in order to further their self-interest. The problem for the classical liberal is how to achieve cooperation if everyone competes. The two concepts (hierarchy and competition) would seem to contradict one another if liberty is also a value applicable to all, for it rules out the coercion that would solve the problem.

This problem is ultimately not resolvable. The classical liberal manages to cope with it through the concept of free association. Free association exists when people voluntarily join together in order to achieve a particular goal desired by all of them. It is essential that each individual be free to quit the association at any time, and that any individual wishing to join it be free to do so, although he or she may have to compete with others to gain that privilege. This is a freedom of opportunity only, since the classical liberal believes in a merit hierarchy determined by constant and unlimited competition.

Free associations are hierarchical, of course, and the conflict between hierarchy and liberty remains. If slavery is eliminated as a means of recruiting and retaining lower members of the organization, why should anyone join at that level? The answer is money and the opportunity to rise in status and wealth. Even so, any hierarchy has a few positions at the top and a great many at the bottom, where the vast majority must remain or the hierarchy would become meaningless. How can the classical liberal explain the continued presence of those at the bottom?

The two answers of the classical liberal are interconnected. First, the people at the bottom deserve to be there, for they do not have the merit to rise, and second, the alternative to employment must be sufficiently miserable (or be made so) to force those without much merit to compete for a place in the free association. Put this way, the free association looks rather less than totally free. If those at the bottom have merit, why should they remain at the bottom of the association? But if they do not have merit then why should they join it at all? The practical difficulty is solved by making sure that the unemployed are miserable, but this hardly seems like free association if a large group of unemployed is necessary to provide incentive for those in the lower ranks of the employed.

The solution is to blame the unemployed. They are, logically, those completely without merit, while those employed but unable to rise in the hierarchy have some merit, but not much. It is necessary that they work, even if their lack of merit is precisely their lack of interest in work. There is a rather curious involution here, for it is precisely the physically hardest and most unattractive jobs that are paid the least. Presumably, people who can and do work in those positions must have quite a bit of merit, but if so their wealth should reflect that merit. The classical liberal seeks to escape the dilemma by an appeal to intelligence: smart people avoid hard physical work. This escape is nonmeritorious if a desire to work is merit. If people are coerced by the alternative to hard physical labor (unemployment) it is difficult to see how the system differs in its essentials from slavery, where the alternative to working is physical punishment.

The problem is one of organization and liberty. If an organization is hierarchical it seems clear that the maximum degree of freedom is located at the top of the organization. The head of a hierarchical organization is in a position to make decisions for the whole organization. In the tory culture, cooperation is assumed and decision making can be decentralized. That is, since everyone in the organization (corporate group) is cooperating for the good of the group and has tenure in the group, decisions can be made by those closest to the problems and the whole organization will benefit. The paradigms of cooperation and tenure are important, for cooperation ensures that all decisions will be for the good of the whole, while tenure ensures that penalties for error will not be so severe that the people involved will refuse to make decisions.

In an organization based upon individualism and competition, decision making will be centralized at the top of the organization because the combination ensures that (1) decisions will be made for the good of the individual making them rather than for the good of the organization, and (2) individuals not at the top of the organization will be reluctant to make difficult decisions for fear of being fired if they decide wrongly. Moreover, a correct decision for the organization may not be a correct decision for the individual's self-interest, which brings us back to (1).

Both of these factors tend to push decisions to the top of the organization, a situation exacerbated by the fact that all decisions made at lower levels of the organization tend to limit the freedom of those at the top. If individual liberty is a goal of all individuals, why should the head of an organization reduce his or her own liberty by delegating authority to lower ranks? But if authority is not delegated, the head of the organization will be swamped by the number of decisions that need to be made.

In order to deal with the problem, the person at the top is most likely to promulgate rules and regulations and require all personnel to adhere to them. As long as the work is purely routine this system may work fairly well, but if it is not then the regulations cannot fit the situations, and long delays will occur as decisions are transferred upward in the organization. By the time decisions or new regulations arrive back at the lower level, it is very likely that the situation will have changed. In this case either an erroneous action is taken or the whole process starts over.

The dilemma is one between an effective organization and freedom for the head of the organization. It is made more acute by the classical liberal belief in rationality. Where both tradition and decentralized decision-making are accepted as legitimate restraints on the leader's power, organizations are stable and, within the limits of tradition, quite flexible.

Where the liberty of the person at the top is maximized and tradition is illegitimate as a guide to behavior, quite rigid organizations result.

The liberty of subordinates is reduced, leading to more paradigm conflict for the individual classical liberal. In order to achieve he or she must sacrifice liberty, but both achievement and liberty are primary paradigms to the classical liberal. To attempt to have both at the same time lessens (if it does not eliminate) the security of the individual. In a culture based upon money, to be fired means misery and starvation. Maslow's hierarchy of needs argues that security needs will generally preempt the needs for self-esteem and self-actualization; in this context the preemption means the individual will tend to sacrifice liberty for security. But if this happens, it will mean that the majority of the members of the organization will agree with those above them even when they are wrong, a situation hardly positive for the effective achievement of the goals of the organization or its leader.

One way out of the dilemma is for no one to work for anyone else (for everyone should be self-employed); but it seems obvious that the greatest wealth is to be gained through large organizations. If everyone desires wealth, then large organizations are bound to be created, especially if there is widespread unemployment. Moreover, the functional specificity involved in large societies requires the cooperation of many people in order to create anything complex. To a classical liberal any such cooperation will both require and create a hierarchy, and we are back to the previous problem.

The combination of hierarchy and individualism in classical liberalism creates organizations where liberty is denied to all save the head of the organization, a situation that parallels that of oligarchy, where all rewards are reserved for the ruling group. A system of free association is obviously under a fair degree of paradigm stress when membership in the association is attained at the price of freedom.

Concept of the Culture

A constant and unremitting competition of all individuals against all other individuals for places in a hierarchy that determines wealth and status constitutes this paradigm. One of its clearest expressions is Herbert Spencer's *Social Statistics*, first published in 1851.[1] In this and other works Spencer argues that constant competition brings out the best in human beings, and that this competition is necessary for the survival of society. No limits such as help or pity for the losers must be allowed to soften it. Only in this way can humanity itself survive and prosper, for the constant struggle will produce meritorious people at the same time it eliminates the inadequate.

This is social darwinism, although it predates Darwin's *On the Origin of Species* by eight years.[2] In its harshest form, this paradigm values the young only insofar as they may be useful to adult individuals and condemns the old to an early death when they cease being "useful." The concept of "nature red in tooth and claw," "the law of the jungle," and "survival of the fittest" are all expressions of this paradigm of individual competition. Social darwinism is basically a theory of human nature, and is fundamental to the logical development of the ideology of classical liberalism.

Darwin himself was interested not in individuals but in species, of which the human race is one. He felt that those species that could adapt or were better suited to changing living conditions would prosper, while others would tend to die out. While species might compete for resources or one species prey upon another, Darwin was not primarily concerned with competition among the individuals within a species.

Spencer, unlike Darwin, was primarily interested in human interaction. He saw self-interest, ambition, and unremitting competition as fundamental to all individuals, whether they were human beings or wolves. Because of this view, Spencer has a difficult time explaining cooperation that is not in the immediate self-interest of the individual, such as charity hospitals, public libraries, or public schools. While his paradigms of individual liberty and pervasive distrust of government (a corporate endeavor which almost of necessity sees society as a whole) prevented him from calling for the outright abolition of such projects, Spencer felt they weakened all those they touched, rewarded laziness and incompetence, and generally demeaned and corrupted humanity.

Niccolò Machiavelli, writing some 250 years before Spencer, had described a particularly successful classical liberal in the first part of *The Prince*,[3] where he describes the tactics of assassination, extortion, tortures, and the like that Cesare Borgia had used to conquer much of central Italy. Borgia clearly believed in the competition of all against all (he even poisoned members of his own family who stood in his way) and, like any successful liberal, had no patience with limited government when he himself was the governor. Interestingly enough, the term "machiavellian" now means an intelligent, ruthless, and greedy person who with amoral cunning will do anything to get power. The term really ought to be "borgian," since the second half of *The Prince*, concerned with how to maintain power rather than how to get it, reads like a tory tract on good government. In the latter part the prince is advised to be honest, to put his trust in an armed citizenry rather than in mercenary (professional) troops, to respect property and traditions, and in general to behave like a good tory monarch.

Classical liberals often cite *The Prince* as a "realistic" description of what is necessary to gain power, justifying the necessity of gaining power by the ends they intend to achieve. They miss the fact that Machiavelli was writing after the Medicis had gained control of Florence. The Medicis were an oligarchical family with at least some classical liberal members (they tended to poison one another). The first part of *The Prince* was meant to flatter them enough so that they would take the second part seriously. Naturally enough, they did no such thing, and the book's main effect was to discredit Machiavelli in the eyes of his fellow citizens of Florence.

The basic problem with constant and pervasive competition as a concept of society is that it fails to explain the cooperation inherent in both the family and the nation. While it is possible to imagine a family in which competition does not exist and a society in which competition is minimal and unimportant, it is not possible to imagine either a family or a society in which cooperation is not present.

Government

Quite logically, the major expression of classical liberal thought is economic rather than political. The emphasis the classical liberal puts upon wealth as a measure and consequence of individual merit and the simultaneous assumption that individuals always compete with one another ensure that money will be the dynamic center of the system. How this combination can benefit the entire society is a question the true classical liberal will neither ask nor be interested in, but it is a very important question. It is, in fact, the question Adam Smith asked.[4]

Smith can be understood as a man with tory concerns who was convinced that a tory culture is not viable. Looking at the conditions of life in Britain in his own time, Smith was convinced that individual self-interest was far stronger, more widespread, and more fundamental to human beings than any urge to cooperate. Believing in a single "human nature" that was individualistic and competitive, Smith could not credit the tory assertions that a functioning society positive for all its members could be based upon the cooperative nature of human beings. Even so, he himself was concerned for the welfare of all. This problem was considered later by the utilitarians, who developed the criterion of "the greatest good for the greatest number" as the best possible goal under the circumstances.

Tories believe in the good of all, a criterion quite consistent with their concept of a society made up of self-managing parts under the guidance of benevolent monarch acting as the parent to the rest of society. Believing that no person can be trusted to guide society for the good of all, the utilitarians saw this system as oligarchy at best and individual tyranny at worst. The solution is to prevent any person or group from managing the economy, since any such management will necessarily be for the benefit of the manager rather than the benefit of society as a whole. The result is "free" enterprise in that the economy as a whole is free from management.

Given the self-seeking nature of human beings in classical liberal thought, it is difficult to see how such freedom from central management would be anything other than the freedom of some to impose their management on others, since it seems self-evident that management and control will result in more wealth for the managers. Smith, however, wished to avoid a situation where just anyone with wealth has the power to govern.

What Smith did was to develop the classical liberal doctrine of self-interest and competition in such a way that it would result in the greatest good for the greatest number despite its tendencies towards management by the rich. Since no previous dominant culture in Europe had extended the principle of individual freedom to everyone in society, Smith was in the position of predicting what would happen in the future rather than explaining or justifying an existing situation. Reasonable people at that stage in European history could hope or expect that individual liberty could or would result in positive benefits for most, but not that it already did.

What did exist was a situation in which a good number of people were poor and miserable, while more and more were becoming so all the time. The classical liberal rejected tory solutions on two grounds: first, such solutions were "against human nature"; and second, they were immoral, since they were paternalistic. "Paternalism" to a classical liberal simply means that everyone in society other than the monarch is forced to live as a child, an intolerable restraint for those who equate childhood with dependency, lack of control, coercion, and low status.

Put another way, classical liberals felt (and feel) that the choice before them was not one among tory, oligarchical, and classical liberal systems of government and economics, but one between oligarchy and freedom. Tory values are fantasies to the classical liberal, and any attempt to base society upon them will simply end in oligarchy. Oligarchy was demonstrably bad for an increasing number of people, and it was increasingly obvious to classical liberals that a continuation of oligarchy would shortly add them to that number. That a classical liberal domination of society would aid them personally was a natural result of policies that would benefit all energetic and meritorious competitors, and was hardly grounds for rejecting the principles involved.

History, which might have suggested that tory values had functioned effectively in the past and therefore might reasonably be expected to do so in the future, came to be considered the history of small oligarchies and powerful individuals which, through the dynamic of individual self-interest, inevitably developed into tyrannies focused upon a single person. The divine right of kings was interpreted not as a limit upon kings but as conferring unlimited power upon them. Tradition became superstition and corporate harmony a mask for domination and exploitation. Freedom for the individual was freedom from the tyranny of government, the institution in society which was supposed to protect and nurture the whole society but which in fact functioned only to protect and nurture the interests of the governors.

The question was, what would happen if people actually were freed from governments' management and control? A century earlier, Hobbes[5] had argued that freedom from government ensured only that human life would be nasty, brutish, and short. He felt not that all people would murder and steal for their own individual benefit, but that enough of them would do so to disrupt any efforts at a more peaceful and productive life by the others. His solution was the institution of an all-powerful government centered in a single individual whose word was law.

A rationalist and an individualist, Hobbes denied the power of tradition and corporate values either to control society or to limit the power of the strong. Attached to the upper classes (he was a tutor to the children of the Cavendish family and later to the children of Charles II), Hobbes did not have the perspective of the middle class. He perceived liberty more as the opportunity to harm others than as a means of avoiding such harm. Believing this, he developed a doctrine that combined individualism and a powerful state. The despotism that would result would be benevolent because the monarch, owning everything, would take care that his private property was well looked after. Where tories see no relevant distinction between public and private because the network of reciprocal responsibilities and rights in tory culture makes such a division impossible, Hobbes identifies public and private in the individual monarch. When all subjects are the private property of the monarch then his private property is the public.

Hobbes's conclusions were sufficiently repugnant to tories, oligarchs, and classical liberals to ensure that they would be unacceptable to the vast majority of the population no matter how logical they were. It is important to remember, however, that they are logical and that individualized tyrannies have existed and do exist. As we shall see later, socialists assume that Hobbes was in large measure correct, and that without the development of socialism, society will end with the kind of domination

Hobbes describes. They do not, however, believe that the absolute monarch will "look after" his or her subjects. Far more logical to them is the assumption that the tyrant will viciously exploit them, wringing from their labor the goods and services that constitute the wealth of the individually owned state.

The classical liberals, while believing in the same concept of human nature as Hobbes, disliked the result. Hobbes's absolute monarch would destroy the freedom of the middle class as surely as would the tories, and middle-class prosperity would be as insecure as when the oligarchs dominated. The problem was to institute a government strong enough to protect private property without being strong enough to take it for its own.

The solution was to create a government that would have the protection of private property as its only function. It would not act to manage society in any way, but would react only whenever and wherever private property was threatened. A government was necessary to prevent the brutal and violent chaos Hobbes envisioned, but the absolute power Hobbes saw as necessary was unacceptable to classical liberals, even if it was in all its essentials based upon their own doctrines of individualism and selfishness. The paradigm conflict between liberty for all individuals and the need to manage and control others in order to achieve individual liberty was too obvious and shocking to be maintained. The concept of a government limited by rational principle was consistent with classical liberal thought and offered the great advantage that it moved the paradigm conflict from government, where it was far too obvious, to the general economy, where it could be more easily ignored.

Before this move could happen, though, some means of convincing the majority of the people that such a development would be good for them was necessary. If they did not believe it they would have to be coerced, but it was all too clear that in the event of a general uprising the only coercive force capable of putting it down would be the government, since any force that strong would very shortly become the government if it was not already.

The solution was to form a government of the elected representatives of the owners of private property. The members would have to be elected for two reasons. First, the traditional governors at the time were still the traditional tories and oligarchs, neither of which could be trusted to limit government to the protection of private property. Second, a system of election by property owners would allow them to vote out of office any member who showed signs of expanding the role of government.

It must be remembered that classical liberals do not trust government, even when it is made up of people they themselves elect. In their eyes its sole function is to protect their wealth from whoever might be tempted to take it. Accordingly, classical liberals are very suspicious of any institution having enough power to threaten their liberty to do whatever they might want with their own private property. The most obvious institution with such power is their own government. The most obvious exception to this rule of distrust of government is the classical liberal leader of government, who can be expected to increase the power of government in order to increase his own wealth and power.

A further complication is that members of a classical liberal government, being individuals, are expected to vote their individual consciences. They are elected by property owners (and in some cases must own property themselves in order to be eligible to run for office) but they do not accept the guidance of the electorate. "Public opinion" should not influence their vote; neither should they look to their leaders to tell them how to vote. They should make their own decisions and stick to them. As a practical matter this principle attempts to isolate the member of government from both "the public" and the aristocracy/oligarchy. As a statement of conscience, it is also perfectly consistent with the paradigms of individualism, liberty, and logic which are so fundamental to classical liberalism.

As both a practical and theoretical matter, however, every individual is supposed to be in a state of unremitting competition for wealth with all other individuals. The strongest position in society is in the government because of the military and police power involved. (Since any institution in society that has military forces stronger than those of the government is in fact a new government, such power cannot be denied or prevented.) How, then, can individuals in government be prevented from using their power to make themselves wealthy? Moreover, since wealth and obtaining wealth is merit, how can these individuals not be considered meritorious? But if they do use their governmental positions to become wealthy (or wealthier), then the government is doing more than simply protecting private property. It is, to a greater or lesser degree, managing the economy for the benefit of the governors, which is the same function it had under the oligarchs.

Classical liberals are caught in paradigm conflict here, and cannot resolve the problem. Generally speaking, their way of coping with "corruption" of this sort is to ignore it as long as it is even semilegal and restricted to individual enrichment. On the other hand, any move toward oligarchy (that is, the inclusion of family members and the subordination of individual interests to family interests) is liable to be exposed and censured. In order to further prevent oligarchy from developing, competition may be built into government institutions. Separate legislatures, executives, court systems, and bureaucracies may be set against one another, in the hope that they will have more to gain from competition than from collusion.

The monarch, rejected by the oligarchs because of his symbolic identity with the whole of society, is also rejected by the classical liberal for the same reason. The combination of individualism, competition, and hierarchy, however, forces the creation of a "chief executive officer." How to have a chief executive officer without allowing the position to take on the attributes of a monarch is difficult. Hobbes more or less works in reverse, too. The classical liberals have no wish to create an absolute monarch, but having created a chief executive officer in a system that assumes every individual competes incessantly for all the power and wealth available, how do they stop him from becoming a monarch?

"By setting interest against interest" is the classical liberal answer, but if there is only one real hierarchy how do they prevent a single winner? Frequent rotation in office and competition among various branches of government is a standard answer, but this pretty obviously makes government inefficient. The hope is that such an arrangement will keep government too weak to threaten private property but strong enough to defend it. In a culture that values individual achievement and efficiency a government like this is sure to be despised as wasteful, yet feared and hated if it becomes more efficient.

The paradigm conflicts that require government and nongovernment simultaneously cannot be evaded by the classical liberal but they can often be ignored. This can be done by assuming that anything really important is economic rather than political. This is really the public/private split under another name, since government is public and the economy is supposed to be private. This split is a way to deal with paradigm conflict but it also has its origin in the nature of logic.

Classical liberals are rationalists. Being committed to logic as a source of truth they are also committed to the separation of roles, since to combine roles or to acknowledge a legitimate overlap would confuse the logic or require the recognition of logically contradictory truths. To assume that politics can be separated from economics (or any other part of life) is nonsense to a tory or an oligarch, but simple common sense to a classical liberal.

Economics

To tories and oligarchs it is obvious that a society's economy will be managed both in production and distribution. The only question is by whom and for whom it will be managed. Classical liberals believe that the entire system should go unmanaged, but that every individual has both a right and a duty to create and manage his own wealth. This arrangement is fine for those who are already wealthy or who have a clear opportunity to become so, but not for those whose chances for wealth are slight or who believe that all members of society should be prosperous. To them such a belief is immoral and illegitimate because it condemns the many poor to subservience to the rich while denying them all rights and privileges.

Until this lack of legitimacy is overcome, a classical liberal culture is very unlikely to dominate. A further problem is the classical liberal's avowed intention to do away with the oligarchy, but with time it becomes obvious to the oligarchs that far more successful classical liberals join the oligarchy than continue to oppose it.

The legitimacy problem remained. It was settled in Europe primarily by Adam Smith. By changing the general goal of society from the welfare of all to the greatest good for the greatest number (thus anticipating the utilitarians) some room for maneuver was gained (especially since 51 percent of the population constituted a sort of minumum "greatest number," although logically any particular set of circumstances could have dictated a greater or lesser number). Even so, the larger question persisted: how could a system based upon selfishness produce any widespread benefits? It did not even have the virtue of oligarchy, which at least provided for the entire ruling group. Wouldn't a system of individual selfishness simply produce a Hobbesian monarch, who would impoverish everyone for his own benefit?

Smith's answer was that "the invisible hand of competition" would automatically manage the marketplace to achieve the greatest possible good for the greatest possible number. Some slippage would occur in the form of failed entrepreneurs, the unemployable, the unemployed, and (in the other direction) the idle rich, but generally speaking it would be the best possible system for all.

In order to bring this about, only one condition was necessary: absolute economic freedom of both production and distribution. People must be free to produce anything they want, in any way they want, and they must be equally free to buy anything they want anywhere they want. What this amounts to is a truly remarkable assault upon cooperation. Smith, believing in the viability of oligarchy but not of tory systems, correctly recognized the problems of the many as being caused and perpetuated by the cooperation of the few. He reasoned that if this cooperation was made illegitimate a new economic system could function, and this one would function for the benefit of the many.

The way this change was to happen was fairly simple, if revolutionary. Free competition was to function to keep a plentiful supply of goods available at the lowest possible prices, another way of saying that the production of goods would be maximized and their distribution would be wide and evenly spread out. The system, as Smith envisaged it, depended upon individual initiative and self-interest. An individual, for example, might invent a widget. The materials in this widget might cost about $1.50 and it might take its inventor about an hour to make one. Being self-interested and not responsible for anyone's welfare but his or her own, the inventor would naturally proceed to sell his newly made widget for as high a price as he could get for it.

Suppose the widget to be immensely attractive (or necessary) so that $100 each can be charged and the widgets will still sell. The inventor is immediately rewarded for his imagination and industry, and some of those who want widgets have them. If the demand (the money people will spend on widgets) keeps up, however, some other enterprising person is bound to see that a widget contains only $1.50 worth of materials and an hour's work to produce. As soon as he does, he will begin to make widgets himself, but will set the price at $95 in order to be sure of selling his widgets. When three or four entrepreneurs get into the widget business the price will soon fall to the cost of materials plus an adequate payment to the maker for his labor. If any entrepreneur drops his price below this level he will soon be unable to feed himself and will have to bring his price back up or cease business entirely. If a widget maker seeks to resurrect the immense profits made at the beginning of the widget trade he will be unable to sell his widgets, and either drop his prices or go out of business.

Since the price thus stabilizes at the minimum necessary to sustain the widget makers at the lowest level they will accept, the price can be said to be a fair price. As long as there is a demand for widgets they will be produced, since any shortage will lead to higher prices and more widget makers. Any further gains for producers of widgets would be made by improvements in the original widget or by efficiencies in its production.

The price of widgets will effectively govern their distribution, other things being equal, and thus function as a rationing mechanism. Price, of course works from the top down: the immensely wealthy can have as many widgets as they want while the destitute get none. Since there is a limit to how much of anything an individual is willing to pay for, the supply of widgets will not be indefinitely bought up by the rich but will soon become available to those who must use some discretion in their purchases. Widgets are thus effectively rationed out to the population through the abstract and impersonal medium of money, while the immediate choice of goods will be made by the individual consumer. Perhaps not all individuals need or want a widget. Given a free market, they need not buy one and production will automatically adjust to this situation.

The system will have short-term imbalances of the supply of widgets and the demand for them. In the beginning there are too few widgets, but after widget-making becomes popular there will probably be too many. At first many people cannot afford widgets, no matter how desperately they desire them, while the subsequent widget glut leaves widgets quietly rotting on the shelves. If widgets are a mere fad they will likely remain there, and all the widget makers will go bankrupt together (except for those who saw it coming and got out of widgets while the getting was good). But if widgets are truly useful to people the industry will soon stabilize and widget makers become solid and prosperous citizens. They will not, of course, become too prosperous, for new widget makers can appear any time the price of widgets rises very much above a fair price.

Generally speaking, the greatest imbalances will occur with new products and those they replace. New products will be continually invented, for the rewards for the invention and production of useful and desirable things are immense. The necessity of actually selling them to other individuals effectively limits these products to those that people desire.

Efficiency in production (the accomplishment of a goal with the use of the fewest possible resources) is automatic, since competition ensures that inefficient producers will be forced out of the market. Even so, the system as a whole will be remarkably stable, a fair price being held day in and day out for most of the products on the market. Society will be generally well fed, well clothed, and well housed if only liberty and freedom can be maintained.

There are three general paradigmatic problems with the free-enterprise system. The first is the simple but intractable problem of the oligarchy. In classical liberal terms the oligarchy represents illicit, illegitimate, and immoral cooperation: all individuals must compete with all other individuals if the system is to work. Oligarchs cooperate with one another. They have strong family ties that not only prevent them from competing with one another (a minor problem since there are lots of middle-class individuals who will compete) but explicitly require them to cooperate.

Since they as a group compete with the individualized nonrulers, what is to prevent them from buying out some widget makers and underselling a fair price until the rest go bankrupt? In fact, if they have enough wealth they can be expected to do so. Having established a monopoly on widgets, they may reasonably be expected to make relatively few of them, thus driving the price up far beyond a fair price and depriving a great many consumers of their chance to own a widget. Conversely, they could fix a high price and then adjust production to supply the demand at that price. Either way, the wide distribution and plentiful production of the free-market system is not achieved. Moreover, inventions and new producers will be greatly reduced, since the greatest benefits will go to the oligarchs while the risks remain with the individualized nonrulers. The oligarchy, then, cannot be allowed to remain if a free-enterprise economic system is to function as Smith envisaged it.

The tendencies of classical liberalism we have previously discussed remain, and it is very unlikely that the oligarchy will be destroyed. What is most probable is that the oligarchs, as soon as classical liberalism becomes acceptable to a fair proportion of society, will recognize its inability to seriously harm them, and will represent themselves as classical liberals. By doing so, they have moved their management of the economy from government (the public sphere) to private business corporations.

These business corporations are safe from government "interference" while at the same time the government is dedicated to their preservation and security (the protection of private property). Their only problem will then be the possibility that the rising classical liberals, acting (quite naturally) in their own interests, will seek to break the oligarchs' power.

If the oligarchy is wise enough to allow the most successful classical liberals to marry into the oligarchy (short of adoption there is no other way) while making sure the moderately successful are both relatively well paid and sharply distinguished from those beneath them, it would appear that the oligarchs have little to fear from the classical liberals. At the same time, the free-enterprise system will not work as Smith envisaged it.

Smith foresaw just such a combination, describing monopolies as disguised taxation on those not in them. In doing so he recognized that monopolies acted as governments in managing the economy, but if the economy is not to be managed at all, how could the monopolies be prevented? The logical dilemma is not an easy one to overcome.

The second great problem with classical liberal economics is the effect efficient production has upon consumption, and therefore upon the distribution of goods. One of the major components of production in any system is human labor and skill. Without these, raw materials cannot be converted into usable products, and Smith emphasizes that it is labor which gives products their value. Therefore the self-interest of the employer and necessity combine to keep labor costs as low as possible: self-interest because, other things being equal, the lower the labor costs the higher the profit to the owner; and necessity because if an employer pays higher wages than his competition, the competitors will undersell him and drive him out of business.

If there are more people looking for work than there are jobs, it is clear that the logic of the marketplace will keep wages at a minimum level. The "minimum level" in a society thoroughly dominated by classical liberals will be one of subsistence only, and there is nothing to keep it from being a hand-to-mouth existence which in the long run is subsubsistence. Malnutrition, poor housing and clothing, and poor medical care will remove the weaker workers as well as the weaker members of their families.

This is so because the doctrinaire classical liberal is a social darwinist. From this perspective, all forms of unearned assistance to individuals are illegitimate. Such aid as food, public health, free libraries, and free schools are considered both demeaning and harmful, since they are sure to destroy the character and moral fiber of those receiving them. To reward people for not working is to stand the natural order of things on its head.

Labor unions are as illegitimate as commercial monopolies. They raise the cost of labor without increasing productivity while denying the individual working person his or her right to bargain individually with the employer. Worse still, they deny the employer the right to run his business as he wishes, since he can no longer hire, fire, promote, and determine working conditions at his own volition. In short, unions and welfare subvert free enterprise. In their presence the system will not work as it is supposed to, and ruin for all will result.

On the other hand, if it does work as it is supposed to, how can it work for the benefit of the greatest number? If the great majority of working people (the lower class as distinguished from the middle class) are paid subsistence wages they will not be able to buy anything other than subsistence goods. These will in the main be food, and probably only one or two types of food at that. No matter how low the price of widgets may fall (or the price of any other nonsubsistence product) the great majority of the population will be unable to buy them.

In this situation, a system of free enterprise will profit only from sales to the middle and upper classes, a situation that resembles oligarchy. In other words, the group benefitting from the exploitation of labor is still the oligarchy and the middle class. The most that can be said for classical liberalism from this perspective is that it has made the upper class more permeable; that successful classical liberals will be able to rise to positions of leadership in society rather than finding their way blocked by an oligarchy.

The situation for the great majority of the population remains the same as it was under simple oligarchy, with two qualifications: first, individuals of exceptional merit may expect to rise with fewer hindrances in a classical liberal culture, and there will be no limit on how far they can rise; second, those who do not rise will blame no one but themselves if they are classical liberals. Having accepted the doctrine that wealth and merit are identical, they must also accept the fact that they must have little or no merit, since they have little or no money.

If there are more jobs than people to fill them we may expect wages to rise above subsistence levels because employers will have to compete with each other for workers just as workers compete with each other for jobs. In this situation, however, we may also expect that inventors will supply an increasing number of labor-saving (or labor-replacing) devices, thus reducing the employer's need for workers and restoring the previous situation where unemployment kept wages low.

Another solution for employers is to either move the factory from a labor-short area to one where unemployment is high or to move unemployed people to the area of the factory. If the new area is in a foreign country or the new people are from outside the country, it is very probable that workers will be divided, a circumstance favorable to the employer.

Labor-replacing devices and moving to high-unemployment or unorganized areas are two devices by which management can overcome union-dominated situations, but a third device can also be used. This is "scientific management," a technique of breaking complex operations down to very simple parts. Workers are hired to do one part only, a system that increases the number of workers needed but that drastically reduces the number of skilled workers required. The object is to make any individual worker almost immediately replaceable by any other individual. Skill and experience are not required and need not be paid for. The result is to maximize the number of people who can do the work. One (perhaps unintended) result of the scientific management is to make bigger enterprises more practical than smaller ones, but the main thrust is to reduce labor costs and increase management control.

All of these strategies are designed to reduce labor costs, and when they work they all have the same result: workers cannot buy the things they produce. Since scientific management tends to make mass production more "economical" than other methods, we are back to the same dilemma: the same factors that make mass production profitable to the individual entrepreneur tend to destroy the market for mass-produced articles in the whole system. That is, the gain of the individuals who own and manage the factories is dependent upon selling what is produced in a mass market, but the same system that maximizes unit profits tends to destroy the mass market needed to sell the units.

There are various "cures" for this problem, but the only one acceptable to the classical liberal is expansion. The difficulty is not that a free-enterprise system cannot produce sufficient goods but that once produced they cannot be sold. At this point, we should distinguish between "need" and "demand." "Demand" is money available to people who wish to buy something. "Need" is the physical or emotional necessity for something. Starving people need food, but if they have no money they cannot "demand" food. As far as a classical liberal economic system goes, they might as well not exist, except for their effect upon wages, which is to keep them at subsistence levels. In this sense, the "market" for mass produced articles is low in countries that have a very few rich people and a great many poor because the poor have so little money with which to buy.

Even so, those few rich in each "poor" country can represent a sizable market if a great many poor countries can be reached. Moreover, countries in which a fair degree of wealth is widely distributed are also good markets. Both sorts of markets involve international trade, so "free trade" becomes the slogan of the classical liberal. Countries with a great many unemployed are also low-wage countries if the government is or can be dominated by oligarchical or classical liberal regimes, so constructing factories there is profitable if the "home" country is labor-short or union-dominated. A further reason for classical liberals to support free trade is that as resources at home become depleted industries must look outside for more of them.

The combination of material resources, low wages, and a world market would dictate the abandonment of the original country as a production site were it not for the action of governments that are not controlled by classical liberals. Radical liberals pursue welfare policies that are both illegitimate and immoral to classical liberals, while tories and socialists both believe in managed economies and welfare states, policies that give the classical liberal no scope for either gaining wealth individually or for exercising the liberty that is all-important to him.

Amid these various decisions and their various consequences, oligarchs retain control over the economy and are staunchly nationalist, since to them their family defines the nation. True, they will hardly defend the rights or living standards of nonrulers. For this reason they often collaborate with free-enterprise systems that benefit them, but they will not become "world citizens" and will function only in the interest of wealthy individuals because of their dedication to the corporate group of national rulers of which they are a part.

Classical liberals must function in a world made up only in part of classical liberals, and they have not managed to dominate the national societies of very many nations. Within these constraints, it is only wisdom on their part to divide their production and distribution facilities as much as possible so that no single government can take over all of any of their operations. Since the nationalism inherent in tory and oligarchical cultures makes international alliances against them unlikely, that leaves radical liberal and socialist regimes as possible problems.

Socialists alienate members of the other four cultures by their attacks on hierarchy at the same time they find themselves relying on nationalism at home to legitimize their domination of the national society. While powerful enough to deny classical liberals unrestrained access to their own markets and labor, they have not as yet been able to unite with non-socialist regimes to do the same abroad. Radical liberals, as we shall see, are generally unable to effectively challenge the management prerogatives of classical liberals, among which are the siting of production facilities and marketing.

All in all, expansion across national boundaries is the most logical and practical response to pressures on wages and low demand. It is equally logical that oligarchs will support this expansion at the same time they ensure that control remains with their own nationalist ruling group. This is the definition of empire: an expansionary system in which control is maintained by the government of the expanding state. That this control denies full individual liberty to anyone not in the ruling group (and is most likely to deny even token individual liberty to those not of the ruling nationality) is a paradigm conflict for classical liberalism.

A third area of concern in classical liberalism is the environment and physical resources, since the emphasis in classical liberalism on immediate and short-term individual profit dictates the exploitation of resources rather than their development. It is always easier to use up and move on than it is to develop a resource in such a way that it will always be available. It is also more profitable to the individual in the short run, and usually over the individual's life span. Since no classical liberal should be concerned about the welfare of any other (even that of his or her own children), nothing in classical liberalism will prevent entrepreneurs from clear-cutting entire forests, single-cropping farmland, strip mining without restoring the top soil, or doing anything else that will lead to immediate profits at the cost of long-term damage to the environment. So long as the individuals making the decisions need not live in the areas affected there is no reason why they should care about them.

The usual response by a classical liberal to questions of this nature (from those of other cultures, naturally) is that as resources are used up it will become profitable to re-create them, to import them, or to find substitutes for them. In any case, these will be problems for others and will be solved by individuals acting in their own self-interest.

Adam Smith, with his interest in the whole of society, would reluctantly agree that such a system is necessary, its only virtue being that any alternative is worse. Classical liberalism would seem to offer no adequate solution to such problems as nuclear wastes, the widespread and toxic pollution of surface water, water·tables, and farm land, and irreversible erosion. The best classical liberals can offer is a faith that technology will save us all, although the more immediate solution for successful classical liberals is simply to live elsewhere or to create separate and controlled environments for themselves, options they can afford. There is no serious paradigm conflict here, a condition which makes this aspect of classical liberalism particularly difficult to influence by nonclassical liberals.

Summary

While the paradigm conflicts of classical liberalism are severe, their belief in competitive individualism prevents them from dealing with societal consequences of their paradigms. In the short run, however, classical liberalism has a fair number of virtues when the society involved is expanding both physically and economically. Rapid individual economic and social movement is possible; people can better themselves through hard work and creativity. The potential for production is immense, while the disregard for tradition and the continuing demand for new and better products leads to a great deal of innovation in both technology and human relations.

Science, too, is liberated from its ties to other facets of society (due to functional specificity and role differentiation) and made more respectable. Its emphasis upon logic, predictability, and freedom from emotion make it particularly attractive to rationalists, while its separation from other aspects of life tends to insulate it from the paradigm stresses inherent in any culture. At the same time, a belief in science as the answer to all problems, an extension of the paradigm that everything is rational, tends to replace religion as the guiding force in life.

Religion, a belief in a controlling superhuman power entitled to obedience, reverence, and worship, is clearly a difficult area for classical liberals, who tend to give obedience, reverence, and worship to their independent, free selves. In Europe the transition from dominance by a tory/oligarchy system to dominance by a tory/ oligarchy/classical liberal combination involved the development of Protestant Christianity. It is widely supposed that without "the Protestant ethic" the free-enterprise economic system would not have become dominant in Europe as much as it has, and this is probably the case.

The transition began in European history with the renaissance, but Martin Luther was the first theologian to express its religious side and have it accepted by at least some of the ruling groups. Luther's basic thesis was that man was saved individually through a direct connection with God. The one thing necessary was the Bible, which is the revealed word of God. Therefore the whole of the Catholic (tory) church was not only unnecessary but a cause of problems, since it came between the individual and God.[6] In our terms, this was a clear denial of the cooperative and corporate paradigms of a tory culture and an expression of the classical liberal paradigm of individual freedom.

The central paradigm conflict of classical liberalism (that between a belief in individual liberty and inevitable and legitimate hierarchy) is developed in Luther's writings in a particularly bold and logical way. Individual liberty is spiritual liberty only. No man should ever let his Bible be taken from him, for it is the means to his own, personal salvation, but he should submit to civil authority in all other respects, even when that authority is unjust.

Luther considered most rulers to be the greatest fools or the worst knaves on earth. Why, then, should any free individual do what they tell him to? Luther's answer is that civil authority is necessary to preserve social order. Even as he argues that there is no legitimate spiritual hierarchy among men he stoutly defends a hierarchy of material goods and political authority. So much so, in fact, that during the great Peasant Rebellion of 1525, Luther was loudly and enthusiastically on the side of reaction, supporting the traditional upper class at the great expense of the lower. Some 100,000 peasants were slaughtered and what was essentially a movement for a return to tory values was ruthlessly put down. The peasants called for the reinstatement of the commons (they had been taken by oligarchs, as was to happen a little later in England) and other feudal rights and privileges that had been abolished by some of the rulers. As might be expected, a fair number of tory rulers sided with the peasants, but the oligarchs won, greatly aided by Luther's classical liberal support of hierarchy.

In his support of temporal hierarchy Luther felt compelled to point out that it was not a hierarchy of merit. Coming at a time of great corruption in the feudal church and in civil authority this was reasonable, but it put the growing number of classical liberals in a position of obvious and severe paradigm stress. It will come as little surprise that most Protestant leaders soon regarded a hierarchy as one of merit as well as power. Calvin became a ruler, while other Protestant leaders sought to change the basis for leadership from heredity to election by property holders. Some, of course, went too far and attempted to do away with hierarchy in the material world as well as the spiritual, but the great majority went in the other direction. Calvin burned "heretics," a clear denial of spiritual liberty to those who disagreed with him. The other side did the same thing (though perhaps with a bit more logical consistency) and the great religious controversy of Europe rolled on.

What it amounted to was a struggle between tories and classical liberals, with the oligarchs supporting whichever side seemed most likely to improve their power position. Very often, in fact, the position of the oligarchs became so powerful that each side was reduced to seeking the oligarchy's support against the other. Protestant theology, designed to free individuals from the "spiritual tyranny" of a tory church, most often ended by making religion irrelevant to daily living. The community of believers became a free association of individuals whose main earthly concern was to get rich. By electing their pastors they could avoid those who made the paradigm stress of their position too obvious, while retaining those who stressed the classical liberal values they most wanted to hear. The accumulation of wealth and power in a secular hierarchy determined by those two attributes became theologically correct: social climbing and getting rich now had the blessing of the church. Moreover, the community of the church could be seen as a replacement of the larger tory community, with the advantage that the church was now a free association that entailed only a limited obligation to the other community members, if it entailed any at all. Morality became a sticky issue, since it was both individual and communal, but many seemed to solve the issue by considering whatever they did to be moral.

All of this, of course, was of immense benefit to the oligarchs in their struggle with the tories, as long as the new culture did not seriously threaten the basis of their own wealth and power. Generally speaking, it did not. The initial fear of the oligarchy that classical liberals would in fact destroy the hereditary ruling class as their logic demanded lessened as it became apparent that successful classical liberals either joined the oligarchy themselves or their children did. The reforms they initiated (free trade, an electoral system that enfranchised all substantial property owners, the abolition of the monarch's power or of the monarch, and the denial of the government's responsibility for the welfare of the poor) were either consistent with what the oligarchy was already doing or could be used to further the oligarchy's ends.

Moreover, classical liberals would work hard and well for oligarchs, secure in the knowledge that it was in their own individual interest to do so. If the lower class could all be persuaded to accept classical liberalism, so much the better. If they could not, it was likely that classical liberalism might claim the most vigorous among them, leaving the rest to work for the restoration of tory values in a system that gave power to the oligarchs.

Chapter 7

Radical Liberalism

For those members of the middle class unable to move up to membership in the oligarchy and afraid of moving downward into the lower classes, the dominance of the oligarchy/classical liberal combination is less than satisfactory. In periods of geographic and economic expansion there is room for small businessmen, minor entrepreneurs, and inventors to prosper, but when expansion slows down these are precisely the people to go bankrupt, since they have neither the financial nor the family resources of the oligarchs. Moreover, it is during these periods that the wealthy have both the opportunity and the motive to take the small middle class over. Mergers, monopolies, bankruptcies, and simple takeovers all make it apparent that at the least a plutocracy is present, and at most that the oligarchy has been there all the time.

In the same circumstances, it becomes apparent that the children of the rich have major advantages in competing for high places in the hierarchy, very much including the hierarchy of government. Conversely, it is obvious in bad times (bad for the poor and the middle class; these are times of great opportunity for the oligarchy and the very wealthy in general) that the children of the poor are at least as disadvantaged as the children of the rich are favored. It is hardly fair to expect a child with malnutrition, poor or no schooling, and inadequate parents to compete equally with even the children of the middle class, let alone the children of the rich. Surely, the parents of the children of poverty are themselves responsible for that poverty, but is very difficult to see how their children are.

The classical liberal simply ignores the problem, largely by neither thinking of it nor looking at it, but the radical liberal does both and feels sick. At the same time, the radical liberal believes in all the paradigms of the classical liberal. The solution is twofold: prevent monopolies and provide welfare for the children of the poor.

In order to achieve these two goals a great many changes are necessary, for while the goals themselves are simple, their implementation is not. At every step, the paradigm conflicts of classical liberalism pressure the radical liberals to make more reforms, but with every reform come new complications, new problems, and more paradigm stress. The radical liberal, by admitting that his or her own actions might and should have a positive influence on others in society (most importantly, on the children of the poor) has come to feel responsible for them.

Since classical liberal paradigms hold that each person is wholly responsible for his or her own life, past, present, and future, the paradigm conflict in the radical liberal (who believes the same thing) is quite strong. Most often this results in "radical liberal guilt," a phenomenon that is mostly a comfort to the radical liberal, since his guilt proves his moral superiority over the classical liberal, who lives much the same kind of life but doesn't feel guilty about it.

Generally speaking, radical liberals manage to give some help to the poor but do not succeed in hurting or changing the way of living of the rich. Once the oligarchs get over their fear of the new culture they may very well "join" it, in much the same way they "became" classical liberals once they understood that appearing to do so was very much to their advantage.

Theoretical Source of Legitimacy

The radical liberal is a rationalist. Radical liberal paradigms on legitimacy are identical with those of classical liberals, and quite different from those of tories and oligarchs. A belief in logic and reason as binding and in science as the ultimate solution to all problems is fundamental to this culture. Physical science will solve economic, medical, and all other problems of the physical world while social science will do the same for interpersonal relations. We are, in this view, making progress toward utopia, defined as a world in which all basic problems are solved, except perhaps what to do with all the leisure time that will result.

If the classical liberal believes that only unfettered free enterprise — under (or over) a government that does nothing except protect the private property of individuals — results (or will result) in liberty and wealth for all meritorious, adequate people, then the classical liberal must be guilty of an error in logic. The radical liberal seeks to correct the error, not to deny that logic is a sufficient basis for legitimacy.

Organization of the Culture

It is logic which tells the radical liberal that hierarchy is inevitable, positive, and based on a single criterion measured by money. A radical liberal approach to organization is generally identical with that of the classical liberal with one important exception: the radical liberal paradigm on voting. This paradigm can be explained as a logical conviction and as a necessity if the radical liberals are to gain enough political power to institute their reforms.

The paradigm is clear enough: all men and women should vote, and all votes should count equally. It is logical that every individual knows his or her self-interest, even if the classical liberal argues that the poor are inadequate in this respect as in every other. The assumption is that the poor have proved their lack of intelligence and character by remaining poor, and therefore cannot be trusted to vote logically and correctly: that is, to protect private property in any and all circumstances and to use government for that purpose only.

The radical liberal responds that every individual has a right as an individual to free expression, and that if liberty means anything he or she should also have a say in his own government. Moreover, the ultimate aim of free enterprise is the greatest good of the greatest number. It is nonsense to assume that the decisions of a minority of self-interested individuals will be to the benefit of anyone but themselves, so the electoral system should be as open to all as the economic system. Just as anyone is free to invent, to produce, and to consume, so all men should be free to vote. If they choose not to, or choose to use their vote corruptly, so much the worse for them.

The radical liberal has another good reason to advocate electoral equality. Convinced that the most wealthy will form a plutocracy unless they are prevented from doing so, the radical liberal is also convinced of two other relevant considerations. First, no poor man will vote for another poor man to govern him. Second, no poor man will vote for the plutocrats who are exploiting him. Logically enough, this leaves the poor voting for middle-class radical liberals. They will vote this way, not only because in doing so they can vote against the very rich and the demonstrably inadequate but also because the radical liberal is in favor of welfare for their children. Interest and principle will coincide, and the radical liberal will gain the political power needed to regulate against monopoly and to give the children of the poor an equal chance to achieve.

The key to the radical liberal position on electoral equality is that the poor will not directly govern. They may be a majority of the electorate but they will not be present in the government, since they will not vote for one of themselves. The fact (to a radical liberal) that the political hierarchy is a hierarchy of merit means that the poor will recognize merit when they see it. Since they themselves have little merit, there is no reason to fear they will elect one of themselves. (There is quite a bit of paradigm stress here, since it may be that the poor's lack of merit will entail an inability to appreciate the merit of hierarchy, but the radical liberal chooses to ignore or discount this possibility.)

In their efforts to achieve electoral equality, the radical liberals often find themselves in a rather surprising alliance with the tories. The tories have been losing in their struggle with the oligarchs and classical liberals, who not only demonstrate the most appalling individual selfishness but insist upon loudly claiming it as their foremost virtue. The tory does not despise the poor, believing that the poor have been exploited and that given a chance they would be as meritorious as any other segment of society. Moreover, tory aristocrats see themselves as the natural leaders of society, and are sure that the poor will respond to their leadership.

While not believing in the necessity of voting, finding democracy a divisive system that sets people against one another, the tory finds nothing wrong with giving the vote to the poor. Indeed, since the oligarchs and classical liberals have risen to dominance it is probably the best system possible, and may have the great merit of returning the tories to power. It can be justified on a theoretical basis by an appeal to the corporate nature of tory culture: if the working people no longer live as corporate groups then the hierarchical heads of their groups can no longer advise the king of their needs. Through the vote, they can achieve the same end, even though the system is far cruder and subject to major distortions owing to the divisiveness and competition inherent in the electoral process. Tory democracy is definitely second best to a tory, but under the circumstances it is the best that can be had.

The middle-class radical liberal and the tory aristocrat combine to extend the vote to the poor, each believing that the result will be to place one of his or her own in power as the representative of the poor. Both believe that his or her policies will be in the best interests of the poor, and they are agreed that the government should be responsible for at least the welfare of the children of the poor. They are divided, however, on the treatment of the rich. Both seek to prevent the abuse of power, but the tory aristocrat has trouble remaining separate from the oligarch, who may be part of the aristocrat's extended family, whereas the radical liberal has trouble separating wealth from merit, since money is still the measure and reward of merit.

Electoral equality is always incomplete, but the logic of the radical liberal forces him to press on. Age is the most pervasive disqualification, the very young not being allowed to vote. This recognition of the human condition would seem impossible to withhold in any culture, but the age of maturity is still open to question. Sexual, linguistic, and literacy qualifications have also been used to limit voting. They are consistent with tory values (as is no voting at all) but not with radical liberal values, which demand universal suffrage as a consequence of individualism.

Basic Unit of the Culture

Radical liberals are individualists, and in this respect they are identical with classical liberals. They also believe in a hierarchy of merit which, while not inconsistent with rationalism or individualism, does put quite a strain on the belief in electoral equality. If individuals are ranked on a hierarchy of merit, why should those with less merit have an equal say with those who have demonstrated more? Conversely, how can a hierarchy exist if all men are equal? These are characteristic paradigm conflicts of the radical liberal, and they cannot be simply ignored.

For liberals, the equality of all individuals is not the equality of people but the equality of money. One man's money is just as good as another's. No individual should be denied the right to use his money in any way he sees fit, as long as he does not trespass upon the private property of another. This last qualification is not, strictly speaking, a logical conclusion. There is nothing in logic to indicate robbery and violence are any less effective or praiseworthy methods of gaining wealth than the production and sale of goods. In fact, the merit of successful thieves and bullies is usually recognized and respected by classical liberals, as long as they are no threat to the rich.

Adam Smith, writing in an age when economics was called "the dismal science" because it condemned so many to misery and want, was essentially trying to put limits on competition so it would benefit society as a whole rather than tear it apart. Competition, said Smith, could benefit society if it could be reserved to individuals. Free enterprise was to be the productive enterprise of individuals, not of corporate groups against individuals.

This tenet is inconsistent with the human condition. We are born and raised as members of a corporate group, not as individuals, and we gain our moral sense from our inclusion in those groups. With corporate groups now illegitimate, where is a moral sense to come from? On the other hand, if people have no moral sense (no feeling of responsibility to others) what is to stop them from organizing in free association to rob their fellow individuals? How can property rights remain sacrosanct when other rights have been destroyed?

As a practical matter, the use of government to protect property rights had the wholehearted support of the oligarchy and the partial support of the tories, who could at least use their own "private property" for the good of all those living on it. Since classical liberals never succeeded in displacing the oligarchy, the government continued to protect private property, even if a certain amount of theft was allowed when the private property involved belonged to the poor.

Radical liberals, convinced that individual self-interest was good for all (including society as a whole), might be termed the first to take Adam Smith seriously. The oligarchs and classical liberals had enthusiastically accepted the competitive aspects of free enterprise, of course, using its tenets to destroy the remaining rights and privileges of tory groups. Since the good of the whole was to be achieved by the invisible hand of competition, they could safely use it to justify the exploitation of the nonwealthy, secure in the knowledge that the visible hand of public authority (the government's coercive forces) would not be raised against them but against those who resisted them.

Adam Smith had warned against this sort of thing, but in classical liberalism there was no way of correcting it. Classical liberal government was too narrowly conceived and too constricted in its sphere of action to prevent the cooperation of the rich, however much that cooperation might be illegitimate according to classical liberal paradigms. The radical liberals sought to expand the role of government in order to ensure that free and individual competition would in fact, take place. In order to gain the power to do the expanding, however, they had to convince most of the oligarchs, classical liberals, and tories to cooperate with them. Since it is not obviously in the interest of classical liberals or oligarchs to do so, the radical liberals' first alliances were with the tories.

Concept of the Culture

Cooperation is inevitably illegitimate in a culture based upon competition, and radical liberals agree with classical liberals in assuming that competition brings out the best in people, that its results are positive for society, and that in any case it is inevitable because all individuals are self-interested. They assume that the individual competition of all against all is necessary and right. However, they have also rationally concluded that limits must be placed on competition to prevent the hierarchy of wealth from depriving those in its lower reaches of liberty and the chance to gain wealth.

Everything is rather confusing once the radical liberal actually tries to apply the limits. Moreover, the logic of hierarchy is that those below take orders from those above. The normal situation in a liberal business organization is one of authority for those at the top and obedience for those at the bottom. Competition between equals in the organization is expected but competition of subordinates with leaders is severely punished. The paradigm stress involved is a major consideration for subordinates, since only the head of the company has the individual freedom that is central to the classical liberal's vision of honor and respectability. Fear of being fired and hope for advancement and eventual individual power keep the classical liberal's nose to the grindstone, but ulcers and heart attacks would seem to be quite normal reactions to the stress involved.

One simple solution to the problem is a system of widespread owner-operated businesses, where hierarchy, and therefore the subordination of one individual to another, can be kept to a minimum. The problems with this solution are three. First, that there is no logical reason why any individual with the power to do so should hesitate to have other individuals subordinate to him or her. Second, a small owner-operated business is always vulnerable to being taken over or bankrupted by the larger and more powerful businesses that benefit from the cooperation inherent in organizational hierarchies, even when those hierarchies are based upon fear and competition. Third, the larger the business the greater the wealth and power of the person at the top.

The radical liberal feels he must cooperate with others to preserve his own liberty as well as theirs. The paradigm conflicts among hierarchy, individualism, and competition become very strong. Rationally it is obvious that a measure of personal liberty must be given up or denied if competition is to be curtailed enough to prevent hierarchy from being exploitative, but in practice liberty is not at all easy to deny. The radical liberal response is to limit cooperation to government, feeling that the more important economic roles must remain competitive. In fact, it is in order to retain competition in the economic system that the radical liberal insists upon cooperation in government.

In the general concept of the society which is to be created and maintained by the radical liberals, an initial equality of opportunity of all individuals is to be followed by intense and general competition. Moreover, radical liberals feel that all individuals, regardless of their age, should retain their access to the competitive arena. Competition insures that some will win and some will lose, but the losers must be assured of the right to try again. Since competition should never end, the problem is how to prevent the results of today's competition from ending competition tomorrow. It is only logical that winners today will use the resources gained to reinforce their competitive position tomorrow, and that today's losers will be even less able to compete in the immediate future. The radical liberal wants to keep competition going when the dynamic of competition favors the winners.

The simplest way to attack the problem is to make sure that every individual starts out equally well equipped to compete. This avoids meddling in the competition itself. On the other hand, children are raised in families and families are corporate groups. It is difficult to help the children without helping the adults, but to do so is meddling in the competition. The paradigm stress involved is obvious, but not as great as the stress at the other end of the scale. Even initial equality of opportunity to compete implies that competition still exists. Monopoly ensures that the only competition remaining will be the competition to join the monopoly. The joining done, personal liberty disappears in hierarchical duties. The radical liberal's solution is to be found in government. Not only the makeup of government but the role of government is to be changed.

Government

Even in government, radical liberals feel competition is necessary and good. Tories and oligarchs believe in fully cooperative government, while classical liberals believe all members of the government (all of them successful classical liberals) should cooperate but that the government's scope should be restricted to protecting private property. The law and order of the classical liberal is fire and police protection, and the latter is primarily a matter of protecting the rich from the poor. The radical liberal, by including the poor in elections, has destroyed the unity of a government of haves protecting themselves from the have-nots. Some other basis for government must be found.

The radical liberal finds this basis in competition. The paradigm stress involved in cooperating in order to compete is very high. "Interest group" politics, the incessant competition of free associations made up of people who are in agreement on a single issue, is a radical liberal construct. The assumption is that everyone will recognize the same limits to competition. The "rules of the game" will be willingly observed by all participants so that the competition will neither destroy society nor end in plutocracy or oligarchy.

By letting the poor into the political process but at the same time attempting to separate politics and economics, the radical liberal has ensured that government will be messy and confusing, to say the least. Now that government may be legitimately used for more than the protection of private property, Pandora's box has been opened again.

There are those, of course, who feel it was never firmly shut. The protection of private property, dear to the hearts (and wallets) of the classical liberals, proved to be an extremely elastic concept whenever it was put into practice. Tories and oligarchs could use it quite as well as classical liberals, and classical liberals themselves seldom found it a bar to the use of government for their own enrichment. Tariffs and free trade, tight money and loose, government grants and government regulations, have all been enthusiastically used by classical liberals when it was to their benefit, and all have been justified in the name of private property.

Nevertheless, the organization of classical liberal government did tend to retain a certain unity. When based upon a voting population made up of the rich (of "successful individuals") it was a government of the haves. The have-nots were very effectively excluded from it, and while the haves might bicker about details or even have really major struggles over the distribution of wealth, their government retained a coherent point of view and, in the eyes of the oligarchy and the successful classical liberals, faced the same visible threat: the have-nots.

By including the propertyless in the formal political process the radical liberal was going against the grain of oligarchy and classical liberalism, but by carefully excluding them from government itself, the consequences of their rash action were minimized. The aim, after all, was to give power to the less successful middle class itself, not to the poor. The poor would be allowed to vote but not required to; they would not vote for each other, but for the radical liberal middle-class candidates; and if by some chance a poor person actually was elected to public office, the rewards of that office itself would quickly convert him or her into a good propertied member of the very class that had devised the system.

In everything but voting, hierarchy was to be preserved. The benefits of government would not be distributed by the poor but by a hierarchical bureaucracy that was clearly middle-class itself, both in salary and in values. A complex system of representative government was to separate the poor from the decisions to be made, even if some of those decisions were to benefit their children. While the radical liberal congressman was expected to vote the interests of his geographical constituency, just what those interests were was a matter largely left up to the perception of the person elected rather than to the voters.

The characteristic single-member geographical district of the radical liberal is the same as that of the classical liberal, and its effects are also much the same. A majority of the voters is represented and the minority is not. If the majority is cohesive, there is no reason to suppose the minority will ever be represented in government, let alone be able to directly determine its policies. The radical liberal assumes that the multiplicity of issues, the consequent multiplicity of associations, and the freedom of all individuals to leave or to join any of these single-issue associations will result in a situation where a permanent majority will not be able to exist. No majority on one issue would necessarily be a majority on another, and it is inconceivable that over the long run any majority would not crumble under the onslaught of cross-cutting issues and individual interests.

It is apparent that the logic here is the same as that which prevents the liberals from noticing oligarchs or tories. It is based upon the individualistic assumption that self-interest is the fundamental component of human behavior and the further assumption that self-interest is the same as selfishness, and therefore competition is both inherent and the determining quality of all human beings.

Neither tories nor oligarchs believe this, and if they are right even for themselves alone, the liberal assumptions about society as a whole are wrong. If some people function as a corporate group, willing to sacrifice their individual differences for the good of the group when that is necessary, they will have an inordinate amount of power in a system in which other groups are constantly forming and dissolving around single issues that both change and oppose each other. When such a corporate group is wealthy, powerful, and untroubled by the conditions of the nonpowerful it is very likely to dominate, particularly if individuals outside it are unable to admit that it exists.

Racial discrimination can also exist in the radical liberal electoral system. Indeed, any minority can find itself excluded from political power if the majority is united in maintaining a discriminatory status quo. While this issue is not compatible with the liberal assumption of individuality, it is very much compatible with the liberal assumption of hierarchy, especially if all the rich and powerful are members of one race while all the members of the other race are poor. While the radical liberal may deplore the situation and cry for reform, it is very difficult to accomplish any meaningful change while simultaneously denying the validity and existence of corporate groups.

Sexual discrimination is also a function of the contradictions between hierarchy and individualism. If men are convinced that their place in the hierarchy of wealth is a result of their merit, then if their spouses are housewives or earn less at their jobs than the men, it must be true that the men are superior to the women. If this condition is widespread throughout society, then it must be the result of some inherent defect in women, for men recognize merit whenever it occurs (witness the wealth of the males). No wealth equals no merit. At the same time, it is obvious that individualism is not individualism if based upon either sex or race, so the male radical liberal has another cause for guilt. Insofar as the female radical liberal is not individually wealthy, it is logical to assume that she blames herself for her obvious lack of merit. In a radical liberal culture there is clearly enough guilt to go around.

Guilt, by the way, is an emotion that rarely results in positive action. The paradigm contradictions inherent in radical liberalism usually result in paralysis. Any action to substantively promote individualism will tend to destroy an equally legitimate hierarchy, and vice versa. Guilt, at the least, gives the person who feels it a sensation of moral superiority over those who are equally guilty but too crass to admit it, while at most it gives rise to symbolic actions that are carefully stopped short of making any substantive changes which would be opposed to the other paradigms involved. Guilty feelings simply are not going to change anything.

The electoral system of the radical liberals is generally designed to en- hance the power of the majority at the expense of the minority. It is identi- cal in its structure to that of the classical liberal. The fragmentation of power involved in separate executive, legislative, and judicial branches is meant to prevent too much cooperation. While the formal hierarchy of the executive branch culminates in the president, who therefore has the most merit, the legislature is far more representative of the individualism of the liberals, for it represents the diversity of the electorate. The protection of private property is already well established by the time the radical liberals are in a position to determine the policies of government. The system of military and police forces, the courts, and the legislature is well designed to protect and perpetuate the rights and privileges of property, and the radical liberal sees little reason to change such a system. At the same time, a fundamental purpose of radical liberalism is to prevent the formation and continuance of monopolies that prevent free enterprise from function- ing correctly. This prevention is essentially a limitation on property rights, so the radical liberal is immediately faced with a dilemma: how to limit the power of private property while at the same time protecting it.

The answer is to create governing bodies limited to single industries — bodies neither chosen by the interests to be regulated nor by the electorate. To allow the industries involved to regulate themselves would be to invite oligopoly (shared monopoly). To allow the majority of the voters to regu- late the industries would, given the radical liberal's electoral system, put the poor (now the majority of the voters) in the position of dictating to the rich. This is an obvious violation of the radical liberal's paradigms of hierarchy, which assume wealth to be the result of merit while poverty is a result of its absence. To allow the poor to dictate to the rich is to invite dis- aster.

True, the poor do not directly rule. Given the radical liberal governmental system it is difficult to claim they rule even indirectly, but they have certainly been given the appearance of doing so, and the radical liberal needs to make sure that they do not. Moreover, the radical liberal still believes in self-interested competition as everyone's most basic motivating force. Given all these considerations, it seems the wiser course to make the regulating body as separate from the elected officials of government as it is from the industries themselves.

The result is the independent regulatory agency. In the United States it is appointed by Congress, usually from nominees selected by the president, and is expected to be nonpartisan (not connected with any political party, which is the same thing as saying not in any way connected with the voters), expert, and dedicated to the good of the whole society. Two problems immediately present themselves, one very practical and the other more philosophical: Where are the regulators to come from? How are they to know what is good for the whole of society?

The first problem is, for a liberal, easily solved: from the executive ranks of the industry to be regulated. It is self-evident that those in the industry know most about it and that those being paid the most money are those with the most merit. It would be foolish to appoint a person to regulate an industry who knew nothing about it. It is possible, of course, to argue that a person expert in the consumption of a good would be the best choice to regulate its production, but such an argument is difficult to sustain in the face of the appeals to technical knowledge of production made by the liberals. Oligarchs are initially against regulation by radical liberals at all, but if they must have it, they much prefer it to be by people from the industry. The liberal trusts their technical merit, while the oligarch trusts both that and their previous membership in the corporate group.

The second problem is (perhaps) more basic. Neither the oligarch nor the classical liberal has any conception of the good of the whole. The radical liberal opposes monopoly and supports equal opportunity to compete, but these attitudes do not amount to a view of society as a whole. The radical liberal cannot put much more content into the concept than either the classical liberal or the oligarch. The tory has a practical and usable definition of societal good, but it requires a managed economy based upon cooperation in a noncompeting hierarchy, which is rejected out of hand by the radical liberal on the grounds that it is unworkable (individual self-interest would prevent it from functioning); and even if it did work it would be immoral because it is paternalistic. The definition of an adult for a liberal is a sovereign, self-sufficient individual; "paternalism" robs her or him of adulthood as well as of individuality.

The result of all this is that the independent regulatory agency of the radical liberal is independent mainly of the government that creates it. Staffed by experts from the industry it is to regulate, it is charged with maintaining both the good of society and the health (profits) of the industry. It is hardly surprising that the regulators most often end by regulating the industry in its own best interests. If this sounds suspiciously like the economic system of oligarchy, it should not be a surprise.

At the same time, the lower ranking employees of the regulatory agencies are very likely to be radical liberals who, if they are not too clear on just what the agency should do, are clear enough on a few things it should not do, among which is aiding the oligopolies of large corporations. If it is a fair statement that regulatory boards tend to become the structures through which oligarchs and successful classical liberals manage a particular part of the economy for their own benefit (a trend that makes them the government in this area), it is also fair to expect at least some of the boards' own employees to oppose this trend.

Welfare for the children of the poor is another difficult area for radical liberals. They are committed to it through a sense of fairness rather than through any great hope that the whole of society will benefit from any change in the number and nature of the poor. After all, in the radical liberal's view the poor are economic zeros. They neither produce nor consume (much) and are therefore outside the economic system. That their numbers and need provide a supply of cheap and easily replaced labor is not thinkable, since merit determines wealth, not the possibilities for exploitation.

The problem with the poor is not (for the radical liberal) that they are exploited but that they are inadequate people. This inadequacy takes two forms: physical and nonphysical. Physical inadequacies are brought about by bad parents and malnutrition. Nonphysical problems are caused by bad attitudes. In fact, bad attitudes are often seen as the cause of physical inadequacies: dope, booze, and junk food all proceed from bad attitudes and cause physical problems, and if attitudes could be changed the physical problems would end.

In other words, liberals feel that if the poor would only accept the cultural attributes and attitudes of the middle class their problems would be over. If the poor had middle-class attitudes, they would soon have middle-class incomes. The oligarch knows better, of course, but is unlikely to enter into the debate. The debate is not over what would cure the poor of their poverty but whether or not such a cure is possible. The classical liberal says that any money or effort spent upon the poor will simply reward their unwillingness to help themselves. Poverty and the fear of poverty are the greatest motivators known to man, and if the poor have not been motivated by their poverty then nothing will help them. Welfare for the poor or the children of the poor is at best a waste of money and at worst a support for laziness, inadequacy, and vice, which could result in harm to their betters.

The radical liberal finds the classical liberal's arguments persuasive but not conclusive, and most certainly not applicable to the children of the poor. Liberals are rather ambiguous about children at any rate, and the radical liberal finds it easy to accept exclusionary statements about the children of the poor which he or she has already accepted for his or her own children.

Public schools, public health, school breakfasts and lunches, aid to dependent children, and the like are all radical liberal measures designed to aid the children of the poor without either aiding their parents or allowing the adult poor to control any part of the programs. The reason is simple: the primary mission of the public schools is the inculcation of the proper paradigms in the young. Any skills taught are extra, if sometimes desirable. The proper paradigms are, of course, those of the radical liberals. This emphasis is natural for radical liberals and very functional for the oligarchs. After all, the more the poor believe their poverty is their own fault and that only individuals exist, the less they will blame or even see the oligarchs. Revolution by the poor is impossible if they blame themselves and find group action illegitimate.

Tories are less interested in a uniform system of public education, feeling that apprentice programs (preferably with the young person's parents) are the best way to transfer knowledge and paradigms. The tory trusts each family and guild to have the proper paradigms and to accept the overall coordination of the tory aristocrats. Since in a tory culture the workers control the technology associated with their work, this arrangement is very sensible. Where tories are not dominant and an oligarchical/classical liberal arrangement of work and technology exists, a tory might well support public schools as a second best approach to aiding the poor.

Since, for radical liberals, the adult poor cannot be trusted or expected to implement these programs, extensive governmental organizations staffed by good radical liberals are necessary to correctly carry them out. These promote a great expansion of governmental bureaucracy, since in the oligarchy/classical liberal combination the only organizations the formal government needed were the military, police, fire, and (maybe) post-office departments. With regulatory agencies for the rich and welfare departments for the poor the number of people employed by the government will greatly expand, and the bureaucracy itself will become a major group in society. It is reasonable to suppose that most of those involved in radical liberal programs will be radical liberals even if their political leaders are not. Once begun, these radical liberal organizations develop a radical liberal dynamic that is difficult to stop.

Partly because of the nature of the clientele (which is either children or adults who cannot be trusted to do the right thing) and partly because radical liberals find it difficult to trust each other (their basic paradigm of society, after all, is that everyone is in competition with everyone else), a radical liberal bureaucracy is process-oriented rather than goal-oriented.

A goal orientation results in the leaders (coordinators) identifying the goals to be achieved and the corporate group responsible for achieving them. After that it is up to the particular corporate group to decide how to do the job and to do it. Resources come from the group itself and, if necessary, from other groups assigned this responsibility by the coordinators. The groups involved are judged by how well the goals are achieved. The whole process is quite easy to understand, but it is equally obvious that the high degree of trust and cooperation involved makes it difficult for liberals to accept it as workable. It is quite unacceptable outside their own group for oligarchs, who depend upon individualization and competition to exploit the nonrulers.

A process orientation requires more explanation, since it is not at first blush as reasonable as goal orientation. In this system the leaders specify not only what the goals of the organization are but also specify (usually in great detail) how they are to be achieved. It is immediately apparent that subordinate members of the organization do not even need to know what the goals are; their job is to do what they are told in the way they are told to do it. Even if their actions are logically related to the organization's goal, their immediate focus is upon the process involved rather than the outcome of their work. Since they cannot be trusted to act on their own, they are required to conform to procedures that must in their turn be checked and enforced by the bureaucracy itself. In this sort of organization it is not unusual for the process goals of all but the highest officials to take priority over the organizational goals they are meant to achieve but that are often hazy or even unstated at the operational level.

This difficulty with operational goals is particularly evident when the goals of the organization involve paradigmatic contradictions. Since this is the case with most of the goals of radical liberals, it is hardly surprising that a process orientation is normal in radical liberal bureaucracies. The goal of public education, for example, becomes less to educate the student than to process him or her through the system. The definition of "education," since it combines the inculcation of paradigms (some of which are in dispute) and the teaching of skills, is hazy to begin with. When this goal is combined with paradigms of individuality that assume that each individual is both sovereign and competitive, the teacher's role is even more ambiguous. If the student must be free to make his or her own choices, and must be allowed to fail as well as to achieve, then the role of the teacher is solely to teach, not to force the student to learn. When it is also assumed that every child must have an education in order to ensure an equal opportunity to compete, the dilemma is complete. No one can be thrown out of school but no one can be forced to learn, either. Social promotion and illiterate graduates are the result. Process goals have taken precedence over the goals of the program to such an extent that the program goals have become the process itself.

It is interesting to note that this situation continues to fulfill the oligarchical goals for public education: those students who fail to learn the skills learn that they are inferior to those who do; that they are themselves to blame for this situation, and that the hierarchy of society is therefore legitimate. The tory approach (you will learn, you will not be allowed to fail, and we will all cooperate in achieving this) is illegitimate to all the other cultures except for the ruling corporate group in oligarchy, and it is most unlikely that their children will be sent to the public schools. While individual teachers may be tory and get away with it (particularly in the lower grades where children are often still tory because of their age), it is unlikely that such a teacher will be promoted to a position of authority. In a process-oriented bureaucracy people are hired, fired, and promoted according to how well they achieve process goals. A tory teacher will be focused on his or her students and their education rather than on forms and procedures. Moreover, the discipline inherent in a tory approach may well be in conflict with the rights of individuals dear to the hearts of liberals, a situation that does not favor the tory teacher.

Generally speaking, the goals of radical liberal governments involve the same paradigm conflicts as does the radical liberal culture. The most common result is a concentration on process, a result that avoids the conflicts of a focus on goals. At the same time, this course carries its own paradigm stress, since the primary goals may be difficult to ignore. The whole situation is exacerbated by the ups and downs of the economy and the diminished or increased number and poverty of the poor.

Economics

Radical liberals believe in the free-enterprise system of Adam Smith but have rejected laissez-faire philosophy, which dictates no intervention or regulation by government. Originally regulation was aimed solely at preventing monopolistic behavior of single firms, but it was soon expanded to cover oligopolistic cooperation of several firms. At the same time, any management of the economy was anathema, since only the invisible hand of competition could adequately connect consumers and producers in a system that could last indefinitely. Consequently, the regulatory agency's goal was competition itself: the consequences of competition were held to be healthy in the long run, whatever the short-term results might be.

Just as it is difficult to help the children but not help the adults, it is difficult to regulate the economy without managing it. To some extent it is impossible, a circumstance that would seem to reinforce the classical liberal's view that any regulation is too much. The ruling oligarchs, of course, could manage their wealth with or without the regulatory agencies. When their wealth is a large proportion of the nation's wealth, they are in effect managing the economy of the nation along with their own, but since their businesses are private, the classical liberal can hardly object.

The radical liberal can hardly object to the process but can find a great deal to object to in its results, especially at times when the business cycle is down. These are times of recession and depression, when unemployment and bankruptcies are high and security for the middle class is low. The response of the radical liberal is to accept Keynesian[1] economics in an effort to achieve stability, and with it security in their income and status. Since the aim of Keynesian economics is to manage the business cycle without managing the economy, we had better begin with the business cycle.

The business cycle refers to the tendency of businesses in a free market economy to respond to increases or decreases in demand by raising prices or firing workers. Demand is money which will be used to buy something if it is available. It should not be confused with needs, as in "people need nutritious food." Even if people need nutritious food there is no demand if the same people have no money to buy it or prefer twinkies.

If a widget manufacturer in a free-enterprise system finds there is a demand for widgets, he will increase his production of widgets but not increase the price, since to do so will result in decreased sales as widget buyers flock to his competitors, who have cunningly not increased their prices. The primary way to increase production, says Keynes, is to hire more workers. Labor-saving technology may be invented and produced in the long run, but in the short run more people is the answer. As more people are hired, more people have money for widgets, and demand also rises. The result is an upward spiral of the economy, with increased employment and production stimulating each other through the demand occurring in the free market.

There is a limit, however, and that limit is reached when everyone is employed. At that point, only higher wages will attract new workers, and higher wages mean higher prices. Moreover, with demand still high the tendency will be for the prices of widgets to rise independently of the increased costs of production inherent in higher wages. The cause is that demand exceeds supply. Since, in the aggregate, more workers cannot be hired (full employment having already been reached), more widgets cannot be made. The price of widgets will rise to the point where people will just do without, rather than pay the higher price, a process much harder on lower income groups than upper. When prices rise with no change in the quality or quantity of the good involved, inflation has occurred.

Inflation tends to benefit the independently rich at the expense of the poor for two reasons. First, the rich will not have to do without as prices rise, while the poor will. Second, since the rich generally control the pricing policies of the businesses involved they will tend to raise prices faster than they are forced to raise wages. The faster and more abruptly these changes occur, the sooner the next phase of the business cycle occurs.

As prices are raised out of reach of many buyers, demand falls and a downturn begins. Rather than lower prices immediately the managers fire workers, thus reducing the supply of widgets to meet the decreased demand. Unfortunately, the price of the materials for widgets remains high, since suppliers also choose to fire workers rather than reduce prices. After all, the object of the exercise for businessmen is to make the highest possible profit: high production and high employment are incidental.

The result is a downward spiral. As more workers are fired, demand falls further, a circumstance that brings as its immediate result the firing of more workers. When a recession turns into a depression is when the process affects the whole society rather than just parts of it, but the nature of the cycle is no different. Decreased demand produces decreased employment, which decreases demand even further.

The rich again benefit, for two reasons. First, as the unemployed working-class and middle-class people find not only their wants but their needs unsatisfied by their lack of money, they first seek to borrow it and then sell what assets they can spare. They borrow it from those who have it, and as things do not get better, they lose the property they have put up for security to the lenders. Moreover, a great many people are attempting to sell what real assets they can and it is a buyer's market for those with money.

Second, as demand falls, smaller businesses go bankrupt and their disappearance as separate firms lessens competition. In this situation, the remaining companies have a tendency to keep prices as they are or even raise them.

In both cases, the rich get richer and the poor get poorer. Although in theory the cycles are self-correcting, there is a limit to how long prices can be maintained as well as to how many people can be fired. Historically these crises have usually been solved by war or the threat of war rather than by liberal economics. War tends to reinforce tory paradigms in society, and the resultant collective goals and cooperation bring back prosperity.

Keynes thought the whole process both destructive and unnecessary. His solution was to use the government to "even out" the business cycle.

In good times with full employment and with inflation the main danger, the government should reduce its spending while maintaining or even increasing taxes. This policy releases workers to find jobs in the private sector, takes money out of circulation and thus reduces demand, and builds up government surpluses for use when the cycle turns down. In extreme cases, the government can raise the interest rates it pays for money (the public debt) in a further effort to decrease demand by attracting money out of the private sector.

In a business downturn, the government should reverse its policies, increasing public spending to provide jobs, paying "unemployment insurance," and decreasing the interest rates it pays on borrowed money, all in order to keep demand up and prevent the next wave of firings. If the process is caught early, it should not be too difficult to even out the business cycle. While the cycle can never be stopped, it can be controlled to such an extent that its effects will be minimal.

In practice, Keynesian economics has some problems. In upturns the government is supposed to withdraw money and jobs from the economy, but this has proven very difficult to do. The pressures to continue needed public works and to expand welfare for the children of the poor are intense when it seems these policies can be implemented without much pain. Classical liberals suffer the agonies of the damned, contemplating a rich government continually getting richer with their money (classical liberals always assume that any wealth is generated by the hard work, inventiveness, and other merits of classical liberals; other cultures are spenders, not producers) and they agitate fiercely for tax cuts. Radical liberals, on the other hand, see the increased prosperity of government as a golden opportunity to abolish poverty and make the whole world middle class.

Oligarchs, who largely escape taxes through their ability to disguise their wealth as business assets and to manipulate both sorts of liberals in government by appeals to merit and the needs of business, do not much care which course is taken. Classical-liberal tax cuts benefit them through increasing demand, and therefore their profits, but radical-liberal government spending does the same thing. Attacks upon poverty in this phase are limited to changing the attitudes of the children, something the oligarch is sure will fail to change an economic system based upon competition and individualism, precisely the attitudes radical liberals seek to inculcate in the poor. As far as the oligarch can see, the middle class is taxing itself (the poor, after all, have little money to pay taxes) to benefit the poor in ways that will benefit the rich, who escape most of the taxes.

This situation is even more obvious in a business downturn. Usually surpluses have not been built up during the upturn because of the classical liberal's aversion to government surpluses and the radical liberal's eagerness to spend them. Both these pressures are exacerbated in a downturn, classical liberals redoubling their efforts to achieve tax cuts and spending reductions while radical liberals argue for tax cuts and spending increases. Since, in this situation, government spending is not limited to the children of the poor but extends to all the unemployed, the many regulations designed to separate the poor from their children tend to be blurred at the same time efforts may be made to aid the new poor (those previously employed) but not the old (those who are chronically unemployed). Since any effort to aid the unemployed will eventually aid the wealthy at the expense of the middle class, thinking oligarchs applaud the whole process.

A complicating factor in a downturn is finance. In the upturn, full employment resulted in greater taxes, but in a downturn, reduced employment results in reduced tax revenue. The obvious problem is the source of money required for increased government unemployment payments and other welfare benefits. If the government borrows the money from the private sector this will further reduce demand, but if the government simply prints more paper currency increased inflation results, a situation that hurts the poor and unemployed the worst. The only solution seems to be to borrow the money from the rich (who are the only ones who can afford to do without it for a time at this point), but in order to attract it, high interest rates must be paid. In order to prevent the middle class from lending their money (which would further reduce demand, which is exactly what the radical liberal government is trying to prevent), the high interest rates are reserved for large quantities of money, quantities too large for middle-class people to do without.

The net effect of all this is to build up a "national" debt which is owed by the (middle-class) taxpayers to the (rich) holders of government bonds. When the interest payments on the bonds begin to take most of the revenue generated by taxes, the radical liberal government is driven to borrowing more to keep up the spending policies inherent in Keynesian economics.

A situation already bleak for radical liberals is made even worse by the fact that the national economy is not a closed system. Tories (and socialists) favor closed systems because of the need to manage the economy for the benefit of all who are in it. Oligarchs favor empire, since while they must manage the economy, the only benefits they care about are their own. Empire, while not necessary, has the great attraction of separating the factors of production and consumption so far apart that the different people involved are hardly even aware of each others' existence, let alone of common needs, desires, or exploitation. Liberals of both sorts believe in free enterprise, which logically includes free trade across national boundaries. Boundaries are illegitimate because they contradict the individualist's belief that all people can and must be seen as individuals without regard to race, creed, national origin, or anything else.

Radical liberals, as usual, find themselves in paradigm conflicts. Their paradigms of individualism dictate free trade, but their difficulties with welfare for the children of the poor and the more general welfare measures dictated by their economic policies push them toward regulations and tax policies that come closer and closer to managing the economy. Embracing policies that would benefit the poor and middle classes of their own country at the expense of poor people in foreign countries is morally difficult, but without some sort of management of their own economy, their welfare measures simply ameliorate the effects on some of their own poor at great expense to themselves and for the ultimate benefit of the rich.

This situation develops not only because of the dynamics of public borrowing, the classical liberals' insistence on tax cuts, and the radical liberals' insistence on spending, but also because of the patterns of investment the system produces. Employing more people is the most direct method of increasing production, but increased employment requires increased investment. In times of full employment, investment in new facilities tends to lag because of the scarcity of new employees. In a closed system, such a situation should logically result in the financing of new technology, primarily in labor-saving devices. It does, but because of another effect of full employment, new technology is not as attractive as it might be. Since profits rise faster than wages there is no great incentive to raise production through new technology, although in the long run it remains attractive.

In an open system, however, the greatest attraction to investment is cheap labor in another, poorer, country. Paying high wages when cheap labor is available is essentially a form of profit-sharing, and neither the oligarchs nor either sort of liberal have any reason to do so. Producing in a low-wage country and selling in a high-wage country has the added advantage of benefitting from the high prices available in the latter. Moreover, a liberal government of either sort is almost certainly going to create tax structures that will encourage investment (benefit the rich) while avoiding "protectionism" which might prevent moving capital (investment) out of the country. To the charge that in the long run such policies are ruinous, the oligarch need only point out that the workers who find themselves unemployed when their jobs are (more or less) exported to low-wage countries will have their buying power maintained by welfare spending at the expense of the middle class.

Since the oligarchs see no reason to protect or to maintain either the middle class or the working class, they have no reason not to take advantage of such a lucrative opportunity. If, in the long run, the entire society suffers, the oligarchy can quite justifiably put their trust in the solidarity and cooperative nature of their own corporate group, secure in the knowledge that wealth and power have been sufficient to protect them in the past and are very likely to do so in the future.

The classical liberals who have enough money to take advantage of the borrowing policies of radical liberal governments and to work for the large corporations that benefit have small reason to complain, even if they may decry spending policies aimed at helping the poor. The only real danger to either group is a violent revolution, and defense spending serves very neatly to block this option, keep government spending high, and reduce welfare payments all at the same time.

The less successful classical liberal sees his or her salvation in lower taxes and cheaper labor in his own country, but finds both to be ineffective, primarily because of the open nature of the system. The radical liberal tends, in the main, to go paralytic, caught among contradictory paradigms which he can neither abandon nor completely follow. If a war does not materialize to allow everyone to revert to tory paradigms in the name of national solidarity and the unusual times, there is a marked tendency for sizable numbers of radical liberals to revert to classical liberalism, abandoning the poor to their no-doubt-deserved fate and the working class in general to the mercies of the free market. Keynesian economics for them has been a failure.

It is important to remember, at this point, that although Keynesian economics has not changed the capitalist system it was designed to save it has managed to do a great deal of good. Unfortunately, the more good is done the more jobs move to cheap-labor countries, and the more good needs to be done. In the face of this dynamic, some frustrated radical liberals turn to socialism.

Summary

Radical liberals are perhaps the most conscious of their paradigm conflicts of any of the cultures. They are often called "bleeding-heart liberals" by oligarchs and classical liberals and rejected as well-meaning but ineffective reformers by socialists. Their frustration is a result of their own conflicts and they tend to wallow in their guilt. At the same time, they are unable to give up any of the paradigms that cause them pain. From this angle they can be seen as classical liberals with a societal conscience. Unfortunately, their basic remedy for the evils of society is for everyone to become a radical liberal.

Their welfare programs do manage to help quite a few people and the public school systems they support at least provide the framework for teaching skills as well as paradigms. They should be judged not so much by their goals, which are decidedly mixed, as by their accomplishments. In the short run they have managed to allay some of the pain in society and to ameliorate some of the conditions that cause it. Those who are not satisfied with this are likely to be the socialists.

Chapter 8

Democratic Socialism

Marx and Socialism

The roots of contemporary socialist thought are to be found in a fundamentally flawed vision of anarchy. European socialism can be seen as an effort to save the values of anarchy while avoiding its inability to hold large societies together. Europeans of the nineteenth century got their information on anarchistic societies in North America from French voyageurs. To Europeans, who were generally loaded down with laws, rules, regulations and other strictures in a time when oligarchy and classical liberalism were constantly getting stronger, societies with neither laws nor governments seemed like paradise. (Liberals as well as anarchists and socialists felt this way. Seen from this angle, liberalism is an attempt to graft the virtues of anarchism onto the class structures of toryism and oligarchy.) If the traditions and customs of the anarchistic Indian tribes were noticed they were most often dismissed as superstition, and the significance of their small size was largely overlooked.

Nineteenth-century European anarchists found the basic problem of European society to be hierarchy. They felt that both nature and the family showed that members of the "higher" species cooperated far more than they competed with one another, and that once free of a hierarchy which allowed exploitation at the same time it encouraged competition, men would freely cooperate with one another rather than compete. In reply to Herbert Spencer and other social darwinists these anarchists pointed out that Darwin had been talking about species of animals rather than the individual members of species, and that Darwin's evidence indicated that the more intelligent and adaptive the species the more cooperative its members were with one another. Contemporary wildlife biologists tend to emphasize both the cooperation and the hierarchy through which it occurs, but in the nineteenth century the evidence for cooperation was the issue.

The Indians of North America clearly cooperated within their own tribe, and compared with European society they had a great deal more freedom. When compared with European hierarchies they were astoundingly egalitarian, too. Anarchists concluded that hierarchy had created the miseries in which working people lived. The obvious solution was to destroy hierarchy, and the obvious place to start was at the top. If the kings, emperors, archdukes, generals, and all the other tyrants died as soon as they gained their positions of power, it would not be long before no one would be found willing to fill these positions, and the whole structure would crumble. Nineteenth-century anarchism became a force throughout Europe, and a fairly large number of powerful people were assassinated.

Even so, the anarchists failed to change society or to grow into a widely supported movement. Most people accepted neither their methods nor their rather simple and purely political analysis of the problem. Moreover, the anarchists could not overcome a major consequence of their analysis: their own inability to organize in a hierarchical manner. Such an organization was entirely against their principles, but without it they had grave difficulties in organizing strangers. The small egalitarian groups of anarchists were highly vulnerable to the hierarchically organized secret police precisely because their members had not grown up with each other and did not have the lifelong face-to-face contact that held the Indian groups together. Relying on rationality rather than custom and tradition while denying any authority other than that of the individual, the anarchists were relatively easy prey to secret police who could infiltrate them simply by appealing to their rationality and individualism.

By the first World War they had ceased to be a major movement except in the anarchist villages of northern Spain. There the ancient anarchist customs and traditions of the small village cultures continued as before. They would become famous during the Spanish Civil War, survive Franco, and continue today. Anarchism is a very strong culture wherever small anarchistic groups can maintain their self-sufficiency. It is not, as the European experience demonstrates, an effective culture for large groups.

Nevertheless, it provided great inspiration to the socialists, who saw the anarchist vision of a society made up of free, equal, and cooperative people as a compelling one. When this vision was coupled with Karl Marx's trenchant and scathing critique of free-enterprise capitalism,[1] socialism became a major movement. Marx, interestingly enough, accepted Adam Smith's vision of free-enterprise capitalism. Where Smith had accepted individual self-interest as inherently competitive, however, Marx saw it as competitive only within the framework of a hierarchical system. Once the possibility of a nonhierarchical society had been introduced by the anarchists, a negative analysis of capitalism became potentially productive. For Marx, wealth and power were based not upon simply supplying the demands of a free market but upon the exploitation of the working class by those whom wealth (capital) gave the power to exploit. To attempt to regulate the business cycle was to regulate greed and exploitation; despite regulation the results would be misery and death. Keynes, two generations later, was to seek a reform of capitalism that Marx had already pronounced doomed to failure.

Marx saw history as moving from anarchistic beginnings to many small, hierarchical societies. In all of these societies the rich (those at the top) exploit those at the bottom (the poor) and the subsequent history of the world has been the history of fewer and fewer rich people exploiting more and more poor people as the rich compete among themselves to see who can become richest. Marx, like Smith, was an individualist who rejected the possibility that the rich could or would form a noncompetitive collectivist group among themselves. In other words, both rejected the possibility of oligarchy but not that of monopoly, which is control of an entire market by a single person through the firm that is controlled by him or her. Marx took it as axiomatic that any government is simply the executive committee of the ruling class, and saw no reason for it to do anything other than oppress the nonruling class. As the ruling class gets smaller its government will simply oppress more and more for the benefit of fewer and fewer people. Eventually the rich will be so few and the poor so many that the poor will simply take over. Since hierarchy by this time has degenerated into only two levels (the immensely rich and the miserably poor) such a takeover will result in a single-class society. In the absence of hierarchy people will freely cooperate, and socialism will be the result.

Marx, a German, lived much of his life in the misery of industrialized England. To him the difficulties of the working class (the proletariat) were identical wherever industrial capitalism had developed. Nations were differentiated only by languages, not by national culture and history, since both of these were destroyed by the new ruling class in their exploitation of the workers. Older forms of society (the many small hierarchies) that had deceived the working class through appeals to an illusory toryism (always a lie perpetrated by the ruling class for Marx, as it was paternalistic nonsense for the liberals) were themselves destroyed by the new order. Industrial capitalism worshipped money to such an extent that the blatant, naked greed exhibited by the new ruling class at least had the virtue of revealing it for what it was. Not even religion, the opiate of the people, could justify the rule of such blatant sinners, and as they grew fewer and fewer the increased possibilities of successful revolution would tend to become more important than the heavenly revolution after death offered by the churches.

A horrid consequence of the separation of the worker both from the technology of industrial work and from the things that were produced was the alienation of the worker, not only from his job but from himself and his fellow workers. Hierarchy, competition, and partial, repetitive, ultimately meaningless work resulted in an individuality so extreme that alcoholism and suicide became rational alternatives.

Marx saw socialism as the new community (hence "communism") but one which would be possible only when the capitalist hierarchy was forcibly destroyed. He saw no possibility at all that men as energetic, individualistic, and violent as the capitalists (witness what they had knowingly done to the working class) would peacefully give up their power and wealth. The coming revolution would be violent, not because the working class was violent but because their oppressors were. Until the workers became the owners of the means of production those who were owners would continue to oppress workers.

While Marx saw industrial capitalism (read classical liberalism) as massively unjust and violent, he also saw it as necessary and productive. It was necessary because it was the stage of history that would result in socialism. Only the bald, cruel contradictions of industrial capitalism could create the conditions necessary for socialist revolutions to succeed. Previous systems of exploitation had been too small and too ambiguous to create the universal revolution necessary, for only a universal revolution could finally extirpate hierarchy and exploitation.

The productivity of industrial capitalism was also necessary, since only industrialization can produce the goods necessary for universal and egalitarian affluence. The problem is with its patterns of distribution, which are not only unjust but will eventually destroy capitalism. This problem is not for Marx so much a consequence of the business cycle that Keynesianism tries to regulate as it is a consequence of competition. Any owner paying his workers more than a subsistence wage will be undersold by his competitors, but if all workers are paid only subsistence wages they will be unable to buy what is produced and the whole system will collapse. The paradox of "overproduction" when the goods produced are critically needed by millions of poor people will eventually destroy capitalism, but only when the capitalists are so few and so concentrated that there is a single capitalist economic system throughout the world. At this point the expansion of the system to new markets, new and more exploitable labor, and new sources of capital will no longer save it because none of these will exist. When expansion (imperialism) can no longer occur capitalism will end.

What would happen at this point was fairly clear to Marx, but perhaps not so clear to later socialists who actually had to deal with the problems and contradictions of socialist governments. In broad outline, Marx expected that workers would remain organized around the physical structures of industrial capitalism (the plants, factories, railroads, and the like) that would be "owned" by everyone. The government would now be the executive committee of the ruling working class, and have as its function the oppression of the old ruling class. Once that class was finally eliminated, primarily through the destruction of all traces of the hierarchy that had given it power, the government itself would wither away, since it would have nothing further to do. The economic system would continue the immense production made possible by industrialization but the egalitarian, cooperative nature of the new society would result in a roughly equal distribution of goods. Only roughly equal, since everyone was an individual and would desire different things, but certainly near enough to equal so that everyone would be affluent while no one would be "rich."

A revolution before industrialization had occurred would fail for two reasons. First, the equality it produced would be an equality of misery, since only industrialization can produce enough goods for everyone to have enough. Second, hierarchy and competition would not be eliminated, since before the rise of industrial capitalism too many small ambiguous hierarchies exist throughout society to be destroyed in a single revolution. Industrial capitalism is necessary, progressive and unjust. Socialism, coming after capitalism, is industrial, progressive, necessary, and just.

Marx died in 1883 before any of the various revolutions had succeeded long enough to have to deal with the problems of a socialist-dominated society. There are now several forms of socialism, each dealing differently with socialism's major dilemma: How is society to be organized if not hierarchically?

Development of Democratic Socialism

Democratic socialists are probably best understood as further radicalized radical liberals who respond to the frustrations of the radical liberal contradictions by moving further toward egalitarianism rather than by returning to classical liberalism. This is most likely to happen when radical liberal solutions have been tried and found ineffective during a period when things are getting worse for the middle class. Lost wars, inflation, depressions, and other catastrophes all tend to increase the number of democratic socialists, perhaps because hard times exacerbate radical liberal contradictions.

The key difference between democratic socialists and leninist socialists (communists) is that the democratic socialists believe that they can create socialism through the peaceful means of the radical liberal political system. The leninists believe with Marx that capitalists will never give up their positions of power and wealth without a violent struggle, and that the visible political government is simply an extension of the ruling class. Democratic socialists believe that government is a separate institution capable of being used by the electorate to change the economic system without a civil war. In doing so they are attempting to use a hierarchical, competitive form of government to create and govern a collectivist, egalitarian economy.

A democratic socialist government has the task of managing the economy for the more or less equal benefit of every individual member of society, whether or not those individuals are democratic socialists. Since the radical liberal experience exposed the difficulties of a government regulating an economy that was privately owned and managed, government ownership of the major means of production is a necessary minimum. "The state," which consists of the bureaucracy and the elected government, now has the responsibility of producing and distributing the basic goods of an affluent, industrial society.

Since violent revolution is seen as neither necessary nor desirable, the democratic socialists must deal with the continued economic and political existence of the other cultures. The general solution is to nationalize only the most important industries. This is attractive to radical liberals, whose position in society is not greatly affected.

Radical liberals generally neither own nor operate large industries, and the small businesses and middle-level positions they do have under a democratic socialist regime continue more or less as before. Indeed, the radical liberals may feel a good deal more secure under a democratic socialist government, for they need no longer fear being taken over by the oligarchs or by the more successful classical liberals. True, they must give up their ambitions to some day join the rich, but if their attempts to regulate against monopoly have been obviously unsuccessful, this may not be too great a sacrifice to make.

Moreover, when the state becomes the entrepreneur (the agent that brings together the factors of production), people who are strongly motivated to create great things are attracted to it. Since the paradigm of the creation of goods as positive and satisfying is common to all the cultures (except perhaps that of the oligarchs, who depend upon the work of nonrulers for their goods), working for a democratic socialist government gives a great many people a legitimate outlet for their energies.

Smaller entrepreneurs, businesses, farms, and the like are generally unaffected. It is the hope of most democratic socialists that a mixed economy is possible, all the large industries being owned by the state and the small ones by more or less equal individuals. The problem is how to deal with competition and individualism while retaining equality, when the state itself is hierarchical. Why shouldn't the bureaucracy (not to mention the elected officials) become oligarchical or even classical liberal, particularly if its leaders find themselves in competition with nongovernmental individuals? How will competing political parties create a unitary, collectivist government?

Most democratic socialists favor parliamentary (majoritarian) rather than fragmented systems of government because of the need for cohesive and vigorous governmental power. But what if the usual dynamic works and there is no majority? Proportional representation is so much more democratic and egalitarian than single-member districts that it seems inevitable that democratic socialists will turn to it as the electoral system, but this will simply make the problem of forming a majority worse, especially when a good many of the members of society are not democratic socialists.

Proportional representation is commonly attempted by devising an electoral system in which any party which gains more than a small portion of the vote (generally 5 percent) is automatically represented in the lawmaking body. It tends to give quite a lot of power to highly unified parties that can hold themselves together no matter what the issue. Their members respond to public issues not as individuals but as members of the corporate group (something the liberals find disgusting). Whenever the major liberal parties find themselves short of a majority, however, there is a great temptation to make some sort of deal with these unified parties in order to govern. They can deliver the votes. At the same time, they can exact the maximum in the way of policy concessions from liberal parties, simply because they are unified.

Proportional representation tends to create unified parties because as long as they can get the votes of more than a minimum percentage of the voters they will continue to elect their members. The party determines the order in which the candidates are listed. That is, if there are 100 seats in the parliament or legislature and the party wins 15 percent of the vote, the first 15 candidates on the party's slate will gain the 15 seats allotted to the party by the voters. Since it is the party that says in what order the candidates are listed, power within the party is more important than individual power. At the same time, an individual who feels his or her party is not giving her or him enough status has the option of splitting off and forming another party. This dynamic practically insures that no single party will have a majority, a result that brings us back to the importance of unified parties in a system of proportional representation.

In a parliamentary system, the chief executive officer of the government is the head of the party or coalition of parties that controls a majority of the votes in parliament. The executive branch of government, in other words, is run directly by the majority of the parliament. This system is quite different from a presidential system of government, where the head of the executive branch is elected separately (or, in some older combinations, is the hereditary monarch) and the congress or parliament is limited to making the laws. The basic principle of parliamentary government is unity: the government is not divided and cooperation is the norm.

While the vision of a mixed economy and an egalitarian affluent society is attractive to radical liberals and may get a good deal of support from tories, who see the hierarchy in government and will most probably be left alone as long as their corporate units remain small, it is clear that major problems stand in the way of the creation of a democratic socialist state, and its internal dynamics will tend to be sources of continual difficulty. The same can be said of all the other cultures, but since all the others recognize hierarchy as legitimate while (except for the tories and fascists) denying moral or civic responsibility for (adult) poverty, their difficulties are neither as obvious nor as immediate as those of the democratic socialists.

Theoretical Source of Legitimacy

Democratic socialists are rational, of course, but their political position requires them to deal with tradition rather than simply denying it as superstition. Since their main allies in parliament are likely to be tories, who see tradition as the very basis of society, democratic socialists can hardly deride it openly. On the other hand, there is no reason why logic and tradition cannot be made to move in the same direction if the democratic socialists are astute enough to make the effort. The small size of tory corporate groups, for example, fits in well with the mixed economy desired by the democratic socialists. If the tories support it through tradition and the democratic socialists through logic, no great harm is done to either side.

Marx, however, was a social scientist battling against the superstitions and fears rooted in tradition. Religion was seen as an opiate with the single function of tricking the masses into accepting and working within the exploitative system imposed on them by capitalists. The older forms of society, such as feudal toryism, were seen as equally exploitative and equally to be condemned. For pure marxists, feudalism is just as evil as industrial capitalism and even less progressive. In their view, by compromising and working with the tories the democratic socialist is well on the way towards ruin. The leninist socialist is convinced the whole effort to work with the other cultures is futile anyway.

Radical liberal political structures are built on compromises, however, and by introducing proportional representation the democratic socialist has made compromise even more certain. Tradition and religion will have to be recognized as legitimate political realities even though the democratic socialist believes both to be illegitimate in themselves. They hope that these anachronisms will gradually die out as the virtues of democratic socialism become obvious to all and as more and more people accept science as the basis for truth.

Legitimacy in societies dominated by democratic socialists is therefore mixed because the political and economic systems are mixed. Contemporary democratic socialist regimes, as a matter of fact, tend to be related more to the history of the country involved than to the pure logic of the culture of democratic socialism. While remaining committed to science, the democratic socialists of Italy, for example, tend to be Catholics as well. This greatly lessens the strains of a working coalition with the tories and does the democratic socialists no harm with the liberals, who have enough internal contradictions of their own to worry about.

Generally speaking, the basis of democratic socialism remains rationality, but this position is softened by the more or less constant need to gain the support of other groups whose traditions and logic are opposed to them.

Organization of the Culture

Equality is the goal of democratic socialists, but because of their commitment to the peaceful road to socialism they must find ways to deal positively with the hierarchies they find in place around them. Just as importantly, by accepting the liberal political framework of election and authoritative government they are committed to a hierarchy of their own.

While it may be argued that this commitment is simply a necessity of the situation and not of the culture, it is also obvious that the situation will never change as long as the democratic socialists are democratic. Coincidentally, there is no reason to expect the democratic socialists not to accept the electoral hierarchy as legitimate after a few generations. This is a major paradigm contradiction that may well have repercussions in other areas.

Economic equality can still be stressed and is the characteristic goal of democratic socialist governments. Their need to work with other cultures, however, as well as their own emphasis upon the need for an equality of affluence rather than of poverty, tends to complicate their economic policies.

The simplest way to achieve economic equality, and the way taken by leninists, is to abolish both rich and poor by having the state control all personal incomes and make those incomes equal. This strategy is not possible for democratic socialists because such a policy contradicts the paradigms of their political allies and would drive their opponents to civil war, something the democratic socialists find unacceptable. Their general solution is basically radical liberal: regulations fixing minimum wages and welfare measures to abolish poverty. The taxation to fund the welfare is mainly on the rich, of course, but it is generally not enough to abolish the hierarchy involved.

Social equality also tends to be difficult to achieve. In countries with very strong tory cultures it is not unusual to find democratic socialist majorities in parliaments that are legally and socially under a monarch. The monarch reassures the tories and, because the power of the monarch is usually far more symbolic than real, he is quite acceptable to the liberals. Given time, the democratic socialists may very well become good monarchists too, even though such a position is hardly logical.

In any event, social differences tend to continue and are generally seen as hierarchical differences. At the same time, differences among people are seen more in the way tories see them: as differences in qualities and tastes rather than as differences in a single hierarchy of wealth and prestige.

If a democratic socialist government is in a particularly strong electoral position it may well try to tax the rich out of existence and to formally abolish the aristocracy and perhaps even the monarchy, but this undertaking generally proves too much for their allies and is not successful. Indeed, such attempts can seriously weaken the coalitions in the parliament and turn the country to ugly confrontations. Far better to let sleeping dogs lie.

In any case, the government and the bureaucracy manage the major industries of the country, so the power base of the oligarchs and liberals is greatly reduced. At this point quarrels in the parliament are generally over personal rather than corporate wealth, and personal wealth is seldom enough of an issue to have a major impact upon the society as a whole.

The great and abiding threat to the general equality achieved by the democratic socialists is that they will be voted out of office, after which the major industries will be sold or simply given back to private interests. If this happens the basis of the welfare state is gone and the welfare system itself will soon be bankrupt. The leninists will be greatly strengthened on the left and the democratic socialists will find themselves correspondingly weaker as they strive to put their electoral coalitions back together and regain power.

Basic Unit of the Culture

The democratic socialists believe in individualism, and their position here is fairly strong. Radical liberals (a major ally), classical liberals, and leninist socialists are also individualists, while the oligarchs will support them in their individualism as long as it is not extended in any meaningful way to the oligarchs themselves. The tories, the other major ally of the democratic socialists, present a fairly major problem because of their belief in corporatism.

The radical liberals, when they were in power, could pass individualistic laws with the support of the classical liberals and oligarchs. Since these laws could be devastating to them, the tories naturally tended to oppose the change, but were generally ineffective in doing so. They were somewhat protected by the usual oligarchs' insistence on loopholes to protect their own families, but often these loopholes were available only to the rich. The democratic socialists, needing the tories as allies in their struggles against the oligarchs and classical liberals, are less able to ignore the needs of the tories.

The welfare laws passed by the democratic socialists make it easier for poor tories to keep their families together and the mixed economy tends to protect their family businesses far better than did the oligarchical/liberal system which preceded it. On balance, the tories are better off with the democratic socialists than with the radical liberals, although both tend to erode tory values through individualism in the public schools, in the tax laws, and in general legislation.

Generally speaking, then, the democratic socialists are able to function as individualists. Free association on single issues, a paradigm of the liberals, is not a paradigm of the democratic socialists and with this they have a harder time. Because of their emphasis on cooperation, democratic socialists believe in free association within functional groups rather than on single issues. The emphasis upon working in groups and accepting the group consensus in making decisions is more restrictive than an issue orientation, and tends to be rejected by the liberals. The tories are no problem in this respect, but the liberals can be very difficult. Since democratic socialists need the radical liberals as allies (and need the peaceful acceptance by the others of policies passed in the parliament), this area can become a difficult one. Generally group loyalty is not a major issue in times of affluence, but hard times will bring this issue to the surface as liberals abandon functional groups in their competitive self-interest.

Individuals are assumed to be cooperative and collectivist by democratic socialists. In this respect paradigm conflict with the other cultures may assume major proportions in times of crisis, and democratic socialists are committed to using peaceful means in solving these crises. Because of this commitment they are essentially dependant upon the cooperation of the other cultures. Whether or not they get it will depend upon the nature of the crisis. If the crisis involves an external enemy they probably will, but if it is internal to the country and the competitive interests of the liberals and oligarchs are better served by noncooperation, the continued dominance of society by the democratic socialists is definitely in doubt.

Concept of the Culture

Democratic socialists believe in collectivism, as do the tories. Their radical liberal allies do not, and this disagreement causes problems. Unable because of their political paradigms to simply impose collectivism on the rest of society (and needing the support of the radical liberals to offset the opposition of the classical liberals and oligarchs, as well as to help them structure individualistic policies against the opposition of their other allies, the tories), the democratic socialists must compromise.

What they would most like is egalitarian cooperation for the good of the whole, but their minimum need is cooperation in running the basic industries of the country. The idea is that if the major industries are noncompetitive and the prices of their products kept low, then the competition in the rest of the economy will do no great harm. This mixture of competition and cooperation is quite familiar to the radical liberals. It simply replaces their attempted regulation of the economy with state management. Once over the shock of accepting the concept that oligarchs and classical liberals have taught them to believe is captivity (not "free"), radical liberals tend to live with this aspect of democratic socialism rather easily, although as long as they remain radical liberals they are never very comfortable with it.

Classical liberals, of course, hate state management of the basic economy, even though it tends to benefit those on the lower rungs of the ladder. Ambitious as ever, classical liberals tend to rise in the bureaucratic hierarchy of government just as they rose in the hierarchies of capitalist corporations, but they yearn for the monetary rewards and the status of the captains of industry of other times. They are as disruptive as they can be, for they compete whenever possible, loathing the cooperation forced upon them by the democratic socialists. They also evade their taxes as much as possible and generally seek to take advantage of the welfare programs that disgust them.

Oligarchs find themselves in a difficult position but not an impossible one. They have lost control of the great industries but probably still control many of the smaller ones. They are prevented from exploiting workers as they would like because of the minimum-wage laws and the extensive state welfare system, but they can still hold their families together and be fairly prosperous. They are very familiar with the general approach of the democratic socialists because it is essentially the same as their own approach to themselves, except for the egalitarian aspects.

Tories tend to be pleased with many aspects of democratic socialism. The state manages the economy and the largest industries for the good of the whole, which does no violence to the tory beliefs in the duties of the monarch, while the freedom to compete at lower levels leaves the tories equally free to cooperate within their corporate groups. They can simply disregard much of the competition in the system and be able to count on state support in doing so, for their collectivist paradigms are much the same as those of the democratic socialists. Simple necessity demands functional groups in order to get things done, and with a minimum of political astuteness the tories can get their own groups accepted by the democratic socialist bureaucracy as constituent parts of the nation.

Government

The general idea of radical liberalism is that all the people should vote and that their elected representatives should govern. At the same time liberals (both classical and radical) generally distrust the judgment and competence of those at the bottom levels of the hierarchy of wealth, and are particularly afraid that the poor will use their votes to take money from the rich and give it to themselves. In order to prevent this dispossession, radical liberals are usually content to work within the structure of classical liberal governments designed to prevent the government itself from doing much beyond protecting the private property of those rich enough to have some.

Democratic socialists reject the liberal structure of multiple governmental institutions with overlapping powers and responsibilities. Where radical liberal political structures typically have four different institutions (executive, legislative, judicial, and bureaucratic), democratic socialists generally have two: parliament and the bureaucracy.

In theory parliament makes the laws and the bureaucracy enforces them, with parliament made up of elected members and the bureaucracy of career bureaucrats protected by a civil-service system that ensures their political neutrality, and therefore their efficient enforcement of whatever laws the legislature should pass. In practice there is a need for a connecting link between the bureaucracy and parliament that is usually provided by the cabinet, a small committee elected by parliament from among its members with a member for each of the major bureaucratic divisions (the ministers) and one to speak for the whole (the prime minister). This committee is known as "the government" and is responsible to parliament for the day-to-day running of the bureaucracy.

Since the bureaucrats heading each division often have far more experience and knowledge of the workings of the law and of the nature of the people affected by it than do the cabinet members, their function often comes down to monitoring the bureaucracy rather than directing it, and a great deal depends upon the cooperation between the minister and the bureaucrat. This cooperation, quite naturally, will be affected by the cultures of the people involved.

On the legislative side, the cabinet members have the knowledge, experience, and authority of the civil service behind them, and because of this tend to be quite a bit more authoritative than their nonministerial colleagues. This authority is increased because of the fragmented nature of parliaments, a fragmentation that is a direct result of the electoral systems generally favored by democratic socialists.

It is not unusual for the solidarity of the cabinet to result in a very powerful prime minister. If the majority coalition is solid enough or if a single party has a majority, this result can be a monopoly of political power by the prime minister, at least for the life of the parliament. National crises tend to reinforce this tendency.

Classical liberals, the first of our cultures to introduce voting as a way of selecting and legitimizing governments, were very careful to limit the vote to the wealthy. Since no self-respecting classical liberal is likely to trust another, however, government had to be fragmented but at the same time protected against any group that would threaten the system of government by wealth. In order to provide a further protection the system of single-member districts elected by a majority was developed. The basic idea was that while some of the wealthy voters might lose their minds and oppose the system, the majority would not. At the same time, the different elites in the country should be represented.

The obvious solution was to have the legislators elected from the different geographical districts (particularly when control of the land was wealth) but to make sure that a majority of the wealthy voters in each district would dominate the possibly hare-brained minority. Single-member geographical districts did this, with the added attraction that older elites not based on landed wealth, such as the guilds, universities, and the church, would have no direct representation at all. Because of these features the single-member district idea was quite acceptable to both the oligarchs and the classical liberals.

The radical liberals found nothing at all wrong with the system and simply extended the vote, first to those who had money but not property (renters), then to all adult males, and finally to all adults. The system still quite effectively suppressed minorities within each district, while the divisions and veto points within the institutions of government ensured that even if a few districts contained majorities of nonliberals they would not be effective.

Democratic socialists regard this system as unfair at both levels. At the governmental level they abolish the division of powers; at the electoral level they object to single-member districts and work for a change to a system of proportional representation. In a pure system of proportional representation all votes are at a national level (no districts) and each party gets the same proportion of seats in the legislature that it has of the national vote. Democratic socialists thus abolish all branches of government except a single body: this is the parliament. It functions as the executive, as the legislature, and as the supreme court, meaning that any law passed by parliament is automatically constitutional and cannot be opposed by the executive, since parliament is the executive.

It should be noted here that democratic-socialist-dominated governments are the most varied in their structure of any of the cultures. Committed to peaceful means to achieve their goals, they are the most likely to be forced to adapt their strategies to already existing structures. What follows is a discussion of some of the different forms democratic socialist systems may take.

In practice, districts are often retained because of pressure from the tories, whose corporate groups are usually solidly based in geographical districts. Compromises with the other cultures involved often result in quite complicated systems, with district elections on both local and national slates, some representing national parties, some powerful or popular individuals, some particularly cohesive districts, and some local parties. Indeed, the general result of proportional representation under democratic socialists is a parliament that has no "natural" majority at all, since no single party has even a near majority of its members.

Moreover, even the most open systems allow no representation for groups that do not obtain enough votes to qualify for a single seat. How many votes will be considered enough and how many members will be elected are constant problems to dedicated democratic socialists, as is the problem of what to do with small parties whose membership is spread across a number of districts. The result is often a combination of district and national voting.

Even with all these problems there is no doubt that proportional representation is more democratic than single-member districts, in that far more voters are able to elect people to parliament who represent their views. Once elected, however, these representatives must find some way of electing the government (the cabinet and prime minister). What happens is that parties with similar goals form coalitions that vote together, and much of the politics of parliaments involves the formation and continuation of these voting blocs. A major problem, of course, is that parties may agree on some issues but not on others. If we assume that each of the various cultures we have discussed will be represented in parliament by at least one party, it is clear that overlapping paradigms may promote coalitions while contradictory ones will promote opposition. Given that each culture has contradictions within it as well as with other cultures, the result for parliaments is continued division and difficulty.

Liberals and others focus upon this aspect of proportional representation when they argue for the single-member district, a system that tends to result in only two parties, each of which must appeal to the less committed middle of the electorate in order to get elected. Generally speaking, however, systems of proportional representation work quite well where there is a national consensus on basic policies, a consensus which generally involves a strong coalition of tories and democratic socialists supported by radical liberals.

Democratic socialists argue further that a real commitment to democracy should accept a chaotic result if in fact that chaos faithfully represents the electorate. The idea is that over time people will work out a consensus which is far more fair and just than that arrived at through liberal methods of election and government.

Even when democratic socialists are able to dominate a majority coalition they must give seats in the cabinet to the other parties in the coalition or risk losing votes to the opposition. The prime minister is always from the dominant party in the coalition but the authority he or she has over coalition cabinet ministers depends upon the value of the their several parties to the coalition, so this is another difficulty in establishing democratic socialist policies.

One major consequence of the supremacy of parliament is that new elections can be called any time a majority votes for them. Generally there is an agreed limit to the length of time a parliament can exist without an election (five or six years is usual) but this too can be changed by parliament itself. In some systems the monarch or an elected president also has the power to dissolve parliament and schedule new elections. This, and the power to form a government when parliament cannot do so (as when there is no majority party and all attempts to form a majority coalition fail), are usually the only governing functions of the chief of state, as the monarch or president is called.

The whole system may sound clumsy and difficult, but experience has shown that parliamentary regimes can work quite well. In Europe most governing systems are parliamentary, although in some the power of the chief of state approaches that of a president in the radical liberal system. Despite the democratic socialists' belief in rationality, it is tradition and custom which allows these regimes to function as much as does any logical assessment of the benefits to be had from them. The democratic socialist/tory coalition brings with it tory legitimacy based upon tradition. The more tory the population the better for the democratic socialist government, although this situation naturally limits some of the things the government can do.

A monarch, in particular, imparts legitimacy to the government. It can be persuasively argued that the great majority of any population has a strong tendency to see the head of state as the nation, and to grant legitimacy not only to the person but to the acts of that person. When a constitutional monarch of the sort we have described here is the focus of this sort of feeling, the parliamentary government is not seen as the nation itself; the monarch is.

People then tend to see the government for what it is: a group of people elected by parliament to oversee the bureaucracy and to chair (and usually run) the parliament itself. Parliament can vote one government out and another in without causing psychological trauma in the nation. Ministers, even prime ministers, who are discovered in wrongdoing can be replaced without any great national anguish over the character of the nation. In contrast, great abuses have been willfully ignored in presidential systems because so many people identified the president with the nation itself, and refused to deal with the problem.

By separating the symbolic father (or mother) of the nation from the government, this system allows people to better assess the actions of the government and to respond to them on a rational basis. Patriotic citizens identify with the nation and the monarch, regarding the government of the day as a device to set policy and run the bureaucracy but not as the country itself. Politicians find it correspondingly difficult to wrap themselves and their policies in the flag; they are seen for what they are, not for what the citizen wishes himself and the politician to be.

Party discipline becomes very important in this system for two reasons. First, in order to have bargaining power within the coalition, parties must have the votes in parliament; if their members refuse to accept the decisions of party leaders in these negotiations then the leaders clearly have no power to negotiate. Second, the parties are responsible to the voters far more strictly than they are in a system of divided institutions. When a party dominates parliament there are no excuses for its not instituting its policies; no other body has a veto power. Neither another legislative house, nor a president, nor a supreme court stands between parliament and the exercise of power. If a party does not deliver on its campaign promises it has no excuse, and will most likely suffer a crushing defeat at the next elections.

Given this situation, it is not unusual for the parliamentary party (the members of the party elected to the parliament) to develop a strong hierarchy and to submit to the authority of the parliamentary leaders, particularly if they dominate parliament and their party leader is also the prime minister. This is a paradigm conflict, and can be troublesome if the prime minister flaunts his or her authority too openly; however, it is a natural consequence of the need for party discipline and is unlikely to change.

Economics

The economic system of a democratic socialist government is as complex as the political system and for the same reasons. Every act of parliament is the result of the coalitions in it, and on economic issues as on any other the coalitions can shift. The government has some influence on the situation through its power to lead the majority, but it is not unusual for a parliament to vote out a government it has voted in. The fall of a government is not necessarily the end of the parliament. It can vote in another government or even return the ousted one, having put it on notice that certain actions will not be tolerated. Party discipline and the need to deliver on campaign promises enable governments to institute their policies, but these policies can be reversed by the next government.

The minimum economic policies of democratic socialists, as we have seen, are state ownership and management of major industries and welfare systems that ensure a healthy, decent life for all. Liberals hold that people work only if they are forced to through threats to their physical security. Since democratic socialism is committed to providing this security it follows (to liberals) that no one will work and that the system will collapse because no goods will exist to be distributed.

As it works out, this criticism does not seem to be justified. Most of Europe is now governed by democratic socialist regimes, yet their industries, both state-owned and private, continue to produce goods as well as or better than those in third-world countries, where threats to security are normal. A lack of hard work and productivity is not Europe's problem.

The major factor not yet accounted for is the nature and impact of the international economic system. In our time the private transnational business corporation has become the basic institution of international trade. Government-to-government economic transactions (many based upon barter rather than monetary units) have been increasing in response to the situation profit-oriented transnationals create, but for nonleninist states the transnationals still dominate the international system.

These transnational corporations are run by citizens of a single state and are oligarchical/liberal. Their purpose is to make a profit, and the primary method for doing so is to produce goods in low-wage, low-cost countries and sell them in high-wage, high cost countries. Transnationals often conceal their profits from taxation by either country through employing bookkeeping fictions to "keep" them in third countries such as the impoverished island nations, which for a fee will happily provide the service. Since no goods, services, or even money actually enter this third country, the transnationals risk nothing in using it. If allowed to operate freely the transnationals can almost always sell their goods for less than those produced in the high-wage, high-cost country and still make large profits.

The results for the countries within which the goods are sold are disastrous. For democratic socialist regimes, both the revenues from the state-owned industries and the taxes from the smaller private industries disappear while welfare costs increase as unemployment increases. A socialist system offsets high taxation with reductions in personal expenses (for example, health and pension costs are paid by the state), but if the products of the state and private businesses are consistently undersold by the transnationals both the public and the private businesses will go bankrupt, as will the state itself a short time later.

Borrowing money at interest from international sources, whether capitalist or not (and if the money is at interest it is capitalist, no matter what the institution calls itself) will not solve the problem, since the drain continues as long as goods and services are being bought from the transnationals. The process is prolonged and bankruptcy staved off, but the end result is the same, particularly if the banks borrowed from are owned or associated with the transnationals selling the goods and services. Eventually the market for the transnationals' goods will collapse, but that has not yet occurred.

What has occurred, mainly in third-world countries so far, is a kind of debt servitude when the international banks begin to dictate the economic policies of the debtor nations. The policies dictated are naturally oligarchical/classical liberal. They are called "austerity" programs, but since the aim is to pay back the banks and provide money for internal investment by private entrepreneurs, the austerity is the fate of the poor and the middle class. The upper class and their banks are the beneficiaries and for them the results are anything but austere.

By requiring these policies from democratic socialist regimes the bankers are simply transferring wealth from the welfare programs to themselves or to other transnationals. Since the money spent for goods and services already goes to transnationals they are simply prolonging the process until they control all the wealth of the country. Long before this happens the democratic socialist regime will have collapsed under the pressure. After the collapse the country will be used for labor and materials available at minimum costs.

The governments of democratic socialists are based upon parties competing for votes and forming coalitions in the resulting parliaments. Since the other cultures are not suppressed, as they are in single-party marxist-leninist systems, democratic socialists generally find themselves pressing for more state management of the economy and stronger welfare measures, while liberals and oligarchs argue for less of both, the former being in favor of free enterprise and the latter, since they do not control the government, favoring the "private" management of the economy by themselves.

The outcome of the competition is greatly affected by two factors: the strength of the tories and the degree to which transnationals penetrate the national economy. The stronger the tories, the more support for state management and welfare measures. The tory/socialist coalition will break down if the socialists seriously attack hierarchy, but if they do not attack it the coalition can be quite strong. In this case, radical liberals tend to oscillate between supporting welfare and calling for more free enterprise.

The presence of transnationals, of course, tends to support the liberals and oligarchs. If the government attempts to counter this pressure by having the state enterprises themselves become transnationals, they soon find themselves caught up in the dynamic of capitalism, whether the government is socialist or not. Radical liberals, in this case, tend to support free trade over internal welfare, and democratic socialist governments can find themselves supporting radical liberal policies. At this point they are often voted out of office, only to be reinstated later when welfare falls even further without them.

Up to this point we have discussed the production and financial aspects of democratic socialist economies. Distribution is the other part, and here democratic socialists tend to find the same sorts of problems. All economic systems ration the consumption of goods, but in liberal and oligarchical systems the rationing is done by the price of the article. This rationing is from the top down, since in a completely monetary system the rich get all they want while those with no money get nothing.

Democratic socialists who gain control of a previously oligarchical/liberal government accept the monetary system that goes with it. They modify it by rationing goods if there is a scarcity, and by instituting welfare policies that make sure everyone has an income sufficient for an adequate living. While some services, such as schools and health care, may be fully socialized (meaning that the service is supplied to all people who require it, staff and supplies being paid for by the state), the usual pattern for democratic socialists is to follow radical liberal welfare patterns but to extend them to everyone.

If goods are scarce, everyone can be supplied with a ration book that entitles them to purchase a particular quantity of whatever is being rationed at a price lower than the free-market price, the difference being paid by the state. If the person wants more, he or she can buy it at whatever (higher) price it brings on the free market if he or she has the money. All people are provided with enough money to purchase everything in the ration book, which itself is meant to cover what is needed for adequate living. If the free-market price falls below the price provided for in the ration book, the buyer will obviously not use the ration coupon and the state pays nothing.

The dynamic here is much the same as for Keynesian economics, but democratic socialists tax the rich as well as the middle class. The problem is that the long-term benefits tend to go to the transnationals, who benefit from low wages outside the country and high demand within it. If nationalized industries respond by locating production facilities in low-wage countries in order to compete, they are then exploiting alien workers and throwing their own people out of work, and must finance the higher welfare costs the increased unemployment produces. The dynamic is the same, although the negative effects are postponed. When they catch up, the democratic socialists are back in the position the radical liberals were earlier.

If the tory/socialist coalition is strong enough to have a permanent majority in the government they may be able to close the economic system, but it is unlikely that they will be able to do so. It is obvious that the oligarchical/liberal coalition which will oppose such a step will receive the support of the transnationals and the governments of their countries. If this includes military and economic support of the opposition groups within the country governed by the democratic socialists (especially in the military), civil war may erupt, something a nonviolent democratic socialist government may have great difficulty in fighting. If a majority of the military enter or initiate the violence on the side of the oligarchs and liberals, the democratic socialist government is very unlikely to survive.

The response of European democratic socialist governments to the dynamic of transnational competition is an interesting one. Beginning in the 1960s many of the European governments converted their state-owned corporations into transnationals and encouraged private businesses to become transnationals. Depending upon the societal dynamics in each country the results were more or less pronounced, but the tendency was the same for all. The corporations that became transnationals were all pressured to move their production facilities to low-wage, low-cost countries and to sell their products wherever they could get the highest prices for them.

The state-run corporations tended to become state capitalist rather than state socialist, and to exacerbate the government's problems rather than decrease them. To be sure, their profits were available for taxation, where those of the transnationals were not, and they could be prevented from moving too many productive facilities overseas, but insofar as these measures were implemented they reduced the government's transnationals' ability to compete.

The obvious solution is for the government to limit access to the internal market. A democratic socialist government cannot manage the economy of the nation if foreign transnationals are free to do what they wish inside the country. Limiting access to the nation is far easier said than done. The governments of the capitalist states are properly horrified at the prospect of not being able to evade their problems through constant expansion, and horrified as well by the paradigmatic attack upon their commitment to the individual freedom of both people and business corporations. They will oppose the democratic socialists' efforts to protect their national economy, and if internationally powerful can cause major problems.

To live entirely on your own resources and still be industrialized is an option available only to the resource-rich countries. Most of the geographically smaller countries, most notably Japan, are unable to do so. Even resource-rich countries would have to make radical changes in their economies and most probably in their way of living. Democratic socialist regimes are not in a position to succeed if they attempt to prevent the transnationals from freely buying and selling in their countries.

Summary

Democratic socialism can dominate a society only if people of the other cultures grant it legitimacy. This will generally happen only if tories are very strong and if the democratic socialists are capable of forming coalitions with them and the radical liberals. Otherwise the oligarchs, and to a lesser extent the classical liberals, will violently remove them from office when they begin passing and enforcing laws that attack the bases of the wealth and economic control of the rich. Leninist socialists can support, attack, or be neutral toward the democratic socialists. In different situations they have responded in each of these ways, and sometimes have done all three at once.

If democratic socialists do manage to dominate the government and economy they still have major problems. They and their actions are subject to reversal in the event of an electoral defeat, which because of their commitment to democracy is always a possibility. Their own contradiction between egalitarian goals and hierarchical government is masked by the belief in hierarchy of the other cultures with which they must collaborate.

Economically, their need to manage the economy is contradicted by the management of the international economy by the transnationals. By managing their own affairs the private transnationals are simultaneously managing the economies of many small countries and partially managing those of the others in which they operate. Such management is rarely consistent with the goals of the democratic socialists and usually works against them. Again because of the electoral system the democratic socialists find it difficult to exclude the supporters of the transnationals, and therefore difficult to manage the economy.

Economic crises, moreover, tend very much to cross national boundaries when transnationals are present, and the democratic-socialist-dominated state is vulnerable to the exportation of these problems. The greater the crisis the more strains put on the government, and the more likely the coalitions that allow it to exist will break. Even if the democratic socialist party has a majority in parliament by itself, military coups, civil war, or other forms of armed struggle can threaten the democratic process to which the democratic socialists are committed.

On the other hand, democratic socialist goals and forms of government are very beneficial to tories and radical liberals, who otherwise might not have the strength to maintain themselves in any kind of security. The coalition of these three cultures is very strong once it has been achieved. The mutual support between tories and democratic socialists is particularly strong. Once formed, this coalition is unlikely to be broken up by anything short of armed struggle. If the radical liberals desert it in a return to more liberal economic policies, it is possible that the oligarchs and classical liberals will again dominate government and society.

Private, profit-oriented transnationals can be dealt with positively by democratic socialist regimes only as long as the government maintains control of the national economy. While the transnationals will deal with and through socialist governments if they have to, their drive for higher profits will cause them to bypass governments whenever it is possible. International debt crises, depressions, high inflation, or any combinations of these or other difficulties generally result in greater control by private transnationals and less control by democratic socialist governments.

In sum, democratic socialist regimes can be strong and stable, but they are always vulnerable to electoral defeat and economic crises. Leninist socialist regimes can effectively guard against these threats but have problems of their own. Situational factors determine the establishment and maintenance of democratic socialist regimes, and not all of these factors can be influenced by the regimes themselves. If they are to be strong, radical liberals must first become thoroughly disenchanted with oligarchy and dubious of their ability to regulate it, while tories must be a strong component of the society and equally disenchanted with the oligarchs and classical liberals.

Once established, democratic socialists may hope to maintain the support of the radical liberal and tory cultures through enacting and enforcing policies that benefit them, but remain vulnerable to an international economy they can neither control nor avoid. While they are in office, however, they probably do more good with fewer restrictions on either individuals or groups than any other type of government. The question is not so much whether or not they are desirable, for their paradigms do the least harm to the paradigms of the other cultures, but whether or not they can be realistically expected to maintain themselves once they have succeeded in establishing their government.

Chapter 9

Leninist Socialism (Communism)

For leninist socialists, democratic socialism is always a cruel hoax, for leninists believe that the rich will never give up their wealth and power without a bloody fight. If this view is valid, democratic socialist regimes are merely facades covering the exploitation of the masses by the few, as the radical liberal governments were before them. Even worse, they give socialism a bad name, making the eventual move to socialism longer and even more bloody than it would otherwise be. Those who have believed in democratic socialism will despair when it fails, and may move back to radical liberalism rather than to leninism.

Lenin, who was thirteen years old when Marx died, was raised and became a socialist in tsarist Russia, a nation with a strong and vigorous secret police. Perhaps because his brother was caught by the secret police and hanged, perhaps because anarchism was especially strong in Russia and therefore its weaknesses especially apparent, Lenin developed a belief in the necessity for a secret, professional, and strongly hierarchical revolutionary organization to guide and channel the socialist impulses of the masses.

Marx was correct in predicting the revolutionary nature of the industrial proletariat and the oppressive, competitive, and violent nature of capitalist governments, but Lenin was convinced that spontaneous anarchistic uprisings of the people were doomed in the face of the highly organized and technologically powerful police and military forces that would be sent against them. The revolution was occurring continually in strikes, takeovers, and even limited military actions, but in order for it to succeed it had to be organized.

Since this organization must be secret it must also be hierarchical. Open discussion and the long process of reaching consensus was impossible in a society dominated by ruthless forces opposed to the revolution and the pervasive presence of the secret police. Not surprisingly, the revolutionary organization was itself modeled on the secret police. Hierarchical, with subordinates knowing only who and what was necessary to carry out their orders, the leninist party gained strength from the same organizational structure as its immediate enemy.

Only necessity could justify such a complete reversal of socialist paradigms, and Lenin himself viewed it as justifiable only so long as it was necessary to achieve the revolution. The existence of a strong and authoritarian organization to lead the people to socialism, however, has become the major characteristic of marxist-leninists. Marxist in their analysis of capitalist society and in their acceptance of socialist goals, they are leninist in their organization and acceptance of hierarchical authority as necessary to achieve the transition from one culture to the other. Even though hierarchy is morally wrong, corrupting, and dangerous to themselves, it is accepted, an acceptance that makes the party stronger than it would otherwise be.[1]

A major problem with marxist-leninist (communist) parties is that they do not tend to wither away. Lenin himself was exceptionally democratic, willing to spend as long as necessary with committees in order to reach a consensus, but the dynamics of both hierarchy and revolution work in the other direction. Hierarchy tends to make the person at the top of the hierarchy authoritative and to define him or her as superior to others. Violent revolution tends to require authoritative decisions even when the initial struggles are spontaneous. When led by the hierarchy, the tendency is even more marked.

Lenin remained democratic, egalitarian, and tireless throughout his life, but this was essentially a triumph of character over the dynamics of the situation. Subsequent leaders of the Russian revolution, functioning within the hierarchical authoritarian party structure of communism, have had less success in maintaining the democratic, egalitarian principles of socialism. While creating an electoral system that is parliamentary, they have limited the electorate to a single party with its candidates chosen by the party. The result is an elected government which is at best analogous to the consultative cabinet of a tory monarch (although much larger) and at worst is simply a rubber stamp. While such an electoral process may serve many positive functions, particularly that of providing connections between the leaders and the led that are not just one-way paths of communication, it is clear that it does not function as a liberal or democratic socialist electoral system functions.

This does not mean that the Soviet Union is not socialist but that it has settled into a particular way of dealing with the major paradigm conflict of socialism. It is clear that hierarchy, control, and authority take precedence over equality, at least in the government, but not at all clear that this leninist structure will inevitably lead to a grossly unequal economic situation despite the anarchist assumption that hierarchy produces exploitation.

It is now time to examine each of the paradigms of communism. We will discuss how stalinism, trotskyism, maoism, and castroism, the major communist systems, have dealt with communism's paradigm contradictions as we come to them.

Theoretical Source of Legitimacy

All socialists believe in rationality as the source of legitimacy, but marxist-leninists have a way of dealing with tradition that does not dismiss it as mere ignorant superstition. They distinguish "objective" reality from "subjective" reality. Objective reality is what the socialist sees as real, using marxist analysis and paradigms. Subjective reality is any other vision, and is produced by nonmarxist paradigms. Religion, for example, is the opiate of the people because it inculcates erroneous understandings about what is going on in this life and what will happen after it. A marxist-leninist does not condemn the holder of erroneous paradigms as stupid or inadequate (as a classical liberal would) but instead agrees with the radical liberal, that such people are not to be blamed but to be educated.

Unlike the radical liberal, the socialist believes the rich have misled and lied to the poor in a conscious effort to inculcate paradigms that will produce subservience and passivity. The cure is to reeducate the workers so they can recognize objective reality when they see it. Before the revolution this is about all that can be done, but after it, economic and political life will be lived according to objective reality; the illusions of the past will be actively exposed as such by the state, primarily through the educational system.

The basis for classical liberal analysis is the economic relations among people. They begin with a concept of human nature that posits selfishness and aggression as basic to all forms of life and proceed rapidly to economics. Adam Smith attempted to channel this drive into the production and consumption of goods rather than robbery. Marx argues that he failed in this attempt.

Socialists, through dialectical materialism, seek to see the material (economic) basis of society clearly and base their action on objective reality. In this they are the same as liberals, who also hold that material goods are central to the dynamics of society.

Materialism, whether it is socialist or classical liberal, is a persuasive paradigm because it has to do with the basic physical needs of life. Maslow argued that people must satisfy their physical needs first simply because if they don't, they die. The other elements in his hierarchy of needs were just as necessary but they were pragmatically secondary. Marx would have agreed. Since the basis of industrial capitalism was the material exploitation of the many by the few, it was necessary to analyze the system in material terms.

The marxist dialectic is a system of analysis derived from Hegel, which states that every thesis (an idea, an economic action, a social movement) will generate its antithesis (a contradictory idea, economic action, or the like), and that over time the two (the thesis and antithesis) will combine in a synthesis. This new thesis will in its turn generate a new antithesis and the process will continue.[2]

Since history itself is dialectical, it is surprising that marxists do not see socialism as generating its own antithesis, and being changed by the ensuing struggle into a new and different synthesis. They do not, however, and their position is that history will end with the creation of a classless society. The reason is that all history is the history of class struggle. When only one class exists after the triumph of the working class, there will be no more history. Logically, of course, a working-class culture (thesis) should generate its opposite (a new ruling class) and history should continue. Most liberals feel this is what has happened in the Soviet Union.

Mao, both a marxist and a leninist, denied the "end of history" idea. He felt that life held many contradictions, and not all of them could be resolved by a socialist society. Some of them, such as the contradiction between the interests of owner and worker, could be resolved (this particular one by making the worker the owner); but others, such as the need for a hierarchical organization to maintain a classless state, could not. We shall pursue this further when we discuss communist governments, but at this point it is primarily interesting that Mao's ideas on contradiction are consistent with prismatic analysis, while Marx's ultimately are not. Mao denies that rationality can solve all our problems, while Marx held that it could.

Mao struggled against tradition and superstition in the name of objective reality but did not believe that socialism, however rational, could result in a cohesive, positive, noncontradictory society. Cohesive and positive, perhaps, but for him the internal contradictions of socialism itself would always tend to produce new syntheses which could change socialism for the worse. The necessary hierarchy is necessarily corrupting to its members, and must be constantly monitored by the people. One logical result is another and competing hierarchy, but Mao believed people were far more cooperative than competitive, and hoped for the best.[3]

Stalin, who succeeded Lenin in the Soviet Union, expected the worst, especially from those who had suffered from the revolution. He put his faith in hierarchy and ruled through the government bureaucracy and the secret police rather than through the party. The result was a return to the traditional bureaucratic government of Russia, a development supported by the traditions of the people.

Dedicated egalitarian communists were, not surprisingly, the first to be gotten rid of, but they expected no better from a hierarchy (even their own) and the threat of war from the still undefeated capitalists was a sufficient argument for the continued necessity of a hierarchy. With the assumption of the duties of governing, the distinction between the party (or guiding and educating organization) and the bureaucracy (a policy-implementing organization) became blurred, and Stalin's shift to the bureaucracy as a power base was sufficiently ambiguous to succeed. The German invasion of 1941 made war actual, and the resultant tory unity more or less legitimized the situation.

Even so, Stalin had never wavered in his dedication to material equality, even though heavy industry was favored because of defense needs. Liberals, oligarchs, and tories could all argue that the Soviet Union had simply experienced a change of elites, but to most citizens it was obvious that material standards of living were rising, and rising in an egalitarian way. "Temporary" problems with a hierarchical government could be expected. The important thing was that positive economic equality was becoming a reality. A few might suffer, but the transition to socialism was not complete, and some suffering was inevitable. Egalitarian economic improvements were worth it.

Marxism and marxist-leninism are ideologies: conscious constructions that explain all of life without contradictions or uncertainties. In order to do this they must be based on a single set of consistent paradigms. When Mao introduced contradictions to marxist-leninism he was moving away from ideology to a more prismatic view of life. The Soviet thinkers have not as yet formally recognized contradiction as inevitable in living, and consequently still have trouble applying their ideology to the actual tasks of governing. Much that is done is extralegal because it is not ideologically correct, but in this the policy-makers have no option. This situation parallels the American, but is far more obvious in the Soviet Union because of the communist government's assumption of authority in all areas.

Organization of the Culture

Equality is the great theme of socialism, and no socialist would think of denying this paradigm. At the same time, it is obvious that people are not identical and that government is hierarchical. Communists, particularly stalinists, have a marked tendency to hold that contradiction is a characteristic of capitalist societies but not of socialist. Since they cannot, by their own standards, claim to be fully socialist (government still exists) they are to some extent spared the necessity of fully confronting their own contradictions.

A characteristic solution is to emphasize economic equality to such an extent that inequality in other areas of life can be seen as not very important — an attractive way of coping with this contradiction because Marx emphasized that the material aspects of life were the most basic and that the relation of people to things was fundamental. All other aspects of life are dependent upon the system of production and consumption of things. Consequently, communists (and socialists in general) are secure in the knowledge that if people in their society are economically equal then other aspects of life will tend to become more equal rather than less. They are on the right track, and as long as they continue to struggle for economic equality and to come at least close to it they cannot be too wrong in what they are doing.

It is a fact, at this time at least, that all of the clearly established socialist-dominated societies (in eastern Europe, the Soviet Union, China, and Cuba) have eliminated poverty and greatly reduced the difference between the most favored and the least favored in society. Judged against the standard of absolute equality they have been unsuccessful, but judged against the income inequalities of nonsocialist societies their success is obvious. At the same time, it is equally obvious that all socialist societies contain hierarchies of some sort, and that those at the upper levels of these hierarchies are also at the upper levels of the economic hierarchy, however small the difference may be between its higher and lower levels.

Sexual discrimination is also against socialist paradigms of equality, and revolutionary regimes in particular usually attack it head on. They often identify the family as the source of their problems. The most extreme solution is to do away with the family. Children will be raised in community (or state) nurseries and boarding schools, and parents will have no special relationship with their children. The object is to prevent the wrong traditions and customs (subjective realities) from being passed on to the next generation.

In no country has this attempt been wholly successful, although the kibbutzim in Israel have probably done the best. In this case, children are considered the children of the whole community, which is small enough so that anarchistic paradigms are possible. In larger communities the family has continued as a strong institution, and with it the respect and acceptance of hierarchy that it engenders.

Basic Unit of the Culture

Despite the continued existence of the family, the basic unit of leninist socialism remains the individual. Because the state assumes the responsibility for the economic well-being and equality of all individuals the direct economic importance of the extended family (aunts, uncles, cousins, grandparents, grandchildren, and so on) is greatly lessened. The nuclear family remains but its members are inculcated with individualism through schools, work, the media, and all the other aspects of life controlled or influenced by government. The parallels with liberal-dominated societies are apparent: in these societies, too, most nonfamily institutions have individualist paradigms.

The individualism of socialism is accompanied by a paradigm of the cooperative nature of people, while that of liberalism is joined with competition, but many aspects of individualism are the same for both. In each, sexism, racism, and nationalism are condemned as violations of individualism. The early marxists saw at once that to found a society on individual equality was doomed to failure if they allowed such blatantly hierarchical structures as sexism and racism to continue. Of the two, sexism was considered the more serious, since men and women occur together in every society. This is not true of racial or national groups, so while these illegitimate divisions among people are serious, they are not as immediate for socialists where they do not occur. Most societies are more-or-less sexist, so this is a constant preoccupation with conscientious socialists.

Racism is often crossed with nationalism, but insofar as it is separable, it is as illegitimate to socialists as it is to liberals. While classical liberals can escape the paradigm stress involved by claiming each individual must gain salvation (wealth) through her or his own individual efforts, and so can be blind to the collectivist nature of racial and sexual discrimination, the socialist does not have the same option. The socialist is conscious of the whole society, or at least feels responsible for it, while believing in the cooperative nature of all people. Unlike the liberals, the socialist cannot believe that the poor are inadequate people: they cannot generally be held responsible for their own poverty, let along be blamed for it. The continued existence of poverty, racism, and sexism is a cause for action rather than for guilt because there is no possibility of blaming the victim. There should be no discrimination of any sort in a socialist society.

Nationalism is theoretically quite as illegitimate for socialists, but its continued existence is less of a problem. While liberalism, like socialism, is universalistic, it is self-evident that nationalism remains strong in capitalist societies. Imperialism is essentially the domination of many areas of the world by a single nation-state. The state (the executive committee of the ruling class) uses its military and political power to allow capitalists of the imperialist country to extend their economic domination to the imperialized areas. In one form, this denies status as independent states to these areas, which are administered from the imperialist country as colonies. In another, puppet governments and armies are maintained but the economic, political, and military domination remain. The neocolonialist states are thus not sovereign in that the imperialist state controls them whenever and wherever it has an interest in doing so.

Only the imperialist state is sovereign. Classical and radical liberals have much the same way of coping with this as they do with poverty, racism, and sexism: imperialism is the fault of the imperialized individuals. Socialists blame the imperialists and support the revolution.

The nature of the revolution, though, is a matter of some dispute. It should, of course, be a revolution of the masses against the capitalist hierarchy that exploits them, whether the members of that hierarchy are from their own nation or from the imperialist nation. Nationalism itself is infantile, analogous to the child's attachment to his family even when this attachment is good for neither the child nor society as a whole. At the same time, most anti-imperialist wars are based upon nationalism rather than socialism. Which is more important? If nationalism, the result will most probably be a continuation of capitalism, with all its attendant horrors; the war will be won but the revolution never even attempted. If socialism, the revolution may well be crushed by the combined capitalist forces, who have far more to fear from socialism than they do from nationalism.

For European socialists the controversy was decisively influenced by World War I. Until 1914, socialism was an international movement that functioned across national boundaries. Socialists looked forward to the day when nations would no longer be the basis of states and the wealth and power of the few. Government would then be unnecessary and socialism universal. World War I was considered, both before and after the fact, to be an imperialist war, fought by the poor to benefit the rich over the issue of which national capitalists would get richer. It was a consequence of the competition among capitalists, and no matter what its outcome the poor would continue to be exploited and miserable. The nationality of the exploiters was ultimately irrelevant.

As it turned out, the masses, both workers and the unemployed, were far more nationalist than they were socialist. They enlisted (or submitted to the draft) in great numbers and many of the socialist parties themselves endorsed the war. International socialism had clearly failed to displace the paradigms of nationalism. The residual toryism of all classes seemed to have triumphed. The workers were killing each other for the benefit of capitalists. Subjective reality had proved far stronger than objective reality.

The slaughter of the war was horrible and in Russia the military was particularly badly led and equipped. Soldiers were being sent into battle without weapons, expected to pick up the rifles dropped by those killed before them. They at last revolted. A democratic socialist government was elected, but proved unable to end the war. In fact, the new government held that it was a point of national honor to continue it. The result was a second revolution that brought Lenin and the communists to power. They ended Russia's participation in the imperialist war and found themselves involved in a civil war that they considered a revolutionary war against capitalism. A great many Russians agreed with them, while the other side was fractionalized and discredited through support of the other war. The communists won.

The eventual result was a leninist socialist regime which succeeded to power over most of an empire that had included numerous non-Russian nationalities. The communists gave up some territory to the Germans in the peace of Brest-Litovsk but did not concede independence to the remaining nationalities, reorganizing the remainder of the empire into the Union of Soviet Socialist Republics (USSR). Given the continuing threat from the capitalist powers (the United States, France, and Great Britain had all invaded Russia in 1919) and the universal character of socialist goals, such a response was both expedient and justifiable, but to many of the defeated nationalist groups the Union was simply a continuation of Russian imperialism. The government has instituted socialist reforms throughout the Russian state, but it is still true that the leaders of the USSR are largely Russians, and the more racially different from the European Russian group any people are, the less they appear in the national government.

Trotsky, the leader of the Red Army, argued that the Russian civil war had been only the first stage of a global war between socialists and capitalists. More correctly, perhaps, it was a war between communists and capitalists, for World War I and the Russian revolution had both proved that democratic socialists not only were unreliable but would actually side with capitalists against their fellow socialists if nationalism was an issue.

Since nationalism was always and everywhere a method of capitalist control and exploitation, democratic socialists might as well be counted among the enemy. In any case, the violence, fear, and greed of the capitalists would cause them to continue the war against communism. Since Soviet Russia was the only communist nation-state (or empire, depending upon your point of view), this of course meant that the USSR was in great danger.

Given the highly developed military technology of capitalism and the tremendous wealth at the capitalist powers' disposal, it would be foolish for the communists to passively await the blow. World War I had shown how devastating main-force warfare was. Despite the success of the Red Army in the revolutionary war, to fight the combined forces of capitalism in Russia alone would invite destruction so extreme that there might be little left to fight over. The capitalists had already invaded twice (first the Germans and then the allies) and could be expected to do so again if nothing was done to stop them.

Trotsky's solution was to encourage communist parties in all parts of the world to initiate armed struggle against the local capitalists.[4] Such struggles might succeed, for the strength of capitalism was in technology and wealth, not in people. Since the wars would all be civil wars the people could be expected to support the socialists, since the capitalists could be counted on to commit atrocities against a despised working class they both feared and hated.

This idea of universal war is quite consistent with a marxist analysis, since Marx had predicted that spontaneous uprisings would occur wherever workers were oppressed. Since Lenin had earlier concluded that the revolution would be more successful in the colonial areas, where capitalism was relatively weaker than in the already industrialized seats of empire, universal war was also consistent with leninism.[5] Lenin's theory of revolution in the colonies is not quite consistent with Marx's analysis but it had the virtue of explaining why the revolution had succeeded in Russia, a largely nonindustrialized state, but not in France, Germany, or Britain, which were heavily industrialized.

Trotsky's ideas amounted to guerilla warfare on a global basis. Stalin disagreed. He felt that the USSR was not especially important to the capitalists. If they could be convinced that the Soviet Union was nationalist before it was communist and that local parties throughout the world were collaborative rather than violent, the capitalists would not invade. Russia was huge and cold in the winter and no invaders had been able to hold it for very long. A strong defensive force, a nonaggressive foreign policy, and nonviolent communists throughout the world would give the Soviet government time to build socialism in a single country. Later, when socialism was well established in the USSR, help could be offered to the working classes in other countries. After all, the great threat to capitalism was the success of capitalism itself, not invasion by a foreign power, even if that power were socialist.[6]

Trotsky's and Stalin's policies could not both be followed. Stalin won and his policies were implemented while Trotsky was driven into exile and eventually killed by a Spanish communist in Mexico in 1940. Stalin died in 1953. Ironically, many capitalist leaders today assume that the Soviet Union is busy implementing Trotsky's policies rather than Stalin's. Socialists consider this assumption a result of the capitalists' need for a universal enemy to justify their attempts at universal domination, as well as a result of their fear of socialism.

Non-Russian communist parties, of course, had little to gain from a strong Soviet Union as such. Only a belief in future help from the USSR and an equally strong belief in the power of local and international capitalism could justify their collaboration with capitalism demanded by Stalin's policy. Coupled with strong party discipline these considerations prevailed. Since the middle 1930s, communist parties allied with the USSR (generally called "orthodox" parties) have collaborated with whatever forces held the government, building strength in unions and waiting for the day capitalism should destroy itself.

Violent struggles against domestic leaders have been conducted by Trotskyites, other marxist-leninists, nonsocialist revolutionaries, and ambitious people of all sorts. To orthodox communists, these have all been "adventurers," although radical liberal movements against oligarchical regimes have sometimes been supported. Generally speaking, orthodox parties have played a very safe game, usually supporting revolutionaries only after it is clear that they will win.

Given the era in which we live, this strategy means they have associated themselves almost exclusively with wars of national liberation. The combination of socialism and national liberation from capitalist imperialism is a strong one, but subject to very severe strains after the war of liberation is won, since it involves a coalition of capitalists (usually radical liberals), tories, and socialists of all kinds. Democratic socialists often find themselves in the middle, and their own internal contradictions do not make this an easy position for them to occupy.

The universalism inherent in socialist individualism demands universal socialism, but the continued presence of both capitalism and nationalism make this difficult to achieve. Marx looked forward to a world centered around work and the workplace, assuming that all people would freely associate in the functional groups first created by capitalism and that government would disappear. Marxist-leninist parties have not withered away with the (partial) defeat of capitalism and show no signs of doing so.

While workers are certainly associated in functional groups, the freedom involved in their being so is even more questionable in socialist dominated societies than it is in those dominated by liberals.

It is also clear that efforts at individual economic equality under communist regimes have been far more successful than efforts at political equality. Poverty has been largely eliminated and, if affluence has rarely been achieved, physically adequate standards of living have.

Concept of the Culture

Collectivism is perhaps the most important of the socialist paradigms in the actual operation of socialist cultures. A rejection of hierarchy is what differentiates them most from the other cultures but large societies require a hierarchical government to hold them together, and socialism in our age has demonstrated that need.

Cooperation is a far more workable value, and all socialist dominated societies have had a great deal of success with it. This is not surprising, since cooperation is far more consistent with the human condition than equality or individualism. Families can exist and thrive without either of these paradigms, but they cannot exist without cooperation.

Mao used cooperation to balance the necessity for hierarchy. Unlike the tories, Mao saw hierarchy as negative, but unlike other marxist-leninists, he saw it as a permanent necessity. Both Trotskyites and Stalinists accept the position that the party is necessary to win the revolution but afterwards will wither away. Both also believe that the struggle will continue as long as capitalists violently oppose socialism, which will be as long as there are capitalist states capable of doing so. In this sense, the issue becomes theoretical and the question answerable only in the future.

Mao created a system designed to minimize the negative effects of hierarchy and to prevent its growth beyond the minimum necessary to hold society together. Egalitarian cooperation was to oppose hierarchical cooperation. In this, Mao directly attacked the most powerful of socialist paradigm conflicts rather than evading it by displacing its solution to the indefinite future.

The Chinese revolution was quite different from the Russian revolution. Armed struggle specifically between communists and the Chinese government began in 1927, when Chiang Kai-shek betrayed them in Shanghai, murdering most of the industrial proletariat that constituted the base of the Communist party. It did not end until 1949 with the victory of the communists throughout mainland China.

The civil war in the USSR lasted only three years. This is important because during a civil war each side must both fight the war and govern whatever part of the country it controls. During the Russian civil war, both the communist combatants and governmental officials were largely members of the industrial proletariat and the middle class. This was not the case in China, where the industrial proletariat had been largely destroyed by Chiang Kai-shek.

Russia in 1917 was largely an unindustrialized agricultural nation, but extensive industrialization had developed around Moscow and Petrograd (now Leningrad) while railroads and the telegraph extended throughout the country. The industrial proletariat was more than large enough to fight the revolution and to dominate the country after it was over. China had no such resource.

According to orthodox Marxism, the task of a communist party in China was to encourage industrial capitalism. It was, after all, necessary and progressive, if unjust. The socialist revolution could only occur after the industrial revolution, and that was a function of capitalism. Stalin was an orthodox marxist, and throughout the Japanese intervention and war in China (1931-1945) supported the Kuomintang, the party of Chiang Kai-shek. This party had been created by radical liberals, and was consequently held to be the party of the capitalists. It was certainly the party of the oligarchs and the enemy of the Chinese communists.

Mao argued that in China, at least, the peasants were revolutionary. Their subjective reality was the same as objective reality. Oppression and exploitation by the landlords had been oligarchical for so long that the peasants had lost hope of resurrecting a tory hierarchy. They were already revolting against the landlords and were ready to understand and accept socialism. Mao's position was that the socialist revolution could precede the industrial revolution: industrial capitalism was not a necessary preparation for socialism.

Such heresy was unacceptable to the stalinists. The Chinese communist party leaders also rejected it as long as they could, but the destruction of the industrial proletariat left them with the peasants as the only possible basis for the revolution. Even then, they might have rejected the idea if the peasants had not already been staging successful rebellions and setting up their own governments. These were egalitarian and cooperative, and as Mao pointed out, the party was in danger of being left behind by the revolution.

Maoism developed along quite different lines from European communism. Where an industrial proletariat was concentrated in cities, the rural agricultural proletariat was spread out. Where industrial workers did not control the technology of industrial production, the Chinese peasants controlled the technology of farming. Where the industrial proletariat is objectively socialist and subjectively liberal, the peasants of China were disillusioned tories. These factors led Mao to develop a revolution based upon the free cooperation of the peasants where the party, while authoritative over its members (leninist), was the guide of the peasants rather than their authoritative leader. Guerilla warfare was a necessity, both because the peasants were dispersed and because the party had neither heavy weapons nor the industrial base necessary to support them. The capitalists supplied the Kuomintang, and even the USSR supported it. The communist party had nothing but the people.

Mao also felt that a large conventional army would inevitably turn the peasants against it, if for no other reason than that it would have to be fed in a land of already hungry people. For all these reasons Maoism developed as a system that depended upon the voluntary cooperation of a people who were not and never had been individualists and who now saw their only hope in equality. The party was necessary but must not be allowed to dominate the people. How it could lead without dominating was the basic question.

The key, to Mao, lay in the collectivist nature of the Chinese. China had been dominated by tory/oligarchical struggles for at least two thousand years. A major problem of the Kuomintang was that its theoretical roots were in western radical liberalism, a situation that had resulted in its domination by oligarchs. Mao had no faith in Confucianism, which was the Chinese formulation of tory values, but accepted its emphasis on cooperation. Peasant cooperation with oligarchs was hardly beneficial to the peasants, but if socialists could gain the same cooperation the civil war and the revolution could be won. The essence of the problem for the party was to prove to the peasants that the party deserved their support.

The structure around which such cooperation could occur was the rural village. Just as plants and factories were the structural units of industrialized societies, the village was the basic unit of China. Small enough to be anarchistic, but for thousands of years part of the larger Chinese society, the village became the basic unit of Chinese communism. It predated the party and was, in the long run, more important than the party. For the twenty-two years the Chinese civil war lasted, the party governed the areas they controlled by providing socialist leadership and the benefits of socialism to the villages. Hierarchy existed but was presented as a support to the egalitarian, cooperative village, a unit small enough so that without landlords equality was both natural and possible.

After the civil war had been won, the party attempted to organize China into communities much larger than the traditional villages, a move that would have greatly simplified hierarchical administration. It did not work at all well, and the villages remained the basic unit of administration in the new socialist state as they had under the tory and oligarchical governments of the past. Equality in the villages continues to be stressed, and the party hierarchy is in constant tension with it. Where Russian communism stressed individualism and party authority, China under Mao stressed collectivism and party leadership. Both have resulted in widespread economic equality, but the nature of government and the economic systems themselves are quite different.

Government

Stalin's governmental structure was remarkably like that of the tsars, including a reliance upon the secret police. Where tsarist Russia had been moving away from managing the economy, however, economic management was a basic function of the new government. Since greater industrialization was consistent with the needs of the USSR's (conventional) military forces, with socialism, and with the industrial workers who were the basis of the revolution, it is not surprising that industrialization was the policy of the government.

Agriculture was to be mechanized and state farms were created. On these farms, not only was new technology introduced but the relation of industrial workers to management was also recreated. Farm workers in this case were wage laborers, and their wage was set by the central government. Other farms were run on a cooperative basis, and in this case prices were set by the central, hierarchical authority. Individual and family farms that had been legitimized by Lenin's New Economic Policy earlier were now abolished as too likely to lead to capitalism. In agricultural and in all other sectors of the economy management was centralized.

In a society as large as Russia's such centralized management has proved possible but very difficult. As heavy industrialization has matured and more, and more varied, consumer goods have been produced, the system has become more and more clumsy and awkward to operate. Agriculture, in particular, has not responded well to a system that has a rather close resemblance to the absentee landlord situation of the capitalist age. Government has until recently remained hierarchical, centralized, and untrusting of the people at the bottom.

Although the individualism that concentrated power in the single person at the top has been replaced by a more collegial leadership, the Soviet Union's socialist government is still a clear contradiction of the socialist paradigm of equality. Justified by the enemy without (the capitalists) and the transition to socialism within, it is now more accepted by tradition than by theory. The third generation of socialist citizens is now maturing and they, like people everywhere, generally accept the system into which they are born. If the government of that system is in contradiction to the

ideals of the nation, that is no harder for them to bear than the same contradiction in liberal states. Internal problems of Russian governments are
more centered around providing affluence than in further justification of
their existence.

From the Chinese point of view, the contemporary Soviet economy is
simply state capitalism. The government is not only the executive committee of the ruling class, it *is* the ruling class. State ownership of the means of
production simply means that the state is the new capitalist. The old distinctions between public and private were largely fictional anyway, and
now the public domain is the private property of the new rulers. The
Soviet capitalists have even reached an understanding with the rest of the
capitalists: they will be left unmolested in return for making no further attempts to poach on the empires already established around them. In the
Maoist view, Russia is another capitalist empire.

This scathing indictment is partly a function of Soviet policy toward
China. After the communist triumph of 1949, Soviet technological ad-
visers were welcomed in China, helping to create the factories needed for
industry and the nuclear capacity Chinese leaders felt necessary for
China's defense. They soon split, however, over the issue of defense itself.
Mao challenged the United States over Taiwan, where Chiang Kai-shek's
forces had taken refuge (much to the dismay of the Taiwanese). The
USSR's reaction was to abandon China on the grounds that the United
States had vowed to use nuclear arms against the USSR in the event of a
major war with communism. Stalin followed the line that Russia was ab-
solutely essential to world socialism, while Taiwan and China were not.

Mao, certain that the United States would never risk a nuclear war over
Taiwan, felt he and all China had been betrayed again by the cowardly
Soviets. Their support of the Kuomintang during the war with Japan had
not been a mistake in marxist theory but the help of one capitalist for
another in the battle with true socialism.

Mao's main concern for China was not that the many would corrupt the
movement towards socialism, something Stalin seemed to believe, but that
the party hierarchy would itself become corrupt. While Stalin was obsessed
by invasion from without, Mao was concerned with a betrayal of socialism
from those most responsible for guiding it: the party officials themselves.
Stalin used the secret police to purge the rest of the bureaucracy, the party,
and society itself of those who opposed him. Mao used the people to purge
the bureaucracy and the party of those who believed too strongly in hierarchy.

"The people," though, is an amorphous concept. The people who
responded to Mao's calls for a cultural revolution against hierarchy itself
were, naturally enough, mainly young people who had been raised with
socialist ideals but who had not yet attained a position in the hierarchy.

They cooperated enthusiastically in what became a purge by young people of older people in positions of authority. Teachers, engineers, party officials, and anyone who had attained visible superiority in any field were brought down, on the theory that any sort of hierarchy was evil. The socialist contradiction between equality and organization was as important in China as it was in the USSR, but in China the forces of equality were more powerful.

After Mao's death, the party reasserted itself, and the new leaders of China vowed that there would be no more cultural revolutions. The villages remain largely self-governing and self-sufficient, while the party intends to lead the country into extensive industrialization. Mao had industrialized, but the structures built up by the engineers were slow to appear in a country dominated by both agriculture and the need for food. Governmental structure, in this case, looks a great deal like tory government.

The USSR, since Stalin, is rather less tory because of the extensive centralization there, but it is clear that at least some tory attributes have remained. Moreover, both Gorbachev's *glasnost* (increased openess in government) and *perestroika* (restructuring and decentralization) can be seen as far more tory than liberal, although Americans have naturally interpreted them as a return to liberal capitalism. The central management of an economy as large and as complex as the USSR's today is clearly inefficient and wasteful, so much so that further progress in standards of living is being stymied. To decentralize economic decisions to the corporate groups doing the production and distribution of goods is clearly a return to toryism.

China, too, is initiating reforms which are designed to return economic initiatives to the producing groups, although they seem to be more individualistic in their approach than the Soviets. The problem for both governments is how to retain control of the economic system without smothering it or allowing it to develop oligarchies and liberalism.

Economics

The great problem with Keynesian economics is that a liberal economic system is not closed. The same problem usually exists for governments dominated by democratic socialists. By forgoing single-party regimes in the name of individualism, they tend to simultaneously deny themselves the power to close the economy to outside influences.

Leninist socialist governments do not have the same problem. Their first and most decisive act is to dominate the military and obtain a monopoly of legitimate force. "Power grows out of the barrel of a gun," said Mao, meaning that if the party did not dominate the military, the military would dominate the party. Most leninist regimes have come to power through victory in a civil war, a circumstance that ensures them enough power to manage the state.

In order to manage it the government must eliminate foreign influences in the economy, since if they do not they will be caught in the situation of the democratic socialists and radical liberals. A difficulty, at this point, is that socialists believe in the superiority of the technology of capitalism. How to benefit from capitalist technology without being controlled by the capitalists is the problem. The usual solution is to purchase the technology of production rather than the goods produced, but this strategy still requires foreign exchange. In order to obtain it something must be exported, meaning that the socialist state must become a part of an international economic system dominated by capitalism.

An extreme response to this problem is to be totally self-sufficient. This is consistent with socialist paradigms but very few socialist governments have chosen this course to date. Albania is completely self-sufficient. Perhaps because of this, information on its internal conditions is scarce. What is available indicates that Albania is moderately prosperous, technologically not as contemporary as other industrialized states, and occupied with attempts to erase the divisions it inherited from its Muslim/Christian history. It is clearly tory/socialist, its government dominated by a single person with the attributes of a tory monarch but an economy notable for an egalitarian distribution of both work and goods. There is also evidence that at least some of its citizens feel the situation is claustrophobic.

Most socialist states fall somewhere in between the Stalinist and Maoist systems. In both, all the means of production are owned by the state and goods are distributed on an egalitarian basis, but whereas Stalinist economies are run by the centralized bureaucracies, the Maoists emphasize management by the functional producing groups. Stalinist systems tend to be dominated by procedural goals and consequent inefficiencies in production, while Maoist systems are good at production but more difficult to control. As long as the Chinese economy is dominated by agriculture, and technology in that field is not highly industrialized, it is a very efficient system, especially since most of what is produced is consumed close to its point of origin.

Mao's policy on industrialization was to spread it throughout the country, keep the plants relatively small, and require that every industry also farm enough land to feed its workers. Such a system minimized problems of transportation and distribution while at the same time maximizing the ability of each functional unit to resist domination by the hierarchy.

The present post-Mao government is emphasizing the legitimacy of hierarchy and the need for stable leadership from the top, but seems to be continuing the policy of local self-sufficiency and democratic management. A future problem may be that of integrating capitalist technology, which emphasizes very large plants and extreme specialization of work, with the broader work assignments and smaller units of Maoism, since the policy now seems to be the more usual one of importing capital goods and even whole plants from capitalist economies.

Distribution, too, differs with the system. Stalinism generally sets wages and prices of goods by the criteria of social utility. Wages are all more or less equal with extra perquisites available to particularly good workers (a system obviously open to abuse) while prices are set according to the social utility of the good rather than its costs of production. That is, basic foods, housing, and the like are kept inexpensive, while luxuries are very expensive if they are available at all.

In the Maoist system, wages are allotted by the workers themselves. Each worker in a unit judges his or her own output on a scale of one to ten. This judgment is open to discussion, and the whole unit must agree on a figure. Once all these figures are settled, proportionate wages and goods are provided by the unit. The self-sufficiency of most units is clearly a major factor in this system.

Cuba has a mixture of the two systems. All basic goods are rationed but everyone receives more than enough in wages or benefits, set by the government, to purchase all the goods in the ration book. The excess can be saved or spent on beer, ice cream, or dining out, none of which are rationed. Major consumer goods, however, are allotted to work places according to the number of workers involved. For instance, if only enough refrigerators are being produced for one out of every 500 workers to get one each month, a work unit with 500 workers would get one a month, while one with 250 workers would get one every other month. Each unit would vote on which of its members could buy the refrigerator. In this way, family size, the presence of small children, and other nonwork-related needs can be balanced against work performance to arrive at a just distribution of goods. At any rate, the government does not have to make the decisions. Management in the Cuban system is also elected by the workers, the whole unit being held responsible by the government for the achievement of its production goals.

Cuba is a fairly small state, and thus escapes many of the Chinese and Soviet problems caused by great size and large populations. It seems possible, however, that this combination of Maoism and Stalinism may be attractive to these states as China seeks to increase industrialization and the Soviets seek to improve the quality of goods and their distribution. The present (1980s) reforms in both states can be seen as movement in this direction, although they are accompanied by a decentralization not seen in Cuba.

In all socialist economies shortages of goods show up as shortages of goods rather than in higher prices. While this is clearly more democratic, it causes long lines at consumer outlets, which means that a great deal of time and energy which might be going into production is instead expended in distribution.

Worker incentives are also a difficult area. Since socialist states provide basic welfare as a matter of course, this source of motivation is not open to them. On a very basic level, socialism responds by making voluntary unemployment a crime. People who refuse to work are imprisoned and used as convict labor. Problems consequently tend to show up not so much in outright refusals to work as in not working hard or with care. Tory cultures consist of small corporate groups, where family pressures, traditions, and peer pressures all combine to keep production adequate. The self-sufficiency of the Maoist work units has the same dynamic, particularly given their method of determining wages. It is in the very large, centralized and bureaucratic stalinist systems that incentive problems are most acute and hardest to deal with.

New technology can also be a problem, as it can be in tory cultures. Tradition, self-sufficiency, and worker-originated and worker-managed technologies all combine to keep tory technology fairly stable and usually labor intensive. Socialist states with large populations are already committed to providing for the welfare of all their people, so labor-intensive technology is also most reasonable for them. A problem with capitalist technology, as we have seen, is that it is most often capital-intensive, especially if it was developed in countries with high labor costs.

In any case, there seems to be no compelling reason for prosperous socialist states to develop a great deal of new technology. Countervailing forces include fear of invasion by capitalist or other foreign powers, comparative deprivation in comparison with goods available in capitalist countries (especially acute when the advertising of those countries penetrates the socialist-dominated society), and the promise of socialism to deliver material affluence at a high level to everyone.

Illegal economic activity (a black market) can be present in any leninist economy. Even with the extreme measures available to leninist governments it can be very difficult to eliminate, especially in large and centralized economies. The smaller the society and the more dispersed the authority the less a problem it is, so long as most people believe in the system. In itself a black market is more a symptom of economic difficulties than their cause, and can at times provide goods and services which the formal economy does not. In eastern Europe and China much of what was previously designated illegal economic activity is now legal, or at least permitted, but these are also the regimes that are dealing with the contradictions of leninism the most flexibly.

Summary

Communism, like the other cultures, has internal contradictions that tend to be most acute when a government of communists is responsible for society. Although the simultaneous denial of legitimacy to hierarchy and affirmation of the need for hierarchy in marxist-leninist parties is serious in the transition from other cultures, it has its greatest effects once the party has come to power.

Democratic socialists avoid the transition difficulties but often find themselves unable to fully dominate society (and their own government) because of their acceptance of radical liberal politics. Maoism and stalinism respond to the paradigm conflict by emphasizing opposite sides of the contradiction, but neither has difficulty excluding noncommunists from government and the economy.

At the same time, communist regimes have been generally successful in eliminating poverty, in raising standards of public health and education, and in eliciting the cooperation of the vast majority of the population in doing so. Revolutionary fervor carries the first few generations and thereafter socialist traditions ensure the legitimacy of the culture.

Severe strains in later generations of communist-dominated societies seem quite usual, centering in stalinist regimes around the difficulties inherent in a process-oriented centralized bureaucracy implementing the policies of a very hierarchical party, and in maoist regimes around the establishment of a fully legitimate hierarchy in a culture that emphasizes equality. In both cases the situation is exacerbated if the society is large, as it is in both the USSR and China. In China's case, the difficulties are multiplied by the continued policy of industrializing an overwhelmingly agrarian system. While it is certainly possible to envision a nonindustrialized socialist society, the marxist assumptions of the benefits of industrialization underlie almost all contemporary communist movements.

It would seem that in the long run successful communist regimes will develop strong tory attributes, while unsuccessful regimes lapse back to liberalism and oligarchy. The tory aristocracy may, of course, develop further into oligarchy, which will then generate its own reaction, but there does not seem to be any necessity in this scenario. Mao confounded orthodox marxists by moving China into socialism before it was industrialized and before it developed strong liberal sectors. Perhaps a stalinist hierarchy may move directly to oligarchy without passing through a tory stage. The dynamics of egalitarianism and cooperation are against it, though, and all socialists, even democratic socialists, are dedicated to egalitarian and cooperative economic systems. Successful communist movements may harm the affluent of oligarchy-dominated and liberal-dominated cultures, but they benefit the poor immensely.

Any transition to a tory political regime implies a transition to tory economics, a transition that would seem to provide the various functional units in society with the opportunity to form the corporate groups characteristic of tory society. If they do, the situation would seem fairly stable, given the strength of tory systems in resisting change, especially if a continued socialist emphasis on equality prevents the power elite of the party from also becoming immensely wealthy.

The contradictions of communism are no more serious than the contradictions of liberalism, but they cannot be ignored successfully by socialists any more than believers in the other cultures can successfully ignore theirs. History will not stop simply because a leninist regime comes to power, but the dynamics of society will certainly be different.

Chapter 10

Fascist Corporatism

Fascist-dominated societies have occurred consistently throughout history, usually as a reaction to liberalism or socialism, but sometimes in response to particularly obvious oligarchies. In our age fascism has been associated mainly with a reaction against communism, although the use of "marxism-leninism" as the evil that justifies anything the fascist regime does is no different from the earlier cry of "heresy" that served the inquisition so well. Put very briefly, fascism is a centralized, autocratic, and nationalist regime under a dictator who institutes nationalistic policies while simultaneously suppressing all resistance to the regime. This suppression usually involves both socialism and liberalism and is done in the name of tory values.

The stated objective of the fascist dictator, in fact, is the restoration of a tory system. The assumption is that tory values are threatened and that a good part of society is not tory. In particular, the great tory value of hierarchy is said to be threatened, and with it the welfare of the entire nation.

In most cases this assessment of the situation is very accurate. What differentiates the fascist from the tory is the fascist's acceptance of a highly centralized, autocratic dictatorship ruling through coercion to gain and exercise power within the society. Such a government contradicts the tory paradigms of the corporate group as a self-governing unit and of the monarch as simply a coordinator and arbitrator among the many corporate groups that make up society. These paradigms have always been bent, if not totally contradicted, in times of great crisis, particularly in time of war. It should come as no surprise to learn that fascist dictators are securing internal support through appeals to nationalism.

Hegel, a nineteenth-century German philosopher from whom Marx received many of the concepts which he would later incorporate in his own analysis of history, argued that war was healthy for the state, since it encouraged collectivism at the same time it justified coercion of opposed groups.[1] For many fascists war is an almost holy occupation in and of itself because of the tory values it promotes within the military and the general population, regardless of the purpose or cause of the war.

Hitler, in his persecution of the Jews, essentially created an internal enemy to justify a war mentality when he could not yet afford to declare war on an external enemy. By declaring the Jews "non-German," even though many of the Jewish families involved had lived in Germany for hundreds of years, Hitler justified the coercive behavior of the secret police (the Gestapo) at the same time he denounced external enemies to justify the rebuilding of the German military.

It is not surprising that "communists" were the other great enemy of the regime (and of "the German people," naturally) and that Jews were assumed to be communists.[2] It is also not surprising that Hitler called his movement the National Socialist (Nazi) movement. By doing so he was able to take advantage of the strong socialism in Germany in the 1920s, which unfortunately for the socialists was split between democratic socialists and leninist socialists. Given the similarity of many tory and socialist paradigms this tactic was fairly successful, particularly when the Nazis definitely increased economic security.

In Italy, Mussolini declared war on Ethiopia to regain the Roman Empire. As a unifying ploy for Italy it was less disruptive to the nation than the persecution of the Jews in Germany, although its effects on Ethiopia were dreadful. Communism in Italy was also an enemy of the regime, of course, but neither the situation nor the methods of coercion were as extreme as in Germany.[3]

It is important to note that fascists come to power almost exclusively in times of great economic crisis. They justify themselves both by their plans to overcome the crisis and their ability to blame that crisis upon "the communists" or some other group. Fascism, like communism, is not a culture suited for peaceful, prosperous times. The secret police and armed repression of dissident groups, which both use extensively, are dangerous even to subordinate members of the dominant culture as well as to those of other cultures. In order to justify these threats to security the regimes must be able to appeal to the even greater threat of what would happen if the repressive measures were not taken.

In good times few people will accept the fascists as legitimate. Economic crises, which threaten the security of large numbers of people, set the stage for fascism and communism, both of which provide specific targets for the anger and fear of the insecure. Fascists have communists and communists have capitalists, and both offer economic security and prosperity. Where the communists depend upon ideology to explain both the situation and the solution, however, the fascists depend upon tradition.

Theoretical Source of Legitimacy

The fascist appeal to tradition as the source of their legitimacy is more than usually theoretical. Tories, because of their acceptance of tradition as defining legitimacy, will generally support whatever system they are in as long as the paradigm contradictions can be ignored. Fascists want to change society, at least at first, and therefore cannot simply accept "the way things are" as legitimate. By picking and choosing where history supports them and simply creating "history" where it doesn't, fascists can represent themselves and their policies as the true traditions of the people.

The history of any nation is diverse enough to permit this sort of thing, and the creation of a history to support the present regime is hardly limited to fascists. What differentiates them from the other cultures is that they use "history" to change the nation itself. Paradigm contradictions are avoided by choosing a past age sufficiently obscured by heroic myth and wishful thinking to allow creativity on the part of fascist historians. If the economic and political crises of the nation are sufficiently severe this evocation of past greatness, harmony, and prosperity may be very compelling.

It would be a mistake to believe that fascists are cynical about their source of legitimacy. No matter how necessary it is to create the past in order to emulate it, fascists believe in the historic basis of their policies and of their regime. To hide from the present in a self-created past may be the historian's temptation, but fascists are busy creating the present in the image of their more-or-less self-created past. The theoretical problem is that in changing society they must rely upon rationality, just as do the other revolutionary cultures.

Even so, fascist "traditions" are consistent with tory culture to such an extent that it may be understood as that variant of toryism which occurs when a nonmonarch attempts to enforce toryism upon a society not dominated by tories. The natural results of the decision to force people to be tories are a centralized government, secret police, the suppression of any dissent, enforced economic coordination, and a constant appeal for solidarity in the face of internal and external enemies. All seem quite normal once the decision has been made to coerce everyone into being tories.

Those cultures that do not accept tradition as theoretically legitimate find this aspect of fascism objectionable, but since much of what the fascists do is actually based on rationality the objectors often find themselves supporting the policies of the fascists while rejecting the stated reasons for them. This confusion in their opponents benefits the fascists. It is most pronounced in the liberals and to a lesser extent in the democratic socialists. The communists are opposed to the fascists on so many other paradigms that a little confusion on this one makes no difference. Even so, if very weak the leninists may surreptitiously collaborate with the fascist dictator in return for their continued existence and control of some sector of society, usually labor unions.

Oligarchs, because of their belief in both tradition and rationality, are in the best position to coexist with the fascists in their ideas of legitimacy. They have had a great deal of experience in masking their dedication either to tradition or to rationality, depending on the situation, and this experience helps them maintain both their existence and their power under the new regime.

Organization of the Culture

Fascists believe in hierarchy, but their hierarchy tends to create paradigm conflicts with tories when carried to the extremes in which fascists believe. "The Leader" becomes almost a god to fascists, and the absolute authority they grant him or her is in contradiction with the tory belief in the separate hierarchies of the differing corporate groups in society. The charismatic qualities of both the leader and the followers tends to work against the weaker corporate groups in society. The authority of the leader is a potential threat to everyone in society, not least to those members of tory corporate groups who emphasize their traditional rights to independent self-government. Fascism is very much a mixed blessing to tories, although many of its negative aspects may be overlooked if the crisis is serious enough.

Oligarchs tend to support fascists in their reaction against socialism, and particularly do so when communists have become major forces. The triumph of any communists means the destruction of the existing oligarchy. It is cold comfort to them that the communists may later develop their own oligarchs: they stand very little chance of being among them. Far better to support the fascist dictator. With a minimum of astuteness the oligarchs have an excellent chance of being accepted as tories in the chaotic situation that fascism both creates and changes, and by the time the new regime is settled in power it is quite possible that many of the personnel in government could be subverted to the oligarchy. Generally the oligarchs must lessen their drive for wealth and also curtail their creation and use of liberals, but both are better than defeat by the communists.

Given time, fascists regimes often become little more than facades for an oligarchy, for the nationalist policies necessary to create prosperity for the people are of course opposed by the transnationals, which continue to dominate the international economy. Since fascism's great reason for existence is the welfare of the nation as a whole, however, the dynamic here is much the same as that for democratic socialists: welfare measures are continued while extension of the system abroad and the intrusion of transnationals at home work against full employment and control of the economy by the fascist government. This is a long-term problem not immediately visible to supporters of the regime and often not to the regime itself for some time. A possible solution, of course, is imperialism, which already established transnationals and their governments find very threatening.

For third-world countries often dependent upon the export of a single raw material for their place in the industrialized world, being cut off from the international economic system amounts to being cut off from industrialization and the products of the industrialized world. Without these products fascist plans for world domination are meaningless, and even regional dominance is usually impossible. Moreover, fascists usually need the support of the oligarchs to give them the economic means to dominate their own country, and the oligarchs are naturally opposed to breaking the ties to the transnationals that make them rich. The high status of many oligarchs and the wealth of the transnationals also tend to make them acceptable to fascists, who usually see poverty-stricken communists as their primary enemies and the wealthy as their allies.

The fascist focus on hierarchy is more than acceptable to the tories and to liberals who are threatened by the forcible introduction of socialist equality by the leninists. Classical liberals have always been uneasy about an elected government because it contradicts their paradigms of a single hierarchy of merit. They may support the fascist dictator both because of his merit (power and the consequent control of wealth) and because of the efficiency of the regime in getting things done. Such support is particularly likely if the dictator presents the movement as nonpolitical, reserving "political" and "politician" for the processes and personnel of the discredited electoral system that has been unable to handle the ongoing crisis.

A problem for fascists, however, is that traditional tory hierarchies have no place for them. Tory monarchs are not dictators (fascist leaders are), already have legitimacy (fascists have not), and do not rule through coercion and a secret police (fascists do). Fascists may justify themselves through appeals to the need for decisive action in a time of crisis, but their claims and the ways they rule and maintain their power are still in question.

Usually fascists create new "feudal" institutions such as Hitler's SS or Mussolini's Black Shirts, which institute more-or-less instant traditions for their members. These institutions are presented to their members and to the people as recreations of institutions from the glorious past, with the added attraction that they allow upward mobility for those who join them. In this respect they are analogous to the medieval church in Europe, and for their members they often become the institutions of the new religion.

Birth is still the basis for inclusion in the oligarchy but the fascist system generally defines citizenship as the only ascriptive attribute necessary for inclusion in the fascist state. Enthusiastic acceptance of the dictator and the new institutions are enough after that. In this the fascists are more like the liberals and socialists than they are like the old tories, whose small corporate groups were determined by birth.

Merit, as measured by the fascists, tends to determine a person's place in the hierarchy at first, and continues to do so at least until the first generation of fascists can be succeeded by their children. This emphasis on "merit" tends to reassure the liberals, although it does little to attract the tories or the oligarchs.

Democratic socialists oppose fascists, not least because of the pervasive focus on hierarchy and the destruction of the only kind of hierarchy they allow legitimacy, that of the elected political system. Communists are even more opposed, perhaps because they have essentially the same political system as the fascists but know it is ultimately illegitimate. People hate nothing so much in others as what they hate in themselves. This aspect of fascism alone would ensure it the undying enmity of the communists.

Basic Unit of the Culture

The corporate group is the basic unit of society for the fascists as it is for the tories. While individual mobility is possible through joining the new corporate groups of the fascist state, once within these groups the joiners find that corporate responsibilities and privileges are emphasized. Liberals are able to rise to positions of power in this system, but they must be very careful to conceal their individualism.

Oligarchs, believing in collectivism for themselves, must be careful to hide their belief that other groups should be broken up and exploited. An exception to this rule may be made in the case of groups outside the nation, but the tendencies of fascists and oligarchs diverge. Oligarchs, as we have seen, individualize and exploit workers, whether their fellow-countrymen or foreigners. Fascists see people as members of their corporate groups, and extend this principle to foreigners.

Imperialism, which is very normal for fascists, generally entails the inclusion of other nationalities on terms dictated by the fascists. The long-term tendency is to treat everyone in the empire as a legitimate member of society, if subordinate, and therefore to strengthen their corporate groups. Communist and fascist regimes have occasionally used imprisoned "capitalists" or "communists" for slave labor, but this is usually a short-term phenomenon.

Liberals of both sorts have trouble working with fascism because of this emphasis on corporatism, as do both sorts of socialists. All four of these cultures believe in individualism. While compromises may occur, as we have seen, and even long-term adjustments may be made to the continuing presence of other cultures, individualistic cultures and fascists do not get on very well.

The fascist emphasis on corporatism and the prevalence of tory and fascist cultures in third-world societies has recently resulted in their being identified as "corporatist" by American political scholars. This is far better than the earlier denomination of "backward" to describe these societies, and has even resulted in the recognition that some elements of Europe are corporatist, but it confuses the tory and fascist cultures. Indeed, at times even oligarchs are described as corporatist. While there is a sound reason for this terminology, it heightens the confusion of cultures.

The corporatism of the fascists may seem a great deal like that of the tories. It certainly seems so to the fascists, but there are important differences. The greatest is that while fascists recognize corporate groups their political system is centralized in the dictator and the new institutions of the state. This centralization means that the corporate groups are not self-governing, or at least that they have no right to self-government. While many of the smaller groups may in fact be allowed to continue to govern themselves, state intervention and control are constant possibilities. Tory corporate groups have traditional safeguards against this; fascist groups have none.

In contemporary times the constant hunt for "communists" also tends to violate the integrity of corporate groups, for the term often means no more than opposition to the dictatorship. Since all the other cultures have paradigms that contradict those of the fascists, they are all vulnerable to this charge. While this can easily make the use of "anticommunism" as a justification for tyranny ludicrous, it hardly makes it less serious.

Actually, the fascists are quite self-contradictory here. Their paradigm of a hierarchy of (fascist) merit implies individuality, while their paradigm of corporatism implies loyalty to the corporate group. While some of these contradictions can be overcome by defining fascism as the corporate group, the result is essentially the same contradiction the communists face: when there are no units between the individual and the state, a single hierarchy of power is necessary to govern. While communists create functional groups in order to get things done, and thereby reintroduce corporatism to society, the fascists create a single hierarchy in order to govern, and thereby weaken their corporate groups.

Oligarchs tend to benefit from this situation more than the others because they can appear to be tories while treating others as individuals. Although their motives are different from those of the fascists, their appearance may be much the same. Moreover, as we have seen, wealthy oligarchs have the power and legitimacy the fascists need, and are therefore in a good position to bargain with them. Hitler allowed the great corporate business families of Germany to run the economy, while the present day fascist leaders of the third world do much the same. The difference is that the oligarchies of the third world are usually subordinate to the transnationals, while the German oligarchies often were the transnationals.

Another area in which fascism differs from toryism is that fascist dictators always have a direct relation with the masses, usually charismatic. Even when it is not, the dictator attempts to make it so through propaganda, mass public meetings, packing audiences with fascist youth organizations, or any other device that will strengthen the dictator's claim of speaking for the masses. Since a tory monarch is accessible to individuals through the right of petition but acts through the leaders of corporate groups, the fascist dictator's more direct relations with the masses tend to weaken the corporatism that fascism tries to create.

Concept of the Culture

Fascists think of themselves as collectivists, fighting to bring back the vertical integration and cooperation for the good of the whole of the tories. Their individualized recruitment, the use of rationality to achieve their goals, and their readiness to take over or exterminate any group they see as opponents works against the collectivism of the tories, however, and may result in tory opposition. In this case the fascists may become even less collectivist than before, in that the alternative to reliance on the disaffected groups is more oppression and more reliance on nontory groups.

Even so, it would be a mistake to think of fascists as anything but collectivists. Their weakness is not in their concept of society as much as in their tendency to declare opposition groups and individuals outside that society, and therefore subject to different rules. The exploitation of political prisoners and the extermination of "outsiders" is hardly collectivist but in the long run the fascists conceive of society as collectivist for everyone in it. As Keynes once observed, however, in the long run we are all dead. Any virtues of fascism may come far too late to make a difference to those who oppose it or are necessary as enemies to the regime.

Oligarchs again tend to benefit from the situation, for their internal paradigms are collectivist, and they have no difficulty in presenting themselves as collectivists to the fascists. Liberals are at the greatest disadvantage, but any positive effect for the collectivist socialists is usually lost in their opposition on other paradigms. The milder the fascist regime, of course, the more likely that the collectivism of the fascists and the socialists will result in some sort of collaboration. This tends to vary with the strength of the oligarchs and their ties with the fascists, since the oligarchs are most opposed to the socialists. On the other hand, the stronger the socialists, the more they will oppose the fascist regime.

Transnationals will tend to support the oligarchs against the socialists, and will generally influence their home governments to do the same. The effect is to make it more difficult for a fascist regime to make collectivism central to the coalitions that support it.

Government

The dictatorship of the leader, charismatic or not, is the characteristic government paradigm of fascists. If charismatic, the most obvious supporters for the dictatorship are the charismatic followers, but behind them is the support of the military. No claim to dictatorial power can be maintained if the military does not support it. Economic support usually comes from tories and oligarchs, although if the situation is so bad that dictatorial government (whether fascist or communist) is acceptable to many people, the oligarchs are probably much stronger than the tories.

Dictatorship is rule by a single person, but any centralized government of a large society needs an extensive bureaucracy to be effective. While a dictator may be effective for a time by appealing directly to the people when his or her support is pervasive and strong, some institutions of government must be created if the dictator is to govern on a day-to-day basis. Insofar as the fascists must control a society they are determined to change, they must create and use strong governmental institutions to do so, institutions that will inevitably be bureaucratic. If they can depend upon already existing corporate groups to work with the state and help the dictator achieve his or her aims, these groups will be expected to govern themselves. If they cannot, the fascists will replace the leadership of these groups with their own people when they do not simply destroy them. In this case leadership must come directly from the dictator, and a bureaucratic organization will result.

In one sense what this means is that a dictatorship will be less intrusive in society in direct proportion to how many corporate groups accept the regime's authority. On the other hand, if matters are so bad that dictatorial rule is acceptable to a majority it is probable that most of the corporate groups in society have already been greatly weakened or destroyed, particularly if the crisis is an internal one brought about by the dynamics of the nation itself.

If the crisis is largely external, like the world depression of the 1930s, a fascist dictatorship may be greatly softened. The "benevolent dictatorship" of Getulio Vargas during the 1930s and 1940s in Brazil was of this type. Third-world nations are by definition far more vulnerable to external factors than are the already industrialized nations, and therefore more likely to develop this kind of fascism.

On the other hand, when the oligarchy is successful in characterizing all opposition to itself as communism, it is often able to collaborate with fascists in such a way that the main immediate goal of the dictatorship is the extermination of the communists, which in this case amounts to the extermination of the opponents of oligarchy. Since the oligarchy is usually collaborating with the transnationals as well as with the dictator, the collaboration gives us the familiar cold-war crusade against godless communism so often waged in Latin America to the benefit of the oligarchy and the transnationals.

This situation is not without its dangers for the oligarchs, for if the dictator is a convinced fascist he or she will be acting in the interests of "the people." If a great many of the people are opposed to the oligarchy the dictator may turn upon the oligarchs in an attempt to better the lives of the masses.

There is no reason why such a move will be sudden or total. It is more likely that it will begin with welfare programs, national industries, and concerns for labor-intensive methods of production. While these are not necessarily against the immediate interests of either the oligarchs or the transnationals, they can become very troublesome. In the first place, they cost money, and great masses of very poor people are not a place to find it: they represent cheap labor, but not taxes. The obvious source of financing for these programs is the wealthy sector of society, which is the oligarchs and the transnationals.

Moreover, increased welfare for the masses tends to increase labor costs, since people are no longer forced to work for subsistence wages. Minimum-wage laws also have the same effect, although monetary schemes such as these can be countered by private banks and other financial institutions generating inflation with the expectation of being able to use it in their own interests.

Such manipulation of the economy, along with the economic power the transnationals have, is directly opposed to the fascist government's attempts to manage the economy for the benefit of all. This dynamic drives them to attempt to control the transnationals and to lessen the range of the oligarchs' power.

In the short run, the fascists have the power to do this, since they control (or are) the military. In the long run, they can maintain this control only if they can produce their own weapons or are supplied by some external source. The most obvious source of weapons is the transnationals themselves, but any frontal attack on transnationals as transnationals is unlikely to get their support. For a time a fascist regime opposed to transnationals in principle may be able to simply buy weapons, but such a course is likely to greatly reduce the international income of the state, and therefore the foreign exchange needed to buy weapons.

Foreign governments are also sources of weapons, but it is unlikely that capitalist governments will either desire or be able to supply them. After all, the government that wants the weapons is using them to deprive the capitalist transnationals of both cheap labor and markets. Insofar as the regime is anticommunist, the communist governments of the world are also unlikely to help.

This leaves the minor nations of the industrialized world. These are usually quite willing to help but can hardly be expected to do so for any length of time, since in order to continue to trade through the capitalist system they too need money. It is possible, of course, to trade without money, bartering so much wheat, for instance, for so many tanks. Barter is not a bad idea, but probably not good enough to overcome the pressures put upon both nations by the transnationals, to say nothing of their internal oligarchies.

It is theoretically possible for a fascist regime to be self-sufficient. For those countries that possess the resources, the knowledge, and the factories to produce their own goods, self-sufficiency is also actually possible. But two factors work against it. First, the changes in life-style and expectations this policy entails will be very difficult for the rich and the middle class, no matter what their culture. Second, the tendencies toward imperialism and war associated with fascism make it very likely that great military resources will be necessary long before the nation can produce them. Even if it can, an international war simply invites the participation of the capitalist states, either directly or indirectly, and the weapons they can supply to the opponents of the regime are very likely to be more plentiful and more technically advanced than those the nation can produce.

An interesting result of this situation is an often successful technique available to the governments of the transnationals' home countries. By offering military aid to anticommunist fascists they may be able to become the major source of weapons, training, and finances for the military. Since the responsibilities of governing society are far more extensive than simply governing the military, the fascist regime may find itself in the position of using the military in such a way that large sections of the population blame the military for the policies. Since military forces are usually uniformed, armed, and very visible when used to oppress dissidents, this blame is a natural reaction. If military leaders do not need the government for support they may well desert it when public opposition becomes severe.

Another pressure can be brought to bear by the transnationals. A response used by both military governments and fascist regimes that are not the military itself is to rely more and more upon a secret police rather than the more traditional military. There are many problems with this course, most of which involve a loss of control of the secret police by the government. When an institution is given great powers and (because of the secrecy involved) is largely unaccountable for the way they are used, it is difficult to keep a clandestine oligarchy from emerging. (The American CIA can be seen as just such a police on the international level.)

Over time, the tendency is for the secret police to use their powers for self-enrichment as much as or more than for political purity. (General Secord, for example, profited from the Iranian arms deal, which was illegal under American law and policy.) Graft, insurance rackets, and the like, basically amount to taking money for not enforcing the law, or to simply using the law to extort money from those who have it. The result is that the oligarchs as a culture are strengthened, the fascist regime loses legitimacy, and the military, insofar as it is the government or is connected with it, shares in this loss of legitimacy.

The resulting situation may well be dangerous for the transnationals as well as for the regime, since the chances of a civil war and the possibility of a communist success are increased. Usually, however, the leninists are decimated, the democratic socialists blocked, and more and more power taken by the oligarchs.

A further factor is the tendency of any ongoing government to move away from identifying with any single institution in society. The reason is that governing the whole society gives the governors a view of the whole society. No matter what the culture of the government, this view will be different from that of any single institution. The difference, especially when the military is not dependent upon the government for supplies, may well detach the military from the regime.

Economics

Fascists believe in a managed economy and a welfare state. Despite their political centralization, they would like to use the older tory system of management by the constituent corporate groups of the society. Where possible, they do so, but where obviously opposed groups or individuals control economic factors the fascists will impose control from the center. The objective is a prosperous economic situation for everybody, with proper differences for the hierarchical system basic to fascist culture.

Extensive social-welfare systems are quite consistent with fascist thinking, and where fascists are changing from a socialist dominated society or even seriously competing with socialists for support, such welfare programs are very common. At the same time, if the socialists have not been able to institute such programs it is the fascist tendency to begin in the urban centers and gradually extend the programs into the country. Socialists are more thorough, instituting their programs throughout society as soon as they have the power to do so.

The difference is more a consequence of different allies than any difference between fascist and socialist cultures. Leninist socialists, not needing to consider the desires of the oligarchs or liberals, have no difficulty here. Democratic socialists can generally count on the support of the radical liberals and the tories for welfare programs. When this coalition is strong the attention of the oligarchs and classical liberals is on control of the means of production rather than on welfare policies, so the democratic socialists can usually institute them without too much trouble.

Fascists, however, often find themselves with oligarchs and tories as their only major allies in economic policy. They lose the liberals because of their emphasis upon managing the economy and they lose the socialists because of their political system. Both oligarchs and tories will support the fascists in their efforts to manage the economy through corporate groups, although for different reasons. The tories will manage their own groups with as much self-sufficiency as possible, relying on the dictator to fulfill the coordinating and arbitrating roles of the monarch. (If the traditional monarch is opposed to the dictator, most of the tory groups will oppose him or her also.)

The oligarchs will support the fascists in their economic policy because they can maintain themselves as corporate groups and perhaps even prosper if enough of the population can be declared opposed to the fascists, and therefore fair targets for exploitation. Convict labor, for instance, fits quite nicely into the oligarchic economic paradigms at the same time it is produced by the fascist oppression of dissident individuals. The urban poor are politically active but not connected with either powerful tories or oligarchs. The rural poor are usually passive and dominated by one or the other. It is for this reason that the fascists begin with the cities.

If the fascists are successful in expanding abroad the oligarchs have obvious opportunities for exploiting the labor and markets taken over. Even if they do not, the oligarchs' ties with the transnationals are useful to them. Generally, third-world fascists find themselves assuring the transnationals of cheap labor, low taxation, easy movement of wealth and money out of the country, and the provision of free services such as sewers, water, and power. All of these provisions work against the welfare goals of the fascists and move the management of the economy from nationalist goals to those of the transnationals.

The fascists hope to retain control of the economy but often find themselves unable to do so. This frustration creates an ongoing crisis that fascists often seek to solve by emphasizing the nationalist policies that appeal to the tories and the anticapitalist views of the socialists and to the antimonopoly paradigms of the radical liberals. The oligarchs and the transnationals are protected somewhat because if the fascists go too far they lose the support of the transnationals without being sure of the support of the socialists or radical liberals. Also, the military situation can easily deteriorate if the country is forced to produce its own military goods.

An obvious solution for the fascists is to go the whole route and produce their own military goods as well as consumer goods. They generally produce the armaments first, however, and thereby tend to lose the support of the radical liberals and democratic socialists, neither of which see any great necessity for a militarized state. The communists see it, of course, but they are unalterably opposed to the fascists because of the fascist insistence on hierarchy and the continued fascist toleration of the oligarchs. Neither care a thing for the classical liberals, who at this point have very little power.

The oligarchs have a further protection in their family ties with the tories and their traditional places as ruling families. The fascist emphasis upon tradition extends to the old families, and many of the fascist supporters come from these families. The oligarchs, of course, have already sent members of the family to join the fascists, and so have influence within the movement.

At best the fascists achieve their nationalist goals and become a fairly self-sufficient and self-managing society. At worst the fascists degenerate into the military and police arm of the oligarchs and transnationals. In this case their economic goals are not attained and their long-term viability as rulers is questionable.

Summary

Fascism is a culture that dominates societies only in response to serious crises. Extreme problems call for extreme solutions, say the fascists, but their solutions call for what amounts to a civil war, usually carried out by the secret police. In looking for and expecting the support of the rich and powerful the fascists clearly run the risk of having their revolution subverted from within. While their goals are tory their methods are leninist. The oligarchs who usually support them are allied with the transnationals and skilled at subverting the tories, the fascists' other major allies. Their chances for taking over the government tend to be as good as the crisis is serious, but the likelihood that they will achieve their tory goals is much smaller.

Throughout the third world fascism is common, but the fascist policies of national control of national resources and prosperity for all within their corporate group are rarely successful. At the same time, the combination of fascists, oligarchs, and tories seems to be an attractive one, for it is not surprising to see a new fascist regime arise from the ruins of the preceding one. Even where fascism alternates with radical liberal governments with an occasional democratic socialist attempt, fascism seems to be the culture that dominates third-world societies most.

Oligarchy and transnationals are usually visible behind the fascist government, which is perhaps why they are so common. In the first world of industrialized capitalist nations fascism is not now the dominant regime in any of the countries, but there has not as yet been a crisis as serious as that which preceded World War II.

It is not difficult to find fascists in any of the first-world countries, although very few call themselves fascists. It is very likely that if a serious crisis were to develop fascism would again be dominant in the governments of many of the industrialized capitalist countries.

Communist nations are not likely to be dominated by fascists through a collapse of the leninist regime. If the government slides into toryism, however, fascism may begin to look like an attractive ally to those tories who reject the socialist aspects of the society. This development does not appear likely in the near future, but as the generations pass it will become more and more a viable option for the unsatisfied.

The internal contradictions of fascism are obvious. The single hierarchy of dictatorship contradicts the self-government of the tory groups the fascists are trying to create or maintain, the fascist system of merit contradicts the tory importance of birth, and the rational re-creation of history contradicts the tradition of the tories. The softer the fascist dictatorship the less these contradictions affect the policies of the regime, since the major area in which they all appear is that of enforcement.

Whether a fascist dictatorship is soft or hard depends upon two factors: internal opposition and external influences. Generally speaking, a soft dictatorship is most likely when the crisis is external and direct influence by foreigners is weak. Such a situation occurred in the third world during the great depression of the 1930s. The depression was exported from the industrialized capitalist countries but it weakened them to such an extent that their power to influence third-world countries was also less.

This combination alone would probably not have been sufficient to bring in third-world fascist groups, but the growing strength of fascism in Germany distracted the other major powers. In this situation it was possible for fascist leaders in third-world countries to lead what amounted to majority coalitions with little interference from the governments of the transnationals.

After World War II, the cold war justified intervention by capitalists into any country in which socialists of any description were strong. This greatly strengthened the position of the fascists in the short run but also made it much more difficult for them to achieve their long-range goals. The cold war in this context is a device aimed primarily at maintaining the domination of the third world by capitalist transnationals, with any protection for the "free" world from the USSR a secondary consideration.

The internal contradictions of fascism are serious, but its contradictions with other cultures are probably the decisive factors in most situations. The most difficult for the fascists is the contradiction between fascism and oligarchy, because the oligarchs are usually their major allies. Tories are also likely to be allies but they are usually much weaker than the oligarchs by the time fascists arise as a dominant force, and are therefore easier to ignore or manipulate. Oligarchs, especially when they are allied with foreign transnationals (usually oligarchical or classical liberal themselves), are very likely to succeed in their strategy of using the fascists to protect them from socialists while preventing the fascists from implementing any economic policies that would seriously injure the oligarchs.

The overt enemies of fascism are the liberals and socialists. Of the two, the opposition of the socialists is far more serious. Classical liberals have difficulties in organizing themselves into strong opposition groups when the oligarchs throw their support to the fascists, and, if the oligarchs are successful in blocking the economic policies of the fascists, have little reason to continue a hard opposition.

Radical liberals are opposed to both the political and economic policies of the fascists (the classical liberals tend to admire the single dictatorship of "merit") but are relatively powerless without an electoral system through which to voice their complaints. Moreover, radical liberals tend to benefit from the oligarch/transnational coalition as long as they are not numerous. The business structure characteristic of transnational penetration always has a few positions for the middle class. If the radical liberals are numerous they find themselves cut out from possibilities of expansion. In this situation they may well ally themselves with the democratic socialists.

Democratic socialists are very frustrated, but their commitments to nonviolence and to electoral methods of gaining power make them weak. The result is often a strengthening of the communists, who maintain there is no peaceful road to socialism. The communists have expected the fascist/oligarchy/transnational coalition, and are prepared to violently oppose it. Without the support of many noncommunists, however, they are unlikely to succeed. Unfortunately for them, their violent methods tend to blur the distinctions between them and the fascists for members of the other cultures. They claim, of course, that if they win their policies will be vastly different and more effective. Both fascists and communists promise prosperity for all, but communists promise equality also. Since of all the others only the democratic socialists believe in economic equality, this promise does not get the communists a great deal of support. Moreover, this is a future policy, and few believe it will be implemented. The situation has to be very bad before a great many people will support the communists, even if they are the best prepared to fight the fascists.

Fascism, then, is fairly attractive to many in a time of crisis, but difficult to implement beyond the process goal of oppressing the opposition. It is fairly easy for oligarchs and transnationals to manipulate the fascists, preventing them from solving the crises that the transnationals have created or used. If the cycle of a new fascist regime followed by continued economic disaster occurs often enough, the position of the communists as the only possible alternative is strengthened. Usually, however, the fall of a fascist government sees the return of the military to their barracks and their supervision of a transition to a radical liberal government. This government also proves unable to cope with the crisis but most often its failure only results in a return to fascism.

Fascism itself is unstable, since it relies on violent coercion to maintain the regime. If it succeeds in doing so there is the possibility a tory culture will dominate, but a return to oligarchy is much more likely. Peaceful resistance to fascism is unlikely to get far in the absence of any restraints on oligarchs and transnationals. Theoretically, if the transnationals were externally restrained the oligarchs would be greatly weakened, and a tory/radical liberal/democratic socialist coalition could emerge as a major force. This is unlikely to occur, however, as is the voluntary disengagement of the first-world governments that support the transnationals.

Fascism offers a combination of prosperity and hierarchy that is attractive to many in the other cultures, but its internal and external contradictions usually prevent it from fulfilling its promise and the bellicosity of fascism tends to create disastrous foreign wars and internal purges. Even so, fascism as a culture continues to be strong and influential throughout the world.

Chapter 11

Understanding Cultural Differences
and Political Change

That the truth will make us free is itself true, if by that we mean that knowing the truth means knowing the difference between what is real and what is unreal. To live a life based upon illusion and fantasy is surely to be the slave of erroneous perceptions: to make wrong decisions and suffer unexpected consequences. On the other hand, truth is paradigmatic, and any truth tends to imprison us in the paradigm that produces it. In this sense the truth cannot set us free from the truth itself. People cannot live in a vacuum, and the very reality of our world constitutes a prison which we can escape only through fantasy or death.

A prismatic analysis of the problem draws the distinction between "reality," which we can never consciously understand directly, and "truth," which is our intellectual perception of reality. We can conceive of a world external to ourselves with which we are connected by our nervous systems, systems that cannot be physically disconnected or shut off except by death. In order to understand the constant incoming information we use paradigms to screen out the irrelevant and to arrange and make sense of the relevant. "Truth," as we generally use the word, is reality itself, but the general usage is confusing as soon as we think about how we know the truth. This confusion explains why most people feel that "How do you know what is true?" is a stupid question. To answer it is to invite confusion and to call the truth into question, something we all find highly disturbing.

"Reality" is and has to be the basis of our lives and our understanding of ourselves. To be constantly aware that we cannot understand reality directly and that our world may not be what we know it is would prevent us from living meaningful lives, even if by that we just mean getting through the day in a fairly consistent fashion. For Americans, who are generally not faced with crucial choices on a day-to-day basis, the need to know the truth is necessary enough. An accurate assessment of reality is a constant matter of life or death to those in the middle of civil wars, tyranny, starvation or disease. The connections between reality and truth that we have discussed may often seem theoretical, but to many people they are terrifyingly actual.

To conceive of truth as paradigmatic and the world and our lives in it as prismatic heightens the importance of knowing the truth rather than lessens it. To know that while we cannot choose what our paradigms are but that we can choose which of our paradigms we will live by makes a knowledge of those paradigms crucial.

To know that others must also make choices, even if unconsciously, based upon paradigms different from our own, is to give us insight into the actions of others that is valuable. Truth in this sense is dependent upon the person who believes it, but it does not follow that all truth is relative and that no values are meaningful except for the single person who has them. Shared paradigms are the basis for human interaction, and without human interaction there would be no next generation.

Cultures

Stable shared paradigms constitute the elements of a culture. The number of people sharing the culture can be as small as a family or as large as most of a nation, but in both cases the existence of the culture means that values are not arbitrary. To simply "choose" our values would set us against our own culture, making communication difficult, actions indecipherable, and alienation natural.

Another and more compelling argument against the idea that we choose our paradigms is simple experience. Young people are often convinced that they can freely choose the values by which they will live (a paradigm in itself, apparently) but older people tend to doubt it. Painful experience has taught them that to change even the simplest and least important paradigm is so difficult that success is rare, while to change the central paradigms of our lives is almost impossible. Broken marriages, self-destructive behavior, and all the other consequences of negative or inappropriate paradigms are testimony not to ignorance or weakness but to the strength of the paradigms that created the situations.

Experiences of this sort can lead to a healthy humility, but they most often result in willful ignorance as we protect ourselves from the pain and disorientation of a loss of faith in our paradigms, which amounts to a loss of faith in ourselves. Humility allows us to retain our paradigms at the same time we recognize them for what they are. In this way self-knowledge may indeed set us free. Ignorance simply ensures that we will continue to have the same responses in the same situations, and most probably to recreate the situations we so heartily hope to avoid.

The key to understanding human dynamics is the concept of shifting roles rather than that of altering paradigms. Paradigms form the basis of roles, and while we may not be able to alter our paradigms we can choose to function with other roles. To understand that roles can be inappropriate or simply destructive, and that we have the ability to change from the role we are living to a different role, is to understand how to structure situations in a positive way, or at least to have a better chance of sorting out the situation and achieving an outcome we want.

The basis of relationships with others is culture. Unless we share paradigms with another person, misunderstanding and confusion are the only possible outcomes. Culture allows us to function as social animals, to achieve things together and to continue being human. Especially in times of crisis the mutual understanding of reality that culture creates is essential to the continuation of the species. At the same time, cultures can separate us. There is no reason to assume that only one culture is functional for continued existence on this earth, any more than we believe that only one personality is possible for all human beings.

Both people and cultures are prismatic. Contradictory and contrary paradigms are the norm within both individuals and groups. This situation is both a blessing and a curse. Self-contradiction and the confusion it produces are perhaps most easily seen as negative, but they also enable people to switch to roles that are more positive within a particular situation. If all our paradigms were consistent and logical there would be no alternative to argument, noncooperation, leaving, or fighting when we find ourselves at odds with others. If we are able to switch to positive paradigms that we both share there is an alternative to conflict which may resolve the difficulty, whether or not we share the roles of which the paradigms are a part.

This option is not necessarily an easy out. Just as we cannot choose what paradigms we have, we cannot always choose to ignore one of them in favor of another. Some paradigms are so important to us that we must live by them regardless of the opposition of others or the cost to ourselves. Prismatic analysis cannot remove paradigm conflict in ourselves, our culture, or our society, but it can make the choices clear, and we can to some extent foresee the consequences of our actions.

Willful ignorance is a problem as well as a solution. When one solves a paradigm conflict by ignoring troublesome information, the consequences may be good. Continued self-esteem, a positive outlook on life, and the

continuation of relationships may all depend upon not brooding on negative information, something which many people can accomplish only by
not thinking of it at all. But if a diabetic willfully ignores his or her condition the results can be catastrophic.

Groupthink

In groups, willful ignorance and role shifts to avoid paradigm conflict
are called "groupthink." What happens is that the role of "group member"
becomes a primary role for the participants in the group. Members sub-
consciously collude to simply not consider information or ideas that would
split the group. It is not even necessary that the process be subconscious.
Any member of a group that has had to make almost any sort of significant decision, even if the significance was limited to the group itself,
will know that many times he or she has consciously remained silent or
spoken up solely because of the group dynamic. Such behavior may well
be positive, since in the long run survival of the species depends more on
the behavior of groups than it does upon the actions of isolated individuals. In the short run, though, we — like the diabetic who denies the
existence of his disease — may very well be dead. Keynes was right: some
short-run behaviors eliminate the long run.

It is important to remember that a person's paradigms are validated by
groups. In a prismatic world our paradigms are frequently challenged,
and one of the primary ways we reinforce them is to seek out people of our
own culture. In these single-culture groups we put forward the challenged
paradigms and are rewarded by finding everyone agrees that they are true.
The more they are challenged, the more the group supports them and the
more we need the group.

Unfortunately, all too often the paradigms supported are precisely those
most inaccurate in describing reality, since these are the most likely to be
continually challenged. If this is true for racist and sexist paradigms, it is
also true for paradigms of universal love, possibilities for world peace, and
an end to nuclear weapons.

Prismatic analysis will not solve such problems or provide a way to tell
the "good" paradigms from the "bad" ones. A paradigm of peace as
desirable may be morally better to us than one that posits white male superiority over all other persons, but such a judgment is in itself paradigmatic. On the other hand, prismatic analysis can make the dynamics of
the process clear and allow us to make useful judgments as to the ap-
propriateness of the role involved and the utility of its paradigms in dealing with a specific situation.

A knowledge of a culture allows us to identify areas where willful ignorance is likely to be particularly pronounced, and to understand the dynamics and consequences of the blind spots. We can even do this for our own culture and ourselves, and the understanding gained will help us see situations more clearly. We will still have to act according to our paradigms, but at least we can do so with our eyes open instead of firmly shut.

In prismatic terms a paradigm's value may be measured by its usefulness in allowing us to deal positively with the people and things in our lives. Within a society what is positive will vary with the culture, and differences in this area create many difficulties. Given that we live in an age of nationalism, it is normal that national symbols will have as their primary function the minimizing of cross-cultural paradigm conflicts within the national society. That this process often involves willful ignorance would seem inevitable, as it is inevitable that members of dominant cultures will manipulate the national symbols in accordance with their own paradigms.

Which culture or combination is dominant and in what areas is therefore important, but the strength and scope of nondominant cultures is also important. The strategies of the dominant elites must depend upon the nature of those who are not dominant if they are to succeed. Moreover, the nature of opposition coalitions and strategies is also dependent upon the cultures involved. The dynamic of each existing society, whether national, regional, or worldwide, depends upon the prismatic situation. Without understanding the nature of the paradigm conflicts involved we will never understand what is going on.

Physical Reality

At the same time, we must remember that many important factors in our personal and national lives are not prismatic at all. About 40 percent of what is now the United States was good agricultural land when the Europeans came; in most of present Latin America it was about 6 percent. This fact alone exerted a tremendous influence over the development of the different areas, as did the fact (again not paradigmatic) that in all of North America there were about 5 million indigenous people, while in Mexico and Central America alone there seem to have been at least 40 million. Factors such as these set limits to what is possible.

Even if physical factors can be changed by human activity they are not often particularly amenable to change at any particular moment. It may well be true, for example, that a strong classical liberal/oligarchical coalition in the United States has resulted in the destruction of much of the farmland here, turning good farms into barren land, but as of now that barren land is a fact. Pollution may well have poisoned a good deal of what is left, but people of any culture, no matter what their paradigms, will have to live with those poisons.

While some of the results of past actions can be reversed, there is no reason to believe that all can be. The poisoning of ground water in the United States is extensive and its consequences in terms of disease are now beginning to be felt, but the idea that somehow this process can be reversed is paradigmatic. Perhaps science can save us. Certainly the liberals and socialists believe it can, but they may be wrong. Perhaps it cannot.

Erosion and pollution, war and empires, the possibilities of nuclear war and the subsequent results for the earth may all be caused by paradigms, but for the people involved in their consequences such things are not paradigmatic. Prismatic analysis will not change that. It may, however, lead to changes that can have profound effects for people. In a different age wood was energy and oil simply a messy goo. When overcutting and population pressures reduced the amount of wood available, the nature of life was changed. With the discovery that oil could be used as an energy source and the development of paradigms that enabled it to actually be used, life was changed again. As we are all too painfully aware, the oil age has its own problems. Perhaps there will be a solar age with fewer problems, and perhaps there won't. There is no historical reason to believe that the transition will be a smooth one or that many will not resist it.

Changes in these physical factors involve paradigmatic changes where people are involved. Animals may be classifiable according to their ability to form paradigms, and it is clear that in this area the human animal is far more capable than any other. Hence nonhuman animals have lesser effects on the environment. Animals may overgraze, pollute water sources, kill one another, and do other things that alter their environment, but they do not have the capacity to blow up the earth. It takes paradigms of a higher order to do that, or to want to.

Revolution

All of which brings us to the question of how to alter society. If things are prosperous for most everyone only a few will call for change, and those few are very unlikely to be heeded or even heard. If the society in question is not prosperous, if many people are living in misery and want, then not only will calls for change be made, but in addition people will listen.

The best definition of "revolution" is that the dominant culture of the society is changed. This means that the paradigms used to govern the nation are different after the revolution has occurred. Revolutionaries themselves go further, feeling that no revolution is complete (or has even taken place) until the masses of the people have the paradigms of the revolutionary leaders. For example, revolution to a leninist or a fascist is not so much the armed struggle which places them in power as the change in the people themselves as they accept socialist or fascist values.

In the United States revolution is almost always defined as any attack upon the rich. This definition is inadequate, for even if the rich were to be defeated, whether or not societal change is involved cannot be determined until after the new government has had a chance to change things. Political speeches are all things to all people. It is only when a new government acts that we can see whether or not a change is occurring, and even then it is often difficult to say.

Elites are fond of saying that change is revolutionary or evolutionary, but that only evolutionary change will be positive. Burke would certainly have agreed, as we have seen, but in the present situation it is difficult to maintain the optimism of the eighteenth century. Evolution in the United States has, after all, brought us nuclear weapons, empire, pollution, racism, sexism, and other assorted evils of our time. If some of these are getting better, others are getting worse. It is no longer possible for thinking people to simply believe that the future will be better than the present.

If evolution is not necessarily positive, then those people concerned with the problems that are getting worse must seriously consider revolution. Whether or not it is justifiable is a question clearly related to the nature of the problems it is expected to solve. Future benefits may be compelling goals, especially when without revolution future costs appear to be enormous.

At the same time, the costs of revolution are obvious. That these vary in their nature and severity with the national society and international intervention is clear to anyone who has studied the Russian, Chinese, Cuban, Chilean or Vietnamese revolutions, but that there are costs is undeniable.

A complicating factor for interested Americans is that many revolutions in the third world have not been called revolutions in the United States. There are fundamental changes in the third world going on now, for example, but they are hardly recognized as such, while any attack upon the rich is immediately labeled "revolutionary." The fascist government of Chile instituted by armed force in 1973 (and supported by the American government), for example, has fundamentally changed Chile. By almost anyone's definition it is now a different country. But this was a movement ostensibly in favor of the rich, and was certainly in favor of at least some of them. The costs involved were brutal tortures and murders of tens of thousands of people, the destruction of democracy, and basic changes in paradigms of government and security held by most Chileans. By labeling the military actions "anticommunist" they have been successfully designated "antirevolutionary," at least in the United States. The costs of the Chilean revolution were higher in blood and violence than the Cuban, but Cuba is called "revolutionary Cuba" by the United States press and Chile is simply Chile.

When Americans think of "revolution," we should realize that our government has supported a great many of them in the recent past and is supporting or creating revolutions now. In "defending the Free World" our government has often aided revolutions such as that made by the military in Chile.

Most revolutionary regimes will attempt to institute a single culture. The fascists want everyone to be tory; the leninists want everyone to be socialist. In exactly the same way, the liberals want everyone to be liberals. Only the oligarchs do not want the masses to have the same culture they do. Perhaps that accounts for their strength.

In instituting the regime's single culture, coercion would seem to be inevitable. Whether this is the soft coercion of a Vargas or the hard coercion of a Hitler depends upon the wisdom of the leader, the society to be changed, and the international situation. Whether the changes last and whether they accomplish what they were designed to accomplish depends upon all the factors we have reviewed in addition to the understanding and abilities of the leaders of the revolution.

The likelihood that regimes of various cultures will attempt a revolution and the probabilities of their succeeding are also open to discussion. Tories, for example, seem rather passive on this dimension. They are inclined to accept what is as what ought to be because of their belief in tradition. This makes them hard to change as corporate groups but easy to manipulate by any government that can claim the legitimacy of tradition. Since most governments are traditional, the tories are unlikely to support revolution but equally unlikely to oppose the new regime once it has been in power for a generation or two.

Oligarchs, with their restricted goals and split paradigms, would seem to be subversive in almost any regime other than their own but unlikely to lead a revolutionary movement of any strength by themselves. Their interests are usually with the status quo, perhaps because they are so effective at subverting it for their own benefit. In any case, it is difficult for them to lead a mass movement when their own interests are so opposed to the interests of the masses. Even if they lie.

During the eighteenth and nineteenth centuries the liberals were revolutionaries and often led armed struggles against the tories and oligarchs, or even against classical liberal dictators who, being successful, saw no reason to allow any competition with themselves. In industrialized Europe and North America, and especially in the United States, the liberals were often successful. From the nineteenth century on socialists have generally been the revolutionaries and liberals, fascists, and oligarchs the counterrevolutionaries.

Violence, Coercion, and the Cultures

Whether or not the results of revolution are worth the costs, or even whether or not any results can justify such costs, depends upon the paradigms of the person making the judgment. Most people feel that the institution of their own culture would justify bloodshed, but that no other culture would be worth it. "Liberty," for example, is worth any sacrifice for many liberals, while "equality" has the same attraction for socialists. To those of other cultures, murder in the name of either value seems unjustifiable. Most people of most cultures, however, seem to have some highly symbolic value that they feel justifies violence. Paradigms differ, but the use of coercion to maintain paradigms or to extend them seems pretty standard.

It would be a great mistake to assume that the use of violence and coercion as governmental policy is limited to fascists and communists simply because their ideologies posit it as necessary. It is perhaps most obvious with these cultures, since both are revolutionary in our times, but it is clear that all of the other cultures have embraced violence as state policy at one time or another. Tories have no great problem with violence done to outsiders as long as it can be justified as positive for the tory society. The Japanese, for example, had no cultural difficulties in waging an imperialistic war when it became apparent that they needed resources controlled by others.

Most important for the United States, however, is the violence and coercion used by oligarchs and liberals to maintain their privileges and options for the future. The present (1980s) wars in Central America are the direct result of the policies of local and American oligarchs and liberals designed to maintain their economic, political, and social positions of dominance there. Lynching, police terrorism, and other violent and coercive methods that have been used to maintain racism in the United States itself are obvious. That many times these methods were used by local governments and groups to maintain local conditions hardly exonerates a national government that both tolerated and abetted them. The antiunion violence which has often overlapped the racial violence is also a clear result of the oligarchical and liberal policies of the national government.

If the definition of violence is broadened to include miserable living conditions, malnutrition, and starvation then it is abundantly clear that the United States is characterized by violence, even though its society is dominated by neither communists nor fascists. It is, quite naturally, the argument of oligarchs and liberals that these conditions are not violence but the inevitable consequence of the qualities of poor people. Once again definitions hinge upon the paradigms of the person doing the defining.

Ideology

Ideology is an attempt to produce a culture without contradictions. It is a conscious construction of theories that explain everything, are not inconsistent, and are presented as paradigms. The truth that will make us free in an ideology is in the end a single truth about human nature, which properly understood is the key to the universe. In other words, ideologies falsify the human condition by denying paradigm conflict and concentrating on a single role. Ideologues are fanatics.

Fanatics, however, have the advantage of a constant focus and simple answers. When other people doubt themselves fanatics can be very effective. There have been many ideologies over the centuries. Marxism is only one of the latest, and certainly not the only ideology functioning today. Capitalism is itself an ideology, although it now has so many variants that the ideology is less obvious than it was two or three centuries ago.

When the revolutionaries win and gain control of government, they then have to deal with a world and people who are prismatic. What usually happens is that the ideology softens and government becomes once again a matter of functional coalitions and compromises among paradigms seen as conflicting but valid. Mao's theories of contradictions both within society and within marxism itself furnish the best-known instance of this trend, but throughout the socialist world it is becoming commonplace. Communists, like democratic socialists, are becoming reconciled to the continuing existence of other cultures as well as to the internal contradictions of their own culture, and their ideology is becoming less an answer to everything than a general guide to proper goals and understanding.

Prismatic Analysis

Prismatic analysis emphasizes the internal and external contradictions we all must live with. Fanaticism of any sort claims that it has no contradictions; that a simple and emotionally secure life can be lived by anyone who just believes hard enough. In ages of great emotional insecurity such movements have a strong attraction for many people who have come to doubt their own paradigms. Whether the movements are revolutionary or conservative hardly matters; they tell us what we need to hear and support us where we most need support.

A prismatic approach to life will not solve our problems so simply. Indeed, it will not solve them at all. It can, however, help us to see them clearly, to recognize that equally valid truths, goals, and roles can contradict one another and that this situation cannot be resolved by declaring a single truth. Paradigm contradiction and paradigm stress are inevitable. The question is not how to get rid of them but how to live with them in the most positive and productive way.

How to do that will vary with the culture. On a personal level we will each do the best we can. The truth that sets us free should not be the truth of the fanatic but the recognition that while there are many truths we have to live by our own. Far better to know what they are and be able to choose among our roles than to blunder around in the dark, creating the same negative situations again and again because we do not know what we are doing. Better to use the freedom we have than to make things worse trying to use a freedom we don't have.

On a societal level we should recognize that all cultures are valid to those who have them. To deny this validity puts us immediately in a fight. If we are convinced that a fight is necessary then prismatic analysis will make it clear what the fight is about and help us wage it effectively. Often, however, a prismatic analysis of the situation will reveal shared paradigms that can be used to resolve the issue with benefits to most sides and harm to the least possible number, and that harm not the greatest that could have occurred. Compromise is not always possible, but cooperation to achieve shared goals may make those that are not shared less important.

A prismatic understanding of the world will not save us from making hard choices or protect us from harm, but it can be used to make sure that the struggles we get into are meaningful, and that we are not ourselves our own worst enemy. Within our own national society we can use prismatic analysis to understand the strengths and weaknesses of our governors, whether political or economic. Knowing these, we can more effectively use our political and economic systems for good rather than evil, no matter what content we give to those words.

Internationally we will be able to recognize the situations of others and the options available to them. Perhaps even more importantly, we will be able to recognize other cultures and other societal dynamics. To believe that basically all nations are alike is natural but wrong. Each national society is a different mixture of cultures, and has different international pressures acting upon it. The easiest way to internalize the principles of prismatic theory is to use them to understand a foreign nation. We know that it is different, especially if a different language is involved, and once we have accepted this difference we can recognize the different cultures more easily than we can in our own society.

The goal of prismatic analysis is wisdom: the ability to choose sound courses of action through a combination of knowledge, experience and understanding. Wisdom cannot itself be taught, obviously, but a prismatic approach to learning avoids many of the pitfalls associated with single-culture analyses of reality. To understand what paradigms are and how they combine in cultures and societies gives us tools which we can use to understand ourselves and those about us. Knowledge of the truth will make us free only if we understand the nature of truth and the limits of freedom.

Bibliographic Notes

Chapter One: The Human Foundation of Politics

1. Thomas Kuhn, *The Structure of Scientific Revolutions*, 2nd ed. Chicago: University of Chicago Press, 1970. This work has been very influential in social science, for it has challenged a great deal of the thinking that more or less posits a "history as progress" school of thought with the United States as the pinnacle of history, and thus automatically better than any other country. It also challenges the marxist assumption that socialism is the greatest and final development of history.

2. Harold Barrett, *The Sophists*. Novato, CA: Chandler & Sharp, 1987. Barrett discusses five of the sophists, emphasizing the liberating effect of their arguments and knowledge in societies just breaking free of the notions that men were ruled by powerful but inconsistent gods. Very much worth reading.

3. Eric Berne, *Games People Play*. New York: Grove Press, 1964.

Chapter Two: Prismatic Analysis and Social Science

1. Thomas Kuhn, op. cit., "Normal Science as Puzzle-Solving."

2. Abraham Kaplan, *The Conduct of Inquiry*. San Francisco: Chandler, 1964. Kaplan is probably the best known exponent of the other side of this argument. He is reasonable, thoughtful, and persuasive, although I do not agree with his assumptions.

3. Abraham H. Maslow, *Motivation and Personality*. New York: Harper & Brothers, 1954. Especially Chapter 5, "A Theory of Motivation."

Chapter Four: Tory Corporatism

1. Edmund Burke, *Reflections on the Revolution in France* (1790), Thomas H. Mahoney, ed. New York: Bobbs-Merrill, 1955. This is well worth reading in its entirety, for much of conservative thought in the United States today is warmed-over Burke.

2. Fred W. Riggs, *Administration in Developing Countries*. Boston: Houghton-Mifflin, 1964, pp. 167–168. This work is one of the most important books we have in political science, but it is unfortunately neglected, usually with the slur that Riggs has "not said anything new." What Riggs does is to posit a "traditional" culture (tory/oligarchy) and a "modern" culture (radical liberalism) and work out the society that results when both are present in a society but neither dominates.

Chapter Five: Oligarchy

1. Riggs, op. cit., pp 187-189.

Chapter Six: Classical Liberalism

1. Herbert Spencer, *Social Statistics*, reprint of 1851 edition. New York: Kelley, 1969. To read this work is to hear every conservative in the United States talk about the welfare state. Spencer says it more clearly and with greater logic.

2. Charles Darwin, *On the Origin of Species* (1859).

3. Niccolò Machiavelli, *The Prince* (1532), T. G. Bergin, ed. New York: Appleton-Century-Crofts, 1947. Machiavelli's *Discourses on the First Ten Books of Livy* (1531) are more direct and open expressions of his own ideas on what government and the state should be. *The Prince* ought to be read, both for itself and because so many people refer to it.

4. Adam Smith, *An Inquiry into the Nature and Causes of the Wealth of Nations*. New York: R. H. Campbell, ed. Oxford University Press, 1976.

5. Thomas Hobbes, *Leviathan* (1651), C. B. MacPherson, ed. New York: Penguin, 1982. Calm and well-reasoned, this justification for total state power is well worth reading.

6. Martin Luther, "Temporal Authority: To what Extent it Should be Obeyed" (1523), trans. J. J. Schindel, in *Luther's Works*, Vol. 45, Walther

I. Brandt, ed. Philadelphia: Muhlenberg Press, 1930. With the background of fascism and communism in our century, Luther's support of state power is familiar and blood-chilling. The parallels with contemporary justifications for supporting torturers and murderers in the name of order and stability are educational indeed.

Chapter Seven. Radical Liberalism

1. John Maynard Keynes, *The Collected Writings*, 30 vols. New York: Cambridge University Press, 1971-1980. Especially "Laissez-Faire and Communism" (1926) and "The General Theory of Employment, Interest, and Money" (1936).

Chapter Eight. Democratic Socialism

1. Karl Marx and Frederick Engels, *The Communist Manifesto* (1848). Port Washington, NY: Regnery-Gateway, Independent Publishing Group, 1982. This short and pithy statement of communist perceptions should be required reading for everyone. Although written more than a century ago, it retains its applicability today, especially for third-world countries. Karl Marx, *Capital*. New York: International Publishing Company, 1967. Dense, huge,and difficult to read, this work is still one of the most influential in the world.

Chapter Nine. Leninist Socialism (Communism)

1. V. I. Lenin, "What is to be Done,""The State and the Revolution," (1918), "Theses on the Fundamental Tasks of the Second Congress of the Communist International" (1920), and "Imperialism: The Highest Stage of Capitalism" in *Complete Collected Works of V. I. Lenin*, Progress Publications (USSR). New York: Imported Publications, 1980. Lenin's clarity of thought and influence on contemporary thinking make these well worth reading.

2. G. W. F. Hegel, *Philosophy of Law*, 1821, trans. by T. M. Knox as *Philosophy of Right*. New York: Oxford University Press, 1942. Rather like Luther in his calm acceptance of brutality and war, Hegel has been the justification for many who see state power as the only way to accomplish their goals.

3. Mao Tse-tung, *Selected Works of Mao Tse-Tung*. San Francisco: China Books, 1977. *Quotations from Chairman Mao Tse-Tung* (New York: Bantam, 1967) is full of aphorisms and bits and pieces which make very interesting reading.

4. Leon Trotsky, *Permanent Revolution* and *Results and Prospects*, tr. John G. Wright, New York: Pathfinder Press, 1969.

5. V. I. Lenin, "Imperialism: The Highest Stage of Capitalism." See note 1 for this chapter.

6. Joseph Stalin, *Marxism and the National-Colonial Question*. New York: Proletarian Publishers, 1975.

Chapter Ten. Fascist Corporatism

1. Hegel, op. cit.

2. Adolf Hitler, *Mein Kampf*. Boston: Houghton-Mifflin, 1962.

3. Benito Mussolini, *The Doctrine of Fascism* (1932), trans. E. Cope, 2nd ed. Firenze: Vallecchi, 1938. *The Corporate State*. New York: Gordon Press, 1976. Mussolini's exposition of the fascist position is a far more coherent and thoughtful approach to fascism than Hitler's. Hitler focused on his own struggle for power and existence and the stratagems and ploys that would help him and his movement gain power. Mussolini was much more concerned with the theoretical basis and justification for the movement itself.

Index

Separation of powers, 98-99
Sex, voting and, 115
Sex roles, in tory corporatism, 62-63
Sexism, leninist socialist culture
and, 165
Sexual discrimination
leninist socialism and, 120-121,
164
in radical liberalism, 120-121
Single issues, in democracies, 42
Single-member districts, 148-152
Slavery, 88-92
classical liberalism and, 88-92
Jamaica system, 80
substitutes for, 80-81
Smith, Adam, 94-95, 100-103, 126,
136-137, 161
Social climbing, in classical liberalism, 88
Social darwinism/-ists, 92-94, 104,
135-136
Social sciences
Plato and, 8
prismatic analysis and, 15-27
in radical liberal culture, 112
Socialism/-ists. *See also* Democratic
socialism, Leninist socialism
anarchism and, 135-137
classical liberalism and, 106
differences among, 140
economics, 130
in Europe, 135-136
Marx and, 135-139
Socialization, 26
Society/-ies
altering, 204-207
classless, 163
comparative chart of, 48-49
cultures and, 29-47
definition of, 29
large, cultures of, 32-33
morality in, 46
in oligarchy, 72
size of, 29-30
small, cultures of, 30-32
Sophists, 7, 11
government and, 8
Soviet Union. *See* USSR
Spain, 136
Spencer, Herbert, 92-93, 135
Spending
in business cycle, 129-131
"defense," 132
SS (Schutzstaffel), 186
Stalin, J. V., 163
China and, 171
government, 173-175

policies, 168-170, 173-175
State, in democratic socialism, 140-
141
Suffrage, universal, 114-115, 119
Supply and demand, 100-107

Taiwan, 174
Taxes
in the business cycle, 127-131
in oligarchy, 77
Technology/-ies
in leninist socialism, 178
in oligarchy, 78-82
in tory corporatism, 56-57, 61-
62
Tenure
in the church, 63
right of, 56, 58-59
in oligarchy, 77
Third world, 187
fascist corporatism in, 185,
194, 195
Theory/-ies, 2-3
defined, 2
paradigms and, 3
truth and, 2
Tories; Tory corporatism/-ists,
51-67
aristocrats in, 53
bureaucracy in, 64-65
in China, 64-66
classes in, 80
classical liberalism vs., 95-99
cohesion in, 51
competition in, 73
corporate groups in, 55
culture contradictions, 62-65
culture in, 53-57
democracy in, 60-61
democratic socialism and, 145
distribution in, 61-62
economics, 61-62, 130
education approach, 126
families in, 54
fascist corporatism and, 181,
184-188, 193
foreign affairs in, 60
government in, 57-61
hierarchy in, 53
historic experience of, 96
legitimacy sources, 52-53
management in, 74-75
merit and, 53
mobility and, 52, 62-65
monarchy and, 59-61
oligarchy and, 69-71, 84, 87-92
ownership in, 55-57